CW00519941

A MOMENT ON THE LIPS

J TAYLOR

This book is a work of fiction. Names, characters, businesses, organizations, places and events are either the product of the author's imagination or used fictitiously. Any resemblance to actual persons, living or dead, events or locales is entirely coincidental.

The moral right of J Taylor to be identified as the author of this work has been asserted in accordance with the Copyright, Designs and Patents Act, 1988. All rights reserved. No part of this publication may be reproduced or transmitted in any form or by any means, electronic or mechanical, including photocopy, recording, or any information storage and retrieval system, without permission in writing from the author.

A Moment on the Lips may not be suitable for the easily offended. Strong language and adult themes throughout.

Trigger warnings: Mild references to weight loss, eating disorders and dieting.

PART I
STARTER

CHAPTER 1

Town Centre, St Ives, Cambridgeshire

It is said that there are two types of people in this world: those who live to eat; and those who eat to live. At five foot three and a size 20, there are no prizes for guessing which camp I'm in, but, after last night, I, Etta Wilson, vow from this point onwards, things are going to change. No more inhaling man-sized dinners and curling up on the sofa in the evening with a glass of wine and a family bar of Dairy Milk, then sloping off to bed with a book and a grab bag of crisps.

Last night was my turning point. My rock-bottom moment. It wasn't as dramatic as the ones you read about in magazines. I didn't have a serious health scare or get stuck in a fairground ride, having no choice but to sit red-faced awaiting rescue as a small crowd looked on pointing, laughing and live streaming it to their friends on Instagram.

My moment happened when I least expected it.

I had left Elm Lodge, where I work as a care assistant, just after 6 p.m. My daughter Chloe is always collected from school by my grandad and his wife Pam on Fridays. So I decide, it being the last Friday in March – which means payday – to divert from my usual quiet route home and walk through town to treat myself to some snacks from the Tesco Express and get myself some tea from the chippy.

As I grow nearer to the River View, our town's hotspot – which, despite its slightly posher décor is, in essence, a Wetherspoons with music – I notice two doormen poised shoulder to shoulder, wearing matching bow ties and frowns. Their frowns are soon replaced by broad grins when a group of women emerge from the nail salon opposite. They look glamorous even with their hair in rollers, trousers rolled up to their knees, and flip-flops on their feet: no doubt to preserve their fresh pedicures and polish.

'Evening, ladies. Looking lovely!' one of the guys calls over while puffing out his chest.

I feel a pang of anxiety deep in the pit of my stomach at the very thought that one of the doormen may extend the gesture to me as I go past. I tug my work fleece down over my bum, fully aware from our long-standing relationship that Lycra, although comfortable, is far from forgiving.

I try to not think about every lump and bump that will be visible as I trudge along. I needn't have worried. When I pass them on the pavement, both men look straight through me, like I am not even there. That's the thing about being overweight: the bigger you get the less you are seen. It sounds ridiculous, but it's true. I always feel the most noticed along-side the most invisible.

I get to the end of the street, to the mini supermarket. I grab a wheelie basket and drop in a pack of jam doughnuts from the display, then notice that they are two for a pound. I don't really need ten doughnuts, but why not at that price. By the time I've reached the checkout, a packet of chocolate buttons, some Haribo and a multipack of Hula Hoops have joined them. I debate getting a bottle of Coke, but quickly decide it would be too heavy to carry home. I use the self-service checkout to avoid any conversation at the till. As I leave Tesco Express, I reach into my pocket and start my well-rehearsed routine.

It is a ridiculous rigmarole. I turn my phone to flight mode. A brass bell on top of the door jingles as I enter the Best Plaice. People glance round at me briefly as I join the back of the queue. I feel a little flushed and my heart races slightly. I pretend to dial a number. I swallow hard and clear my throat.

'Hello, I'm in here now, so what do you want me to get you?' I say, pausing for a few seconds as if I'm listening to the reply. 'Large chips or normal?' Another few seconds' pause.

'Okay, so a large cod and chips? No, I'm just going to get a battered sausage and share some of yours. And what? Oh, scraps. Yes, okay. I'll ask. I won't be long. Love you too. Bye.'

I pretend to end the call, feeling equal amounts of utterly ridiculous and thrilled that everyone will now think that the food I am about to order isn't all for me.

'Hello, madam, may I take your order, please?' says a teenager in a monotone voice. He is wearing a baseball cap embossed with 'This Plaice is Ace!' and a disinterested expression. I smile at him.

'Can I get a large cod and large chips, and he also asked for scraps if you have them please?'

'Yes, we have scraps, no problem. Anything else, madam?' he asks as he rings up the order on the till.

'Oh, I'll have a small, battered sausage as well. That's all, thank you.'

I pay and walk over to the waiting area. A woman smiles as I sit down on the plastic chair next to hers.

'Mine's the same. Could eat a horse. I don't know where

he puts it!' she says. 'I'm like you. A handful of chips and a fishcake does me.'

I chuckle along with her, inwardly cringing.

An awkward silence follows.

I stand up and peruse the noticeboard; nothing overly exciting. Still the same poster for a missing Yorkshire terrier called Mindy, a few new adverts – garden services, maths tutoring – nothing I'm interested in.

When the woman leaves, I sit back down and watch through the shop front window as she climbs into the passenger seat of a car parked right outside. A man who must be her husband leans over and takes the bag of food from her lap. He rummages urgently through the bag that's now balancing on his belly, shovelling handfuls of chips into his mouth as he goes. When he passes the bag back to his wife and starts the engine, placing his, no doubt very greasy, hands on the steering wheel, I notice that a jumbo battered sausage has found a home between his teeth.

An elderly man who had been waiting for his order of cod roe and small chips – that he paid for using a seventy-five-pence-off voucher cut out from the local paper, and a stack of twenty pence pieces – had also been watching.

'Couldn't even wait till he got home! Heart attack waiting to happen! Needs a manual job like I had in my day,' he remarks to no one in particular as he opens his two-wheel trolley and places his order inside.

I clutch my hot paper bundle close to my chest, breathing in its delicious aroma, rather like a mother does with her newborn, and pause at the road, waiting for the traffic lights to change. My carrier bag of goodies swings on my wrist as I impatiently press the button again. I just want to get home now and start silently planning in my head what I will do when I get there. Feed the cat, quickly change out of my clothes, put on my comfy onesie. Then I'll sink on to the sofa. My mouth starts watering at the thought of the sausage, fish and the salt-and-vinegar-soaked chips piled high on my plate. I am just thinking about what I have recorded on my Sky planner to watch when I spot him.

He is standing on the opposite side of the road. He isn't alone. The lights change, but I don't move. I am planted to the spot, gawping at them as they saunter across. He is all tanned and broad shouldered. His slight stubble and curly raven hair are in stark contrast to her pale skin and lithe frame that's encased inside a pillar-box-red body-con dress. She's slender and taller than me. She reminds me of a race-horse. All legs, cheekbones and angles.

I feel a stab of jealousy as he protectively takes hold of her hand. She says something to him. He laughs in response and playfully ruffles her champagne locks. She has one of those blunt fringes; the ones you spot in glossy magazines. The type you rip out to show your hairdresser when you want to reinvent yourself. A glossier, more glamorous version of you.

I am still standing there in a daze long after they've been greeted like old friends at the entrance of an Italian restau-rant and have disappeared inside. I bet she drinks something classy like White Angels and purrs into his ear, 'Well, if it was good enough for Audrey Hepburn…' between ladylike sips. I feel like I want to cry. I don't remember walking, but I must have done because suddenly I am on the footpath alongside the river. I stop at a bench and slump down. I no longer feel the urgency to get home.

I sit and stare out at the water, replaying the last hour in my head. I wince as I think back to the chip shop, but, seeing them together, that's what's really affected me. Robert

11

Ward. The father of my child. The man I wasted so many years chasing in an attempt to make him love me back.

Maybe it was seeing how happy she was with him. All dressed up, slim, confident, living a life that I can only dream about while I stood watching on, wearing a pair of market leggings that are baggy at the knees, holding a carrier bag full of binge snacks on one arm, and hugging enough fried food to feed a full-grown man and his wife in the other. I can no longer fight back the tears.

A lump in my throat burns as I try to swallow my sobs. Warm salty tears start to stream down my cheeks. I then lose the plot a little. I hold my head, my fingers entangled in my hair, right at the scalp, and let out a sound that I didn't even know I had in me. A banshee-like screech; an ear-piercing scream. 'How have I let myself get to this?' I rant. I can't even pinpoint the turning point when my weight went from curvy to out of control.

That's the thing with getting bigger. You don't go to bed a size 10 and wake up a size 20. It's the bigger portions here, the takeaways there, the treats after yet another bad day, the comforting slice of cake that you inhale with your mug of cappuccino. It all becomes normal. Soon treats are no longer treats; they are your daily diet. Nothing is out of bounds. Granted, you notice that your clothes are getting tighter and your face rounder, but you make excuses: the tumble dryer shrinks everything; you'll start losing some pounds after Christmas.

Then you tell yourself your life is too stressful or you're too unhappy to start eating better and exercising right now, but you will definitely start when things have calmed down. Or my personal favourite: you tell yourself you'll start on Monday. It's always Monday, but Monday never comes.

Then sooner or later reality hits. You're no longer a bit chunky, you're obese, or several stones well on the way to it.

In that moment you know. You simply cannot continue to turn a blind eye or make half-hearted attempts to change the shit show that is your life.

It may sound a bit dramatic, but my weight has affected my whole life for as long as I can remember. Not just physically but mentally, even down to the outfits I wear. I choose clothing based on how well it covers me. I don't even like most of the clothes I own. I stick to dark, stretchy fabrics, hoping that I will blend into the background wherever I go. Less chance of nasty comments that way.

Even when I'm ignored, I still worry that people are making assumptions about me. The worst one for me is the 'you have such a pretty face' compliment, which translates to 'nice face, shame about the rest of you'.

Food is not like other addictions; it can't be kept private. It's out there for all to see. That is why I stopped socialising. I feel too exposed.

All I do is eat, feel bad about eating, and then think about what food I want to eat, and then around the circle I go again. There must be more to life. I acknowledge that some overweight people are happy with the size they are, but I am not. So, for my own happiness and for the sake of turning my existence into an actual life that I am content with, and a body that I feel comfortable in, and for my seven-year-old daughter, I stand up, holding the now stone-cold fish and chips, and launch them into the bin.

CHAPTER 2

Evie Cottage, Farm Drove, Hemingford Gray, Cambridgeshire

When I first moved here, the darkness terrified and exhilarated me in equal measures. It still does. The early morning skies always seem bigger, more vivid, and the nights are not like the ones in residential areas. There are no street-lights, no cars; just a wall of black as far as you can see. But it is the silence that makes the darkness so tangible.

I live in a tiny detached cottage in the grounds of my landlord's farm. Tom is from Ireland, and, despite having lived in Cambridgeshire for the last sixty-plus years, he sounds like he left his hometown, Kilkenny, yesterday. He has a thick, fast accent; the type that makes you frown and squint as you try to concentrate in order to pick out enough key words to get the gist of the conversation.

We are only a fifteen-minute walk from town, but we could really be anywhere. Once you pass the private road sign and get to the crossroads, there are two handmade wooden arrow plaques: one pointing left to Shamrock Farm; the other for Evie Cottage points vaguely in the opposite direction, down the long farm road, more of a dirt track really – the only entrance and exit to my home. One side of the track is lined with imposing English oaks and horse chestnuts. On the other side, there is an overgrown ditch, which acts as a soakaway to the open fields that Tom's farm manager harvests each year.

Being a creature of habit, I use my phone torch to light my way, although, due to a lesson learnt back when I hadn't long moved in, I always carry a backup mini torch.

I had been walking home one evening in late October, after an overtime shift that I had taken on to save up for Christmas, when my phone battery died halfway down the path. I have a new respect for anyone visibly impaired after that night. Even walking the short distance in a straight line, with only the soft, warm outside lights that illuminate my cottage acting as a beacon in the distance, in an otherwise maze of darkness, was terrifying. It is amazing how disorientated you get when you cannot see in front of your nose. Every little noise from the wind or wildlife seems amplified.

Even now, each time I approach Evie cottage I feel incredibly lucky, especially during the colder months when smoke is escaping from the chimneys and the glow from the lounge table lamps welcomes me home.

It really is a special place to live. So romantic and cosy – as long as you have a torch! But it is hard sometimes; there is no getting around it. Putting your bins out is a major effort and, when it snows, you're pretty much stuck. Not that I have a car, but, if I did, I still wouldn't be going anywhere, and I can't watch any remotely scary films any more. I made the mistake of watching a film called *The Strangers* one evening, and I was petrified for weeks, going to bed at the same time as Chloe, triple-checking the locks, my heart racing with any creak of the house.

Like everything, there are pluses and minuses to living here. It's not for everyone, but I've grown used to the privacy. So much so that I am sure that I would struggle to live anywhere else now.

As I reach the cottage, I am met by a particularly bolshy rhododendron bush that is currently at war with my garden gate. In a few weeks, the bush will turn its efforts into producing mug-sized, ruby-red blooms, but, for now, all its attentions are focused on conquering as much space as possible. It's a battle that's currently being won on glory. The poor picket fence gate as good as groans as it scrapes open, only to bounce back, admitting feeble defeat as soon as it makes contact with the dense, determined, foliage wall. I vow to start pruning tomorrow.

As I make my way up the uneven cobbled path you would be forgiven for thinking that I had just missed someone's nuptials. Pink sodden petals from the cherry blossom tree have coated everything, from the grass to the doormat. Even the daffodils dotted in the wide borders have rose quartz sprinkles. Nature's confetti at its finest. I exhale. I feel calmer. I always do coming home.

The small but perfectly formed creamy stone cottage has been my sanctuary since the day we moved in five years ago. When I am huddled by one of the open fires, book in hand, or hanging washing on the wooden drying racks that are suspended over the ancient but functional scarlet Aga, as the fairy lights that are wound around the oak beams twinkle away, the damp, the avocado bathroom – complete with carpeted bath panel – and the draughty single-glazed windows never seem to matter as much.

Tuesday to Thursday my grandad and Pam pick up

Chloe after school and bring her back here. Sometimes I will leave a beef stew or chicken casserole simmering away in the Aga. If not, Pam cooks tea. She makes the best dinners. Proper comforting meals like toad-in-the-hole, ribeye steak and chunky chips, minted lamb chops and creamy mash potato, always from scratch.

When the clocks go back and the nights draw in, my grandad starts the ritual of always making sure that the log and kindling baskets are stocked, he then goes from room to room – the lounge, the kitchen, and my bedroom – lighting the fires and opening all the internal doors 'to spread the warmth'.

It's a massive help, and generally makes coming home really lovely. I appreciate the help so much and, without them, I couldn't work full time. Well, I could but Chloe would not be as happy as she is with our current set-up. Plus, I can barely meet the rent now, let alone if childcare costs were thrown into the mix.

On Fridays, I work until six, not four-thirty, so Chloe has a sleepover with Grandad and Pam at theirs. They say it's to give me a rest, but really it's because they can't get enough of Chloe's company. She is a tonic to them, as they are to her.

No roaring fire greets me today, but at least I have Alice, our ragdoll cat, who looks up sleepily, peering at me with her inky-blue eyes as I open the kitchen pantry and dump the Tesco bag inside. Out of sight, out of mind.

I laugh as I watch her unfold her enormous cream body and chocolate paws from the warmth of her radiator bed. She stretches, letting out a slow, exaggerated, yawn. Chloe and I fell in love with Alice during one of our afternoons at the local RSPCA centre.

We weren't even looking for a pet. We used to go and have a look around, drop off some blankets and towels that we picked up from our jaunts around the local charity shops in town, and there she was. She wasn't like the other cats, rubbing themselves against the glass viewing screen, vying for attention, or perched on one of the cat trees, grooming themselves nonchalantly. Alice was hidden inside a velvet igloo bed, making herself as small as possible. If it weren't for the incessant meowing, which sounded more like a distress call, I wouldn't have even known she was there.

'Don't come out, that one,' said a volunteer, closing the door to the cat pod opposite as she eyed me reading the details: a kind of bullet-point life rundown. It read 'Alice. Ragdoll, aged seven. Shy. Owner passed away. Cannot go to a home with other pets. Fine with children over three. Needs outdoor access'.

'Came in a month back now. She could have had a home a few times over, being a pedigree, but she is just too snooty, and she needs to go somewhere where they are not on a busy road, cos she likes to go out. We have some ginger kittens in the nursery. They might be better if you're looking?' continued the volunteer.

Maybe it was the thought of Alice finding herself alone, in a strange place, or the fact that she had quickly been labelled 'snooty' when she was clearly just incredibly sad and bewildered but, either way, I couldn't leave her.

We reserved her before we left, and then called in on Tom on the way home, to check if it was okay for Alice to join us at the cottage. Thankfully, he happily signed the adoption form to say he accepted pets without any hesitation, albeit with a slight look of bemusement as to why I'd even asked.

Later the same week, we had a home check, and, as we had no other pets, and lived next to open fields, we got the green light. By the following weekend, she was home.

After the initial settling-in period, us giving her space and her spending most of her time hiding in the larder, under the cheesecloth skirt of the butcher's block table, she slowly came around. And then, one night, I found her asleep next to Chloe in her bed. Eventually she started to join me on my lap in the evenings, happily kneading my thighs as I gently groomed her in an effort to maintain her thick luxurious coat.

That was nearly three years ago now, and we have never looked back. Despite her beauty, she isn't precious. She loves to play fetch – much like a dog – retrieving balled-up tissues or hair scrunchies that we throw for her, us then laughing as we watch as she swaggers back, proudly dropping them back at our feet, like a lioness presenting a kill to her pride.

Tom is also regularly graced with her presence up at the farm. He fusses around her, lighting the log burner in her honour. He adores Alice. He doesn't just show it with words – although you cannot fail to smile at the blatant delight in his gruff, gravelly words in the voicemails he leaves me: 'Tom here. Our ladyship is at the farmhouse again in case you get home and add her to the missing list. I've fed her and she's warm, so she'll be grand.'

It is Tom's small heartfelt gestures that are especially telling of his affections. Often I come home to find a carrier bag on the gate from him, full of vegetables. Without fail, amongst the muddy potatoes and bunches of carrots will be a small brown paper bag, like the ones fruit used to come in back when it was purchased from a greengrocer. The bag will sometimes contain a toy, a mouse that squeaks, or a ball that jingles; other times a can of mackerel. Regardless of its contents, the words 'For Her Ladyship' in thick green felt-tip pen will be written across it.

She is a lovely cat, the opposite to snooty and unfriendly. Today she rubs around my legs lovingly as I open a can of tuna and fork it into her bowl. She wolfs it down with a contented purr that could be mistaken for a swarm of bumblebees.

With Alice fed, I heat myself up some cottage pie that was left over from yesterday's dinner and eat it at the battered oak table in the kitchen. I knew I had a perfectly good meal here waiting for me as I headed into town this evening.

Another fact about one's life revolving around food: you eat for taste and comfort; not for nutrition and wellness. There is no doubt that the vegetable-dense, lean, minced beef dish that I fork into my mouth is better for me than the take-away; the thought of which I had salivated over all day at work, then discarded by the river this evening. That said, I really did fancy those vinegar-soaked chips. A chip shop chip really is the champion of chips.

After washing up, I pour myself a glass of white wine. I traipse up the steep staircase and shake off my work clothes, emptying my pockets on my bedside table before placing my uniform in the washing basket. I debate lighting the fire in my room but decide against it. It's getting late, and I'm tired. Probably emotionally drained from earlier. I opt to flick on the plug-in heater for ten minutes to take the edge off the cold and dampness in the air instead. While my bath is running, I flop on to the end of my bed in my towelling dressing gown and call Chloe to say goodnight.

I exhale as I plunge into the steamy hot water. If it were a spectator sport, bubble bath would be what I reached for – due to the coverage – but, as it's just me, I prefer a good glug of scented oil. I press play on my iPad that's perched on my bath board together with an ESPA candle, which I got for Christmas, and my phone.

About five minutes into *The One* on Netflix, my phone alerts me to a message – quite a lot of messages it would seem – from the relentless beeping and flashing. I lean over the side of the bath to reach for my towel to dry my hands then pick up my phone. I'm expecting to see Pam's name, together with a group of smiling photos of Chloe making butterfly cakes – the ones she told me about on our call when I asked what she had been doing this evening.

But the messages are not from Pamela.

CHAPTER 3

I have been added to a WhatsApp group. I scroll to the top of the page and find the first message. All the names are saved in my phone, and they're all work colleagues. I'd only switched my mobile from flight mode when I got upstairs after eating, so it must have just reconnected with Wi-Fi. I sigh, hoping that June, our manager, hasn't set up a work WhatsApp, although she moans so much during work hours I doubt she has anything left to say. That said, I wouldn't put it past her. I drain my wine glass as I start to read:

Val – 20:07
    Dear Fellow Women,
    I apologise for the boldness of this message, and the late hour it may find you. It has taken me a few brandies and a tense hour thereafter on the phone to my son Andrew, whose technical knowledge sadly does not match his patience to share said knowledge to set up this group. So, if you are reading this, you're one of the chosen ones (just joking!). It's Val from work and I've created a group for us to chat. This is

far too long for me to type so I've done the rest as a voice message.

I press play on the audio message, which is several minutes long:

'I'll just get straight to the point. Well, the thing is, ladies, you are kind of all I have at the moment. I mean, I do see my sister who lives in Milton Keynes every month or so, but we have never been close, and she can be quite judgemental.

'Apart from her, there's no one really. I mean I have people I'm friendly with but not friends, like my neighbour, who, when we see each other in passing, will stop and have a chat with me, about mainly (always) her son and how ashamed of him she is.

'The latest is that he recently obtained a bride from Thailand. She strongly suspects he paid for her using a loan she gave him – on the pretext it was to pay for repairs to his bungalow roof; something he vehemently denies. But her argument is the roof looks no different. After seeing MANY pictures of his roof on her camera roll, I can confirm this to be true! As much as it's riveting stuff, and I enjoy her sensational updates, they are few and far between. Of course, I do have my sons, Richard and Andrew, but to be frank, men for company isn't the same, is it? And they are only around nowadays when they want something, and even then there's no conversation. They mainly grunt at me or ask what I have to eat as they're "absolutely starving!".

'They're much like their father in fact, which brings me to the reason I am in this position and reaching out to you all. Tim, my not-so-darling husband of thirty-one years, has left me. He packed his bags this week. I wish I could tell you why, but I got no explanation. Everything had been normal. I left for work, leaving him some lunch in the fridge, and came back to a dark house; the fish pie untouched.

'A letter, that was more of a note, written on a piece of kitchen towel, which, thinking about it, is a good representation of his effort level for the whole of our lives together. No explanation; just stating he will be in touch in due course and that I should move on and do what makes me happy.

'Honestly! It was as casual as if he had left me a note to remind me to put the bins out! Cowardly right to the end, and what does that even mean, I ask myself? I have been a wife for thirty-one years; a mother for twenty-eight. Their happiness was my happiness. With them all gone, I am lost as to what my happiness even is.

'I don't know why he has left – a midlife crisis prompted by his retirement, an affair, illness? Your guess is as good as mine. So, it's a peculiar time for me, and I could just do with some friends for some advice on how to deal with it all, but also some company.

'I know I'm a bit older than you all, but we always get on well when we have chats on our breaks (I'm aware that sounds "tragic as tragic gets", as my son so kindly put it this evening when I told him about my plan), but what do I have to lose? So, this is me reaching out, because the alternative is me working, rattling round at home watching *Grand Designs*, out of sheer habit – I don't even like house renovation programmes (Tim always chose what we watched in the evening) – and comfort eating, and gosh am I comfort eating!

'Which is just making me feel worse, and not helping my ongoing battle with my waistline. I have eaten two packets of cheese and onion crisps this evening, a Turkish Delight and half a tray of Ferrero Rocher, after a curry from the local takeaway; because…well, just because.

'So, I need to know what do you all do with yourselves out of work? You all always seem so happy and full of life. We have all worked with each other for a while now, but we don't really know much about each other, do we? Sorry if you find this a bit strange and using your numbers for non-work purposes, but I didn't want to put you all on the spot. I just thought maybe we could have some work nights out, or supper at mine now and then? And maybe you had some ideas on what I should do about Tim? If you would rather not socialise out of work, feel free to leave the group. I won't take offence, but I do hope some of you have got time for an old girl who still has plenty of life in her yet. Well, some life anyway. Right I've garbled on enough. Hope to hear back soon. Love, Val.'

Yana, the newest member of our care assistant team, having joined us last year when she arrived from Russia, is first to reply.

Yana – 20:41

This is so terrible, Val. You should have told me when we at the work! Of course I would love to do some things. I do the night school, to improve my English. Simon my husband takes me to date night one time per month when he gets his work pay, so I am always wanting night out with you girls! And you can always be welcome at house of Yana! xx I am trying to lose the weight as well. Val, if I were you, I would investigate your husband. I think that I will be good at helping you with this if you wish me to xx

Nicky – 20:45

Hello, everyone, Nicky here. I am in much the same boat as you, Val. As you probably know I am divorced and live at home with my cats, Sammi and Pinkie. They are rescued Siamese brothers. I don't go out much, mainly to work, food shopping, and to see my son. I have been trying to diet (again!) but getting nowhere fast. Jenna is on a diet as well – we were talking about it at lunch today. If I were you, Val, I would take matters into my own hands...You deserve answers xxx Yana, your English is coming on brilliantly.

Jenna – 21:03

Yep, I am on a diet – or was!!! I've been so good and eaten nothing but Special K and bananas for two days, now my Jason has just come back from footie training with a kebab and chips, and I am halfway through it! I never say no to nights out (or in as long as it is at someone else's) because my two boys are driving me nuts – they never go to bed! Up and down all night I am! Val, men are such dicks. Don't let him get away with it. We can help ya xx J

I reply:

Etta – 21:17

Hi everyone, sorry to hear about your husband, Val. I would be up for meeting out of work. As you all know I have my daughter Chloe and live alone, but my grandad and his wife Pam are always happy to look after her xx I also am on a diet, starting now. I had a meltdown today on my way home from work and decided I need to sort myself out. As far as Tim goes, Val, I completely agree with the others, you deserve answers. I will help any way I can as well xx

. . .

Val – 21:18

Thanks, everyone. I appreciate you all being so kind. I really need to know why he has done this. Any help greatly received. Etta, oh no, what happened? I might join you all on the dieting. Maybe it's something we can all do together? It's so hard with no support, isn't it? Especially when we all have so much going on. Food is my go-to comfort. When I read Tim's note, the first thing I did was pour myself a brandy and work my way through a multipack of Twirls. I've always put my size and health on the back burner, too busy worrying about everyone else. Maybe it's time to worry about me, put myself first for once.

Jenna – 21:21

YESSSSS!!! Defo do together. Boredom eating is my thing. I just can't stop snacking on anything, even things I am not that keen on. I ate my boy's Power Rangers jelly beans last week, then helped him look for them the next day knowing I had scoffed them the previous evening…shit parent award lol. I did get him replacements though ha-ha xx also what happened this evening, Etta??? Are you okay xx?

Etta – 21:25

Sounds good to me! Yes, I'm okay, just saw my ex, for the first time since Chloe was a baby, so shook me up. xx

Yana – 21:25

I try to lose the weight because I soon go the party of my stepson. Felicity ex-wife of Simon is party host and she is, what you say, a smug skinny cow!!! So now I am thinking that I must join the group diet with you. Last time I am with

Felicity she wrinkle her nose at me like she smell curdled milk and say, 'Oh hello Yana – oh dear, did you not get the message that it was smart clothes? No matter, as long as you're comfortable, I suppose! And that top always looks nice on you, I love black, but I find it swamp my tiny frame.' Felicity is queen bitch disguised in Boden. Very nasty lady. I also had drama on Monday. Very bad drama. So I need to get healthy xx

Nicky – 21:31

You know the saying, a moment on the lips a lifetime on the hips? Well, I have ten stones worth of moments on the lips to shift so I am in too! Ten stone to lose sounds so daunting. I should weigh around twelve stone, not over twenty, so I will join you all dieting! And if you need some help finding out what's happening with Tim, Val, I would be happy to help you. X

Jenna – 21:34

It's doable: Nicky, my nana's friend, lost eleven stone when she got diagnosed with diabetes. I have about two stone to go before I get married. I am still eating kebab as I type this lol. I need some motivation, you would think a wedding would be enough, but it isn't. I am so good at investigating! I will help too, Val!

Etta – 21:35

I need to lose about five stone, maybe more. I haven't weighed myself in ages; ignorance is bliss, or so I thought. Either way, it's a lot fml and I want to do it asap! Also, what happened on Monday, Yana? Xx

. . .

Val – 21: 38

I have no idea where to start in finding out what Tim is up to, so, yes please, I need all the help I can get! X

Yana – 21:41

You all come for evening at house of Yana on Sunday? My husband's at the work from 6 p.m. (he do nights as a train driver). This is good as we have no work on Monday so drinks and we decide on the diet? When you come I tell you all detail of my bad Monday – it was very terrible! I do not have weigh scales; but I know in my heart I need to lose many stones.

Val – 21:51

You ladies have made my day. Thank you so much. Sunday sounds great, you have all really cheered me up xx

Nicky – 21:53

Sorry, I was doing the cats' trays again! Sammi (the seal Siamese on my tote bag I bring to work every day) has anxiety diarrhoea! This is the best thing that has happened to me this year!

Jenna – 22:09

Aahhh xxxxx I'm in!! My Jason can babysit. He can't moan because he is going out in town with his football mates tomorrow. We can decide on a diet plan, and we can investigate Tim as well, I'll bring wine xx Nicky, I love cats. What's he anxious about?

·   ·   ·

Nicky– 22:10

Sorry, I meant us deciding to do this is the best thing to happen to me this year – not Sammi's toilet issues! And life in general, I think, Jenna xx

Yana – 22:14

Come to 23 Popes Lane next to the fire station for 6 p.m. x

We all send a round of thumbs-ups and say our goodbyes, and I heave myself out of the lukewarm water. I now have the incredibly attractive combo of goose pimples head to toe and prune-like palms. I climb into bed with newfound hope. This couldn't have come at a better time. I don't feel so alone. I need this and I think they do too.

CHAPTER 4

The next day, I make a list of why this time I must succeed in losing weight.

Reasons I want to lose weight

1. No more summer chafing of inner thighs or under-boob rashes.
2. I will be able to shop in the main section of clothes shops and buy clothes based on if I like them, not on how well they cover me and if they stock my size. I also won't want to die each time I go to the counter, and the queue behind me watches the size 20 hangers being heaved off, and the tiny size 6 shop assistant disappearing from sight, as she holds up the tent-like garments to fold them. It may just be me, but I find that so mortifying.

3. I will be able to take part in Chloe's school sports day. Last year I had the humiliation of Pam, aged sixty-six, take my place in the mums' race.
4. Not to feel that I have to avoid mirrors/shop window reflections for my own mental health.
5. Feel comfortable walking down the street/in social situations.
6. Be stared at for a reason other than my size.
7. Not be treated like a second-class citizen. Fatism is as disgustingly real as racism.
8. Not feel tired all the time. Carrying around many stones of extra weight is hard work.
9. Prove that bastard Robert that I am, in fact, not only good enough for him but far too good.
10. Be proud of who I am.
11. Be healthy, so I can always be the mum Chloe deserves and needs.
12. Maybe find a man who isn't a complete shit and feel confident enough to start a new relationship.

When I think back now, I blame my ex, Robert, for a lot of my weight problems. I mean, he didn't force-feed me; he did something much worse. He always made it clear that I wasn't quite good enough for him, always commenting on my size and how I would be 'completely stunning' if I just 'lost *all* the weight'. His comments may have prompted some woman to slim down, but they just made me balloon even more.

Robert made me feel worthless, and that just triggered my emotional eating. Individuals who have never had food issues may look at me and think, what a lazy slob. Just stop eating so much and move more. I wish it were that easy. I know what I need to do to lose weight, but my attachment to food makes something that sounds so easy so bloody hard.

I have always been chunky. I was a size 14 to 16 when I met Robert, but I was tanned and toned. I was young, having just had my eighteenth birthday. Too young, really. He was thirty. Looking back now as a thirty-year-old woman, he should have known better.

I never stood a chance. I mean, what does an eighteen-year-old girl know about love?

It was the old saying: don't let someone be your every-thing when to them you're just an option.

I just couldn't see it for what it was at the time. Actually, that's a lie. I did know deep down that I wasn't Robert's first choice. Still, I was so consumed by him that I chose to cling on to any shred of affection that he showed me, because back then I was robust enough to take the many knocks he threw me along the way, and naive enough to think that one day he would feel for me as I did for him.

I'd chase him relentlessly. He'd disappear for weeks on end and then reappear, with neither an explanation nor an apology. I would pathetically welcome him with open arms, cook him meals, wash his clothes, drink in every little drop of his attentions and then he would be gone again. In reality, I was more like his mother than his lover. I even resorted to trying to buy his affections, spending what little money I had on him.

Side note to anyone currently being someone's bank or to anyone who may ever contemplate trying to buy someone's affections in the future. Take some advice from someone who has been there: don't. It never works. Save your money, your time, and, most importantly, your heart. Real love never comes complete with a price tag.

Anyway, our fucked-up relationship – if you can even call it that – went on in a miserable cycle for about five years.

Then Chloe arrived, and so did even more extra weight. I had held out hope that Robert, who had blanked me as soon as my belly swelled and the pounds piled on, would fall in love with me when the baby arrived and I became the mother of his child. I cringe at my stupidity.

When he resurfaced a month or so after Chloe was born – having turned up unannounced on my doorstep late one evening, as he often had over the years – his first words were not 'I am sorry for being on the missing list during your whole pregnancy', and definitely not 'Can I see my daughter?' but 'God, you're massive! Christ, you look rank! Like, really terrible!'

I am a good few stone heavier now. Imagine what he would have said about me if he had spotted me on Friday in town.

Robert had stayed just long enough to help himself to a chicken and bacon sandwich from the fridge, and to ask me if I had any money I could 'lend' him. Which was code for could I give him some cash that I would never see again.

Off he went ten minutes later and twenty pounds richer, passing me without so much as a peck on the cheek on his way out. I'd lied when Grandad and Pam resurfaced, after they had made themselves scarce to give Robert and me some privacy to talk. When they asked me what Robert had said about the baby, I lied to them because I was so mortified.

'He absolutely loved her,' I replied, my watery eyes not quite meeting theirs. Pam, who is a lot more observant than some may think, had given me a small, kind smile, sidled up to me and squeezed my shoulder.

'He is an idiot, darling. Shall we have a nice cup of tea and a Blue Riband?'

It was a bad time in my life. The first-time mum of a colicky baby, realising that the man I loved was a complete scumbag. I was permanently tired, tearful and angry. Angry at Robert, but also at myself, for the situation I had got myself in. It was during the long night hours when Chloe wouldn't settle that I was forced to take stock of the situation. I reflected on all the times Robert had let me down.

The times I sat waiting for him and he stood me up. The naked photos of a woman I had seen on his phone (a phone that I had paid for!), and the way I had pathetically allowed him to tell me that I was mad when I had confronted him when I knew I wasn't. I could go on all day. There were so many warnings that I chose to ignore.

He had put me down all the time and made me wish I were more how he wanted me to be. As much as my heart still wanted him, my head knew that for Chloe's sake things had to change.

I made the decision to delete his number so that I had no option but to stop calling him. Robert carried on never contacting me. He did come around a few times in the months after, but, as I stopped giving money to him, and as I still looked 'a right mess', he soon disappeared altogether from our lives. I moved to the cottage later the same year, and didn't give him my address. A few months later, I did reach out formally to offer him a relationship with Chloe. He wasn't interested.

That was nearly seven years ago. Since then, my only toxic relationship – or any relationship for that matter – has been with food. Despite all this, I'd be lying if I said that seeing him yesterday didn't floor me. It has really knocked me for six. I don't want him, but I kind of want him to want me. I want him to desire me, so that I can tell him to dream on.

I do feel guilty that Chloe is stuck with a father like Robert because of my choices, but, without him, I wouldn't have her, so for that reason I have no regrets. Chloe is the best thing to have ever happened to me. That said, he did look good on Friday; he hasn't aged at all. Not from a distance anyway. Why do men always have skin and eyelashes they don't deserve?

This evening I have had chicken soup, a granary roll (no butter), a fruit salad, and one of those low-calorie jelly pots. I almost ordered one last Chinese, but I stopped myself. The days of starting my diet tomorrow are in the past. I never want to feel how I did yesterday evening, or in fact how I have felt every day for as long as I can remember again.

CHAPTER 5

Sunday always means a roast at Grandad and Pam's house in St Ives. This Sunday is no different. Their house is where I grew up. I didn't live there, so to speak, but I may as well have done. I was there more often than my mum's. After my nan divorced my grandad, she moved to a bungalow a few towns away while Grandad remained in the house, because he is like me: sentimental.

I am a self-confessed collector of memories. A shell lifted from a beach in Hemsby during a family holiday in 1993, a cinema ticket stub from a rare date that Chloe's dad took me on. I keep everything because the objects I collect are much like a smell that transports you back in time to a long-forgotten place. It can be from years before, but in that moment you are back there reliving the past in your mind's eye.

Someone shuffled past me a few weeks ago and their trail of Clinique Aromatics Elixir stopped me dead. I was, for those few seconds, no longer in Superdrug buying tampons; I was with my nan. Not how she is now, of course – I don't think she even wears perfume anymore – but how she was back when my grandad used to buy it for her without fail, every year for Christmas and birthdays. Times when she smiled and meant it.

Songs can also be as powerful as that whiff of a lost love's aftershave; both of which are capable of triggering that ache in the pit of your stomach and a nostalgic smile to form at your quivering mouth. Even now I can't hear Ashanti's 'Foolish' without being involuntarily transported back to 2002 to my eleven-year-old self, during what was the hottest, most relentless, summer, when all I did was play that song that I had recorded from the Q103 radio station on a cassette tape on repeat.

I can still almost taste the soda stream concoctions that my friend Teri, who lived opposite Grandad's, used to knock up, while I kept a lookout; her not yet being permitted to mix it without her mum's supervision. We thought we were the height of sophistication as we lay out on the wilting grass, reeking of Sun In hair lightener, taking sips of what were honestly quite shit versions of Coke and Cherryade, while doing *Bounty* and *Mizz* magazine quizzes and gossiping about everything and nothing.

It's funny how you hold on to memories containing people that you would never otherwise give a second thought to. I haven't seen Teri for a good fifteen years. I don't even know anything about her as an adult; if she's married or if she became the vet she had always aspired to be. Yet there she is in one of my most happy childhood memories.

If I've learnt anything working at the care home it's that anything or anyone that triggers a memory is not to be undervalued, because it's those memories that are the difference between existing and living.

Happiness really is just memories when you think about it. Everything we do, from a trip to Disneyland to birthday parties, is for the memories. The tiny fragments of euphoria, the nanoscopic snippets of our lives that we package safely in a nook of our brain, where they linger, patiently, ready to be recalled upon for us to reflect on with love.

They are often the little things, like the dinner I am at today, the family caravan holiday, which was a bit crap at the time, the walk in the woods where the rain lashed down as you took cover, huddled together, laughing, silently pocketing a single leaf as a memento. It's only as time passes and the leaf wilts and things change, you grow up or loved ones are no longer there to cook you meals that memories become so precious.

That is why I am a collector of things. The objects are my insurance, I like to know that I can revisit my special moments, even if I grow to forget how precious a particular memory may be. I take comfort in knowing that my objects will act as prompts; a gentle nudge to the life I had before. I know what you're thinking. I could just take a picture. And you're right. I could, but I find that you see more when you are not too busy looking.

My grandad and Pam's house hasn't changed much since I was a child. Their road is fairly prestigious; not quite middle class, more an 'if you own a house there, you are doing okay' kind of road. There are no bankers or judges; more IT consultants with trendy beards, who climb into their Prius cars each morning wearing cords and Kings of Leon T-shirts, clutching their reusable coffee cups. There are also a lot of older residents, like my grandad and Pam, them also having purchased when it was still possible to buy a decent-sized family home without having a deposit and a joint income to make your eyes water.

It was different for their generation, so I am always told. During the seventies, eighties and early nineties, it was a main priority to own your own home. No one cared as much about flash cars or designer clothes. The message was clear:

invest in bricks and mortar, pay off as much as you could, as fast as you could, and, other than that, you only bought things you could afford, and, if you couldn't, you made do until you could.

For people like my grandad, it paid off. Number 31 Willow Road is typical English leafy suburbia. Four bedrooms, two bathrooms, a spacious living room, sun lounge, a kitchen – complete with a serving hatch that opens into the dining room – a single garage and a good-sized but completely overlooked rear garden. The model detached seventies house. Pristine. The lawn is always perfect, the kitchen always gleaming. It smells of Cif and Shake n' Vac. It is my safe place. If the world was ending, you would find me in that house.

Despite having the dining room, any cooked meal is eaten in the conservatory – or sun lounge as it has always been called – 'to save the carpet, darling!' Pam sets the table like it is Christmas day for every meal. Each setting has a placemat, four forks, three knives, two spoons, two wine glasses and a crystal tumbler – on coasters, of course – together with a napkin 'for the messy eaters!' Always fabric – 'paper is for picnics and truck stops!' – each one folded and carefully threaded through a gold napkin ring holder. The napkin rings were another one of Pam's QVC purchases and came with a mini candelabra that wouldn't look out of place on the set of *Downton Abbey*. It was all very grand, while it lasted.

The candelabra's reign ended abruptly on New Year's Day last year, due to an incident involving my sister, who had, as usual, indulged in quite a few too many Proseccos and found herself with a sudden need for a second helping of pigs-in-blankets. Luckily, my grandad took his position of fire safety officer at work very seriously and therefore knows 'stop, drop and roll' like the back of his hand.

By the time I had thrown my hand to my mouth and muttered 'Oh fuck!' a few times and Pam had scooted off in the direction of the kitchen in enthusiastic pursuit of the fire blanket and extinguisher, he had sprung into action – disaster averted – but, after the near-miss, the centrepiece, together with the job lot of one hundred peony-scented dinner candles in colour Meadow Bloom Pink have been banished, location unknown. Three cream, battery-operated, flame-effect pillar candles have since taken its place. Not as fancy, but less chance of burning down the house and/or oneself.

Safety first and all that.

My grandad is the most placid man you could wish to meet. Not in a weak way but in a 'never moans, nothing is too much trouble, puts the happiness of his loved ones before anything else' kind of way. For that reason, he gives in to most of Pam's requests. The garden-shed-sized hole in the middle of the back garden lawn is the latest testament to that. The soon-to-be 'koi carp pond, fully stocked, wider, deeper and better lit than Karen's at number twenty-four!' is well underway.

However, despite his agreeable nature, food is not something he is prepared to compromise on. He supports Pam in her choices – wholeheartedly – but he draws the line at healthy versions of a roast dinner. So usually me, Grandad and Chloe tuck into the tasty version – goose fat potatoes, thick slices of juicy beef topside, homemade giant Yorkshires, roasted vegetables – all swimming in thick meaty gravy, while Pam looks on longingly as she nibbles her skinless chicken breast, three Frylight potatoes, steamed carrots and peas.

Compared to our feast, her plate always looks a bit like the plain friend in comparison.

It would seem that misery does indeed love company as Pamela was absolutely delighted when I asked via text this morning if I could join her with the healthy roast lunch option. It wasn't that bad, to be honest.

'What's all this in aid of then?' Grandad asks, gesturing to my bowl of Müller Light and chopped strawberries in-between mouthfuls of his sticky toffee pudding and custard.

'I'm going to lose some weight,' I reply sheepishly.

He rolls his eyes, not unkindly. He has heard it all before. Pam is much more enthusiastic, spending the rest of the afternoon repeatedly telling me how I should come back to Slim With Us diet club; even trying to use the fact that they now get badges if they have a good week to persuade me.

'Like I get from Miss Thompson when I get my spelling right?' asks Chloe.

'Yes, darling, sort of, but with these badges, when you have ten of them, they can be redeemed for a fat-free chocolate brownie! Or an apple tart vegan protein ball pack!' replies Pamela more avidly than any sentence with the words 'fat-free' and 'chocolate' deserves. I ummed and ahhed but there is no way I'm going.

I tried it before, years ago now, not long after I stopped seeing Robert – his words still ringing in my ears – but having unlimited grazing rights on foods including so-called sin free chips and burgers just isn't for someone like me, who eats until they are full, and then keeps on eating. I know that it must work for some people, but having these so-called unlimited free foods was just a green light for me to overeat even more than I did usually. Not only did I put on weight but I also got a standing ovation for it. All right, they didn't stand, but they are all so happy-clappy at that club.

You have never seen anything like it. When I had

rejoined the circle having been weighed after my first week of dieting, it was announced that I had gained two pounds. This was met by a sea of applause 'for great effort and determination', led by Mandy, the slightly snidey diet club leader. Who I couldn't help noticing had a very substantial bottom of her own under her ankle-length pleated skirt.

Pam, upon seeing my cheeks colour, had ramped up the moral support and yelled out 'and muscle weighs more than fat!' as an alternative excuse for me. One that I knew wasn't true, but I appreciated the gesture. I just sat there, eyes to floor, completely defeated, willing the frenzied clapping and frantic nods of solidarity to draw to a close, so that I could get home and order myself a cheese burger and chips.

In reality, it was a waste of time going to the club because my heart wasn't in it. I'd been just kidding myself all week. All I had done was scoff kilos of peeled potatoes, sprayed with one calorie oil replacement spray, oven baking them like they were going out of fashion, and wolfing down home-made burgers, telling myself that the ketchup that I was smothering over them was fine, as were the buns I sand-wiched them in – healthy add-ons! – perfectly legal according to the Slim With Us bible.

When I think back, I wasn't even that big then – about twelve stone – so it shows how much things have spiralled over time. I don't even know what I weigh now. I was four-teen stone a year ago when I was weighed at the doctors. I was a size 18 then, so I must be a bit more now. Anyhow, Pam and the rest of the slimming group seem to treat the Slim With Us club more like a social gathering to have a natter and show off their latest outfits than real dieting support.

Pam has routinely gained and lost the same seven pounds since I have known her. Even though she makes herself the Slim With Us version of meals most days. Then each Tuesday after her weigh in, if she has lost anything she will buy herself a cake or have a bar of Galaxy Ripple as a 'naughty treat'. Plus, on Saturdays, she has a 'little chill from her weight-loss journey', which to date is about twelve years and counting, and so will have a takeaway, which usually Chloe and I have with them as well.

No, I need a new approach. A way to cut out all the rubbish without falling off the wagon after a few days (or hours!), like I usually do. Hopefully, tonight when I go to Yana's we can come up with a plan.

By managing to divert the conversation away from me rejoining the diet club, I find myself somehow agreeing to join Pam power walking. Starting tomorrow. Lucky me! Not long term, just while Sally – Pam's usual fitness partner – is out of action due to having an operation that, depending on who you are speaking to, is referred to as either 'women's problems' (my grandad) or a 'small routine hysterectomy' (Pam who I feel, it is fair to say, has grown extremely disgruntled about the whole inconvenience). Her view is that Sally is milking it a bit now. Pam had sympathy until she popped over with a box of Milk Tray and a Fenjal bath set earlier in the week.

'Propped up on the sofa she was. Watching daytime TV, remote in one hand, tube of Pringles in the other, while her husband ironed his own work shirts! There seemed nothing wrong with her!' Pam recalls, shaking her head in disgust at the memory.

I joke that it sounds like most of my evenings, minus the major abdominal surgery and a loving husband to run around after me, of course.

'You work full time and are a single parent! Sally has no excuses. She's just let herself go!' said Pam, tutting. 'So, anyway, where was I? Ah yes. So I said, "Now come on, Sally. Let go of the crisps. We don't eat non-Slim With Us approved snacks in the week! You are better than this, darling", but she gripped on to the tube and whined, "My surgeon has said I can't diet while I am recovering, and that I need my calories to repair!" Plus...!' announces Pam as she sidles up to me, lowering her voice as though she is about to share a state secret, 'she was in her bed coat! I mean, I wouldn't mind, but it was almost midday!'

I try not to think about all the times Pam has called round mine in the afternoon and been met with me in no bra and bleach-stained loungewear. For some reason, I seem to be largely exempt from her high standards; maybe because I am family or maybe she just thinks I am a lost cause.

'Anyway,' continued Pam, 'I called an emergency meeting with the club ladies, and we all agreed that Sally must be clinically depressed. We are meeting again in Costa Coffee tomorrow. Jessica is printing off some helpline numbers to get advice on how one goes about staging an intervention. We decided that we have to try everything before we involve professional bodies!'

I nod because I cannot swallow a laugh and speak at the same time.

'Professional bodies?' I ask, still trying to suppress the snorts that are desperate to escape.

Pam nods sensationally, her eyes bulging, eyebrows raised to the Artex ceiling as she mouths the words 'possible sectioning'.

I then sit through a ten-minute account about how Jessica, who lives at number 29, will be leading the 'circle of trust' due to her previous experience; her having been summoned to collect her grandson from his private boarding school in Berkshire back in January. Apparently, Raffety, Jessica's fourteen-year-old grandson, was found wrapped in a roll of catering tin foil under a flapjack stand in the campus canteen.

'Super skunk, the headmaster said it was called. You don't expect it when you go private, do you?' Pam asked me, while I shook my head in bemused agreement. 'I mean they wear such smart blazers and these adorable little hats. Jessica said that her son-in-law, Rafferty's father, has pulled back his funding of the schools new Olympic-size swimming pool. And I cannot say I blame him. What that poor woman went through on the train journey home, no one should have to go through that!'

'How long has it been then since Sally had her operation?' I enquire when I have composed myself. I watch as Pam pulls out her tangerine leather Radley diary, licking her finger as she flicks through the pages.

'Three weeks on Wednesday. Two weeks of belly dancing I've missed now. I'll be really miffed if she doesn't pull herself together by our next session. I could go on my own, but it's her turn to pay so I am holding out. Three pounds is three pounds at the end of the day. But at least it frees up my schedule, so I can concentrate on training you,' beams Pam.

In typical Pamela fashion, my agreement to walk with her has already been ramped up and is now being referred to as her 'training' me. This gives me anxiety. I've seen what she wears to Fit After Fifty aerobics in the WI hall on a Thursday lunchtime.

No, I have decided that if she comes out dressed like Jane Fonda, all leg warmers and flammable materials, I am not going. There may well be a time and place that calls for that attire – admittedly I cannot think of any now – but what I do know is this: I am not emotionally robust enough to join Pam walking the corgis around the housing estate, before taking the path next to the main road towards the town centre.

I know what will happen; I can see it now. We will be cheered on by the endless beeps of car horns that Pam's outfit of magenta shiny tights, glittery high waisted belt and thong leotard will without doubt attract. The horns will sound one after another in a mixture of amusement, horror and disbelief. Pam being Pam will bathe in her popularity, waving at them, grinning like a Cheshire cat, while prancing like a jubilant show pony, before turning to me and uttering with mock embarrassment, 'Oh, this is getting silly now! Goodness, they are all obsessed with me!' She will then thrust her diamante-cased mobile phone at me, and her instructions will be clear. 'Film how much they all love me so I can show everyone at club! Make sure the sound's up, darling. I want them to hear all the horn hoots! Gosh, I bet this is how Lady Di felt!'

CHAPTER 6

I had a bit of a wobble before leaving for Yana's house in Needingworth that evening. It started with me having mum guilt for leaving Chloe at Grandad's for another sleepover.

I had no logical reason for this because she loves staying there and was especially excited today when Grandad announced he had a new Sylvanian Family set to add to her doll's house. Plus we have had all weekend together.

I then started fretting about what to wear, then it was what I would talk about, would I make a fool of myself, would the others roll their eyes behind my back and wish I hadn't come. Which is ridiculous, because I see and speak to these women practically every day at work. I know they wouldn't care what I was wearing, and they are not the kind of women to be bitchy. In the end, I pulled myself together and left wearing my usual black leggings, an olive-green over-sized shirt and flat ballet pumps on my feet.

My taxi driver didn't help with my anxiety, with his huffing and puffing when we had a bit of a problem finding Yana's house. 'Bloody maze these new builds are. The numbers are all over the place,' he whinged, head out of the window, as his filthy silver Mondeo crawled along. 'Half of them still only have plot numbers! We'll be here all day. I'll have to radio in and give my next job to someone else at this rate.'

He caught sight of my face in his rear-view mirror and threw in a small, forced chuckle, but his passive-aggressive message was clear.

I found myself saying that I would just get out and find it myself. It couldn't be far away, and I could always ring one of them if I had no luck. When I handed him a ten-pound note, he made a show of digging around in his jeans pocket for my four-pounds change, even though I could see he had two fifty-pence pieces and at least five pound coins in the centre console. There was no way I was tipping him after his attitude. After an awkward stand-off he as good as threw four coins into my outstretched palm and drove off without a goodbye.

The estate had that just out of its wrapper appeal: shiny letterboxes; no oil-stained driveways; the uniform turf on their small strips of front garden still a lush, deep green.

Yana must have spotted me from her kitchen window, as, before I even notice her, she is on her doorstep calling over to me. 'Etta! I am here, hon!' she greets me warmly, wearing Betty Boo PJs and pink fluffy slippers. 'You look very different with your hair down, like the exotic mermaid. I wish my hair was like that!' she said as she ushered me inside.

My cheeks flush, never having been good at accepting compliments, which have been very few and far between in the last few years, and nearly always about my coal-black curly hair, which hovers near my hips.

'Your home is lovely!' I enthuse, changing the subject away from me as I place my shoes on the rack. Yana proudly gives me a mini tour. Everything about 'The house of Yana and Simon', as per the sign fastened to the front of this red-brick semi, is a Mrs Hinch dream.

A fresh linen aroma lingers in the air, courtesy of the wax burners in every room, and on top of the gleaming cooker hob in the kitchen is a silver glass tray, polished so well that I can see my reflection. On it is a vase crammed with faux cream peonies.

After Yana makes me a drink we join the others in the living room. I grip my vodka and coke a little tighter as I imagine myself dropping the contents all over the pristine mink-grey, deep pile carpet.

'Yay, you're here!' beams Jenna, who's sitting on a fluffy ice-white beanbag, next to a mirrored coffee table. I give a little wave as I take off my cardigan. Jenna notices my shirt and lets out a little laugh. 'Good taste!' she says, gesturing to her own mustard version. 'Sainsbury's have some proper bargains, don't they?' she adds.

This perks me up. I can't be that frumpy if Jenna is wearing the same top as me, I think; albeit a different colour. I take a seat, sinking into the velvet sofa next to Val. Instinctively, I hug one of the many scatter cushions to my torso to cover my belly. I notice that when Yana sits down she does the same.

Nicky is in the chair opposite, engrossed in her mobile, but she flashes me a smile. 'Hiya, Etta love. Right, they are settled so I can relax now. Phew!' she announces to the room.

'Nic's been worrying about her cats for a change,' Val teases as she sips from her tumbler of what looks to contain a very generous measure of brandy.

'The boys don't like me leaving them at night. You all know how they are, but I've left an audiobook on for them, and I have the pet cams on interactive mode, so I can soothe them if they get too agitated,' Nicky replies, like she is trying to convince herself as much as us.

'If anyone can soothe them Marian Keyes can,' said Val, who seems to sense that Nicky is more uptight than usual and so changes her tone from teasing sister to reassuring mother.

Jenna shoots me an amused look and rolls her eyes as if to say, 'Oh, here we go again!' We are well used to Nicky stressing about her cats. All day at work she frets; it's endless. Anything and everything is a cause of anxiety for Nicky where they are concerned: if they have been asleep too long; if one is bullying the other; do we think them both being asleep in a ball means they are too cold; should she pop home at lunch and close the blinds in case the window cleaner comes three days early and makes them jump...

We thought her having pet cams installed would calm her nerves down, but they seem to have had the opposite effect.

As soon as we are all settled with drinks, I ask Val if she has heard any more from her husband. She nods.

'I have,' she says, shaking her head. 'He's only gone and got himself a solicitor!'

CHAPTER 7

Unfortunately, it's not good news. Val received a letter yesterday morning from a hotshot lawyer stating that he was acting on behalf of Mr Timothy Green. It had tersely stated that Val needed to provide her legal representative's details to commence proceedings 'as a matter of urgency'.

'I've been trying Tim's phone non-stop,' says Val. 'It goes straight to voicemail. I even rang his brother Clint yesterday. I thought he may have headed down to Devon to stay with him, but he isn't there. Clint didn't even know he'd left me. My sons have both spoken to him, but, other than saying that he's fine, they refused to go into it.'

All four of us gasp and agree when Jenna says that sons should always take their mother's side. From what Val has said, her sons are trying to keep out of it.

'When I rang Andrew again today, to ask him where his father was staying, he sighed and said, "Mum, I'm staying neutral, like Switzerland",' Val told us. 'I got a bit cross then and said, I had a three-day labour with you, my boy – three days! I deserve some support!'

I ask Val what he said to that. If he gave any clues whatsoever. She shakes her head; the frustration in her face clear. 'No. He put the phone down straight after I asked him if he knew what an episiotomy was.'

We all hoot with laughter.

'I can give you the details of my solicitor. She's ace. I wouldn't have kept my house if it weren't for her,' Nicky offers Val. 'Although, that reminds me, I must ask her if she also does criminal law. I might be soon needing some representation – due to my actions against my ex-husband.'

'You're not planning to off him, are ya?' jokes Jenna.

Nicky replies, 'No! Nothing like that. What happened was, I'd been checking up on him on Facebook, not like a stalker – just a few times a day – just to see what he is up to, and I accidentally liked a few of his posts. Then I happened to bump into him at his badminton club on a few occasions, and he goes and threatens me with a 'before police action' legal letter, accusing me of tracking his movements, demanding that I "cease my harassment and comminatory behaviour". It was extremely aggressive and said,' Nic adds casually, 'that they are still considering applying for a restraining order and filing criminal charges against me.'

Jenna then asks what comminatory meant. When Val tells her, Jenna says, 'Fuck him, Nic! Don't let him stop you playing a sport you enjoy!'

Nicky then explains that she had only gone to the health club to bump into him casually and not to play badminton.

To which Jenna replies, 'Free fucking country, mate. Seriously, don't worry about it. They're just trying to shit you up. I mean, does your ex own Vivacity Leisure? Does he fuck! And if he don't want you looking at his precious Facebook, he can set it to private. Problem solved!'

The rest of us exchange amused side glances and raised eyebrows. She does have a point, to be fair.

'Do you think it is definitely final then, with you and Tim, I mean?' Yana asks Val gently.

Val exhales, taking a few seconds to decide what to say. 'I was hoping it would blow over, that he would come back, and things could get back to normal, but I know I'm kidding myself now I've had a chance to think it all through.

'He had obviously planned it all. He'd left his keys for the doors and garage on the side. Everything of his has gone. Even the computer, which is technically ours, though I never used it. The sneaky so-and-so must have hired a van; the garage is completely cleared out. I'm not even sure I want him to come back now. He must have been lying in bed in the days leading up to it, knowing full well his intentions.'

I cannot even imagine being with someone for as long as she'd been with Tim, let alone being with someone that long and then one day them disappearing without an explanation.

'I was just a glorified cook and housekeeper. Plus, the more I have really thought about it, we had nothing in common by the end. Maybe it's for the best. At least now I can do as I please. It's still bugging me, though. I need to know what made him do it. Why now? There must be a reason. Something, or someone. Once I know, then I think I'll be able to draw a line under it all, but I need answers,' Val says decidedly.

I can understand her viewpoint. Tim must have known when Val left for work that morning as he kissed her cheek, and said, 'Love you, see you later' that he was lying on both counts. Because he knew that he wouldn't be seeing her later, and people who love someone do not treat them how Tim has Val.

Still, it cannot be easy. Val said herself she doesn't even remember what her life was like without him in the centre of it.

Yana busies herself, refilling our glasses with Stoli Vodka

and Coke as she says, 'So I think about this since Friday, Val. Have you checked phone records? That will be the way to find the truth.'

Nicky agrees, telling us that it was some phone and bank records that she'd managed to get hold of that had proved that her ex had been having an affair before he'd left her.

Val drains her brandy then says, 'I wouldn't even know where to start with that. But I know one thing: he isn't just getting away with it. I intend to find out everything.'

CHAPTER 8

Jenna, clearly a good multitasker, had been listening intently, while also sending her fiancé Jason voice notes detailing strict bedtime instructions. 'Jase, I don't care if you've already done it shitloads of times or that you're tired, mate. Don't you dare let them in our bed! Keep taking them back to their own room. I mean it, Jase! Don't you dare! I'm leaving you to it now. Don't wait up. Have fun. Love ya!'

As she places her phone on the arm of her chair screen down, she rejoins the conversation. 'Val,' Jenna says, touching her arm, 'don't worry about all this shit with Tim. I'll help us get to the bottom of this for you. It'll be a piece of piss,' she adds reassuringly.

'Trust me, mate, this is my area of expertise. Just the other month, my mate Porsha's boyfriend Lewis was acting well sketchy, so we hacked his phone. We found that he was on a dating site, posing as seven years younger he was, and claiming to be an accident and emergency consultant doctor called Tommy.

'He had filtered his face so much we didn't even think it was him till we enlarged it. He had about ten layers of filters!

So, anyway, we set up our own account, created a fake profile, we did, using a photo of some belter of a model from Ukraine. Then we sent him a message and started being all flirty, proper putting it on him, saying we wanted him to get our pulse racing, give us a full body MOT. Really cringy stuff.'

Jenna is snorting with laughter now, as are we.

'He is so arrogant; he fell for it wholeheartedly. My poor mate was fuming. She didn't let on, though. After a few days, we arranged for him to meet Shakira.'

I notice Yana pressing her lips together to suppress her laughter.

'Shakira Kournikova was my idea. My mate said for me to choose the name. Something sexy to really get him going, like, and it doesn't get sexier than them two knockouts, does it? So anyway, he was eager to treat Shakira like a princess, the location was chosen, and he had taken care of everything.

'Lewis, the sneaky little fucker, says Shakira is to meet him at Prezzo's in Cambridge high street, wearing something "short and sexy, to show off her crackin' legs, tits and arse!" In return, she will be rewarded with dinner, and not just pasta but three whole courses! She will then accompany him back to the Premier Inn that he will pre-book "for a night of filthy fun" his words, not ours!' She is shaking with laughter now. 'The cocky perv really thought he was getting the equivalent of a high-class escort all night in exchange for a twenty-pound-a-head early diner deal and a forty quid room.'

I have tears rolling down my cheeks as she picks up the story.

'Anyway, we deliberately made their date a day when he was supposed to be taking my mate to see her cosmetic nurse, just to fuck with him really because Porsha can't drive after, cos her eyes swell up after the cheek fillers, so he had promised he would take her.

'Porsha was all like, "No Lewis wouldn't stoop that low! He knows how hard it is to get an appointment with Nurse Katiya", but I knew he would, so I said, "Mate, you need to get on to Nurse Katiya now and get it rebooked, cos he's gonna bail on ya". And I was right.

'He really went to town. Made up some dramatic story of how he had to cover for another teacher on a school trip to Wales, because this so-called sick colleague, who'd had a sudden violent reaction to antibiotics, was now in hospital. Then he acted like a martyr saying he would be gone overnight and how he would miss her!

'His expression when we turned up at Prezzo's! We'd been watching from the pub opposite, and he'd arrived early. His beady eyes were scanning the door, waiting for Shakira to shimmy in. You should have seen his face when my mate strode over and plonked herself down all calmly opposite him.

"Hiya, Tommy", Porsha said as his face kept alternating from looks of confusion to sheer horror. "Good job you've got medical training because you look like ya about to have a fuckin' heart attack, babes!" Porsha thundered at him.

'The funniest part was when he pleaded with her. "Baby let's talk about this, somewhere else, before the person I'm meeting arrives. I can explain; it's all been a huge mistake. She means nothing to me." The dozy sod still thought Shakira was en route. His face when Porsha loudly brought him up to speed!

'Then I picked up a platter of gross-looking sliced meats and olives that a couple were sharing on the table next to his and tipped it all over him, even the dish of dipping oil thingy. The waitress marched over, and I was expecting a bollocking, but instead, she said, "Good for you! Women supporting women! Yeah, the future is female!" Then she glared at Lewis and gestured to what was left of the meat plate, most of which was still hanging off his cheeks and round his feet, and spat, "As for you, I will be charging that to your table!"

'Lewis nodded sheepishly as the waitress turned away with a flick of her high pony only to reappear with a dustpan and brush, which she thrust into his hand, pointing at the floor, then she volleyed the bill on the table with a sarcastic "Thank you for choosing Prezzo's".

'Me and Porsha left him on his hands and knees sweeping up stuffed mini peppers and all that rank stuff raw meat comes with. Shell-shocked and teary eyed, he was,' Jenna said, cackling at the memory. 'I mean, how thick can you get? What woman would agree to go out for pasta before heading off for a night of passion! You'd just want a lie down and watch a bit of tele, wouldn't ya? Although the fact that he, a forty-four-year-old balding PE teacher, had so much self-arrogance that he believed a twenty-one-year-old stunner, who would make most Victoria's Secret models feel frumpy, couldn't wait for him to "ravish her" is quite admirable in a way. Fucking deluded, but admirable!'

When we all stop wheezing with laughter, Nicky asks Jenna how she managed to hack the scumbag's phone in the first place.

'Yes, do you know how to hack?' asks Val hopefully.

We are all looking at Jenna in awe, like she is about to reveal herself as some technical genius.

'Well,' Jenna says, smirking, tapping her fingertips together. I remember my doctor did something similar, right before he broke the news that my BMI had entered the obese range. He had then spouted off all the possible side effects; each one more dire than the last. Basically, if the type two diabetes didn't get me, the fatty liver or strain on my heart would.

In light of my terrible news, I walked home crying. I

then proceeded to chomp my way through a pack of six cherry Bakewell tarts while still sobbing and watching body transformations on YouTube, promising myself that would soon be me. Soon, but not that soon, as I was due to have an Indian takeaway for my birthday the following weekend, so no point starting until after, I had kidded myself.

When Jenna is sure she has our undivided attention, she continues to indulge us. 'So, I persuaded my Jason to invite Lewis the shitbag out in town, knowing anyone who goes out with my Jase and his mates will come back bladdered. When Lewis got back home, he was as we expected: completely shit-faced. Passed out cold.'

Jenna, who, like all of us, is several large drinks deep, is really getting into it now, miming Lewis lying on his living room floor, mouth open, dribbling.

'Anyway, we get his phone out of his pocket, and he had one of those fingerprint locks on it, so I said to my mate, "Porsha, babes, you're gonna have to hold his hand up while I try all his fingers." So, she does, but his hands are too clammy, so off she goes to get a tea towel from the kitchen. But she can't find one, so I say, "Mate, just take off his sock. That'll do".

'So then Porsha pulls off his trainer and unpeels his sock and wipes his fingertips with it. After a few goes I try his thumb, and, bingo, we were in! We did put him in the recovery position when we were finished, though Porsha didn't wanna bother. She said, "Fuck him! Leave it to fate!" But I didn't want that on my conscience. It's one thing being a bit sly to help ya mate out, but I'm no monster and she ain't either. She was just pissed off. You know what it's like.'

We nod in a 'we know exactly what it is like' way. I'm aware I'm biting my lip to stop the giggles that are desperate to escape, and everyone else is doing much the same, so I know I am not the only one who finds Jenna's graphic story-telling hilarious.

'Oh, I almost forgot,' said Jenna. 'We also used his quick cash app to send us both money from his bank savings account. Just fifty quid each. I wasn't sure, but Porsha said if the piss-taker can afford the dating site fees he can afford to pay our expenses. So, I said "Yeah. Fuck it! Go on then".

'I bought myself a new black trench. Lovely it is. Zara always does a shit-hot mac. Porsha spent hers on a night out in town where she met her new fella. He's taking her to Disneyland Paris in May. So that's two good things that came out of it.'

Tears of laughter stream down our faces. I know that I should be appalled, but I am awestruck. What a woman! Who wouldn't want Jenna on their team?

CHAPTER 9

'Now I tell you about the worst Monday of my life,' said Yana as she takes some big gulps from her glass and places it back on a silver coaster.

'Well, Simon, my husband, he think that I have poly-cystic ovaries and the lazy thyroid, and that is why I get very big. He thinks this because I tell him this, but it is lie I just made up, so he believe it is not my fault I gained the weight. I think he will be disappointed in me if I tell him the truth, so I hide it.

'I always have curves, but then I meet Simon, and he loves food from my home country very much – kotleti, pirozhki. All his favourites. Delicious but very fattening, so I cook for him, and I eat it too. Then when he go to the work I am missing my sister and mother so I binge eat food. I buy multipack of sausage rolls, crisps, biscuits. You know the type of food at the English supermarket Tesco. I love the tastes, so I eat lots at one go. I say to myself, "Yana, this must stop" but it never stop.

'Then I start to eat secret food when Simon is not at the work. I yearn for these foods very much. So, I wait until he is sleeping. What I do is this. I go downstairs and get all the food from where I hide it in the ironing basket. No chance of Simon finding secrets in there,' she jokes before continuing.

'I remove the wrappers off the foods so there is no rustle rustle, and he does not wake. Then I open many bag of crisps and tip it in a big bowl. Then I hide the wrapper, until Simon leave, and I can put it in the rubbish in the outside bin under other rubbish.'

Yana's eyes scan our faces and, satisfied that none of us is overly shocked or horrified, she carries on. 'After I eat in bed next to him while I read or watch television on my iPad with my headphones in. First I am happy but then after the food is gone and I very depressed and sad. I always then say now I will stop, but I do not stop because I am addict of the food.'

I know exactly what Yana means. The amount of times I have binged and promised myself both before and after that it will be the last time I've lost count of.

Yana pours herself a shot of vodka and carries on. 'Well, I told you all also about the posh old wife of Simon, that she is arranging their son's twenty-fifth?' Yana asks us as she throws back her neat spirit like a seasoned pro.

We all nod and smile encouragingly.

'I panic at thought of coming face to face with her. She is not nice lady but very thin. So I think Simon wish I was also like this so I go on the soup diet. But that did not work. Then I start to swallow fat-binding diet pills that I got online. They send me them from Russia.'

Everyone gasps as I have visions of Yana being duped into taking Christ only knows what.

'You need to be careful with them, mate! My auntie bought some of those once. Didn't sleep for three days, she didn't. My uncle had to rush her up the hospital after she fell off a ladder when she got an urge to clean their guttering out at four in the morning! Turned out she had been sent high purity speed!' said Jenna as Yana nods in agreement.

'Pills of Yana come from Russian doctor. He tell me I have to also do the low-fat diet. I said to him "yes, of course" but I did not.

'Instead, I carry on eating pirozhki and all my secret foods, so I have very bad IBS flare-up. Because of this I knew it was not a good idea when Simon said we will have dinner out on Monday because I had been on and off the toilet all of the morning. But because I am very greedy, I say yes anyway.

'I ordered the double cheeseburger with bacon, curly fries and the coleslaw. I knew it was a big mistake before I had even finished it. My stomach started this weird loud rumbling, and I say to myself, Yana, you're in some big trouble. As much as I tried not to, I let out the fart.

'Simon's face was very shocked; but this is not even the beginning. Then I had the horrible knowledge that it was not just the fart. So, there I am sitting in the busy Frankie and Benny's, knowing in my heart that I had shit myself! I think, Yana you must get to the toilet, so I shuffled with my husband's coat wrapped round my waist. Actually this is lie. I had to hold it in place with my hands because I was too wide for the coat to tie round me.

'Before I shuffled off, I say to Simon, "You now must rush to Asda next door and buy your wife the pair of jogging bottoms, the baby wipes, body spray and the bag for life". I then want to cry when he ask me what size to buy. I have no choice but to tell him the size twenty-two. His face was shocked because he think before this I am the size sixteen. I lie to him, and I cut out tags so he does not see the truth. Now he know.

'So, this is why I want to lose the weight. It does not get worse than having bad accident on yourself in public and husband knowing you have size twenty-two arse.'

We all pulled empathetic 'oh fuck' faces. Poor Yana's putting on a brave face, but we can all tell that it has really affected her. I don't really know what to say. Be too sympathetic and I risk looking patronising. Say too little, she might take offence that I haven't taken an obviously highly traumatising event seriously enough.

'And I thought I had a bad week,' I say in what I hope is a comforting way. Jenna also tries to make Yana feel better, telling her that diet pills are well known for those types of accidents. Val agrees and tells us about a similar story she once read in a *Take A Break* magazine in the hairdressers.

'I have a question,' says Jenna when Yana has perked up and the conversation is more upbeat. 'Why a bag for life, mate?'

Yana flashes a small smile and replies, 'The free bag have holes, and it was to transport my clothes home. I was worried about the spillage.'

Yana manages a throaty laugh, though none of us joins her as her watery eyes give her away. We all try to comfort her, saying it could happen to anyone, and that Simon won't be fazed by it.

'I shit myself in front of Jase when I had Frankie. Honestly, they don't take any notice. My Jase was more worried about getting an exact birth ETA off the midwife so he could arrange to meet his mates in the pub to wet the baby's head!' reassures Jenna.

I know what's coming next before Yana even says it.

'Etta, now you tell us what happened on Friday?'

I feel like a teacher has just asked me to read aloud to the class. I take a deep breath and begin.

CHAPTER 10

'Well, it's a bit embarrassing really,' I mumble, my eyes not quite meeting hers. This tickles Yana, and she breaks out into an infectious giggle. 'Etta, I think you forget that I shit my knickers in family restaurant, and Jenna get her friend's boyfriend very drunk to steal phone, and then she spy on him wearing coat that she buy from Zara with money stolen from man's banking account!'

Yana is laughing now.

'It was a mac, and I didn't wear it to Prezzo's actually,' interjects Jenna comically.

'Sorry, my mistake. It is mac!' chuckles Yana before continuing. 'And Nicky has police injunction for stalking husband of Nicky, who is not now husband of Nicky, and she also have many cat-based panic attacks a day! Have I missed anything, ladies?'

Val raises her hand. 'Yes, you forgot me! The one whose husband was in such a rush to leave her, that he didn't even eat his fish pie; the pie I spent two hours making. He always was an ungrateful bastard!'

They all have a good point. So, everything comes flowing

out. How I regularly have pretend phone conversations in the chip shop and the Chinese on Fridays on my way home from work, so I don't look as greedy as I actually am. How I have no social life or relationship. I even tell them in great detail about seeing Robert in town. How I pulled my hair in frustration, screamed like a maniac by the river, and threw my dinner in the bin. Then I surprise myself even more and divulge further. I tell them all about how my relationship was with Robert. I don't even feel embarrassed.

'I can't remember not feeling like this. Uncomfortable in my own skin, I mean. Since a child, I have always been chubby. I have never felt confident with my body. But my eating really started getting out of control after I had Chloe and I stopped seeing Robert. It was the living alone and knowing what he thought of me that tipped the scales, literally. At first, I was always tired so I ate rubbish to keep myself going. Then in the evenings when Chloe got older and started to go to bed and sleep through, I used to eat to comfort myself, like you, Yana. Not one chocolate bar or a packet of crisps but two or three, or sometimes more. And I started eating lots of takeaways, and I have been doing it ever since. I have put weight on every year since then. I don't have a lot else in my life. I mean, I have my family, but no real friends. Food has been my emotional crutch.

'The friends I did have I grew apart from. Some of them did try, but there is only so many times someone will invite you somewhere. When the answer's always no, they all quite rightly gave up eventually. Maybe I've been a bit depressed,' I say, grimacing at my words. How could I only just be realising this now?

For someone like me, who doesn't share my struggles surrounding my body image, my feelings, or my relationship with food for fear of judgement – and because I haven't had anyone to confide in even if I wanted to – tonight is a revelation. Being able to speak openly has come surprisingly easy to me.

Maybe it is because these are women who understand my plight because they are going through similar. I know they wouldn't dream of judging me, as I wouldn't them. I explain to them how seeing Robert on Friday was what triggered me into losing my shit and deciding to lose weight. For myself, because I want a better life, but also because I want him to want me, and for me to have the upper hand to tell him to piss off, as childish as it is.

It is very liberating. What's the saying? The truth will set you free. And it's true. Me admitting out loud all I have felt and bottled up all these years, and all the shit I have been through with Robert, and acknowledging that I do struggle with food, and why, feels like I have released a stress valve inside me. I feel purged.

'I think men make us all go a bit mad,' says Nicky out of nowhere; no doubt after reflecting on what we have discussed.

'It is so hard, isn't it?' sighs Val sympathetically. 'If Tim had social media, I would be the same as you are, Nic. I mean, it's a bit callous to expect you to move on just like that, after a split from a long-term marriage.'

Jenna accepts an apple sour shot from the tray Yana is strutting around the room with. I watch as she then downs it in one without a flinch, as if it was Evian.

'How long have you been separated from your ex-husband, Nicky?' Yana asks as she hands me a shot glass with 'Ouzo Loves Ya Baby – ZANTE 2017' printed on it. I try and copy everyone else's down-in-one technique but, as it hits my throat, I gag and start to retch.

No one notices though. All eyes are on Nicky, awaiting

her response. By the time she has finished sticking out her bottom lip and sucking her teeth and muttering things to herself like, 'Um, so we had the extension done in twenty ten,' she finally declares, 'About nine years and seven months, I think. Give or take a few weeks.'

I think she is joking at first, and, from the unsure guffaws from the others, I think they do too. We all look sideways at each other, like inquisitive meerkats waiting for Nicky to break into her booming laugh, but it never comes.

Jenna is the first to decide that Nicky isn't joking. 'Bloody hell, Nic! I thought you was going to say last year or something, not nearly a bloody decade! You need to find someone else, mate. Time to move on and get online dating before it seals up babes! If it ain't already!'

Jenna is outspoken, but she has this genuine warmth that makes what she says never sound too harsh.

Before anyone can say any more, Yana declares she is 'dying for the fag' so we all join her on her patio's sunken seating area, despite only Val, Jenna and our host being smokers.

We sit huddled shoulder to shoulder in a circle. I sip my drink while Nicky picks up the conversation we left inside.

'You're right, Jenna, and I would love to meet someone but who would want me?' Nicky gestures down at herself, it all then comes flowing out. It seems her ex is more than a bit of a shit. Two days after their son left for uni, Theodore announced he was moving out.

'I didn't see it coming at the time but, looking back, there were little warning signs that change was afoot. I remember standing mashing potato for a cottage pie a few weeks before, and he had scolded me harshly, saying that there was no need for all the butter I had spooned into the pan and no wonder I was the size I was.

'He had also taken up badminton and had a bit of an

appearance change. New clothes, expensive aftershave – when he had only ever worn Lynx all through our marriage. Then he upgraded the Citroën to a convertible Lexus.'

'That's textbook glow-up,' interjects Jenna.

I have no idea what that means, but I resist asking for fear of interrupting Nic's flow as she continues.

'It was just before Theodore was due to leave for work on a rainy Wednesday morning when he had announced he was leaving me. He told me between slurps of black coffee that I needn't lay a table place for him that evening, as he wouldn't be coming home. Then I saw his wheelie suitcase was in the hall. "I can't take another day with you," he said coldly. "I've fulfilled my obligations to our son, so now it's time to part." I begged him, pleaded with him for reasons why, and for him to reconsider.

'I will always remember the look of disdain when he replied, "My reasons? Take a look in the mirror, Nicola. I can't take the embarrassment any more. I didn't sign up to have Heather Trott as a wife. I don't love you and I haven't for an awfully long time." When I asked him where he planned on staying, he said, "Not that it's any of your concern but Louise has kindly offered to put me up temporarily in her smashing little townhouse."

'Louise was his assistant, the reason Theodore started eating Pret salads and pots of prepared pineapple for lunch, rather than my cheese and onion bloomers and slices of coffee cake that he used to rave about.

'When I asked was something going on with her, do you know he had the cheek to roll his eyes and shout, "That's right, Nicola! Make it everyone else's fault! Louise said you would do this. *You* are the reason I am leaving. You only have yourself to blame."

'That was in late September and, by the December, my son was having Christmas dinner with his dad and his new fiancée Louise.' Nicky paused briefly to take a good slug of her drink before continuing. 'I fucking hate her! She is so smug with her superfoods and Bikram yoga. I mean, what kind of fucking idiot eats sunflower seeds as a treat, unless they're a fucking cockatiel!' she raged, as we all pulled trying not to laugh grimaces at each other. Not because what she has just told us is remotely funny but from the shock of hearing Nic swear. Nicky never swears. She nearly sliced her finger clean off after she trapped it inside a sliding door at work – blood spurting everywhere, there was – and all she said was, 'Oh fudge.'

'He sounds like a right bastard, mate. You're well shot of him. Loads of men would give their right bollock for you,' declares Jenna. 'We're going to pick your confidence and self-esteem off the floor and then, when you're ready, we will help you find someone. A decent bloke who actually deserves to breathe the same air as you.'

I decide I really like Jenna. I was always a bit intimidated by her. Not that she ever gave me reason to be, never having been anything other than chatty and kind. She just has a real glamour puss vibe about her that makes me feel self-conscious. It's a reflection on me, not her. All the oldies at work say what a ringer for the movie icon Grace Kelly she is. It's true. Jenna has a Roman nose, a symmetrical face that is framed perfectly by honey-blonde hair extensions, and her signature winged eyeliner always makes her look really sophisticated. But it's not just that. Some people just have that aura that makes you gravitate towards them, and Jenna has that in bucket loads.

I think back to the first message Val sent to us, though, which was only a few days ago, but now seems like an age. Something she said replays in my head. The part when she commented that we all seem so happy and full of life, and she's right. We are all walking, talking examples of why appearances can be deceptive. How easy it is to draw conclusions about someone.

Each morning this week after Val's husband left, she got up, plastered a smile on her face, gave herself a good dousing of her signature Youth Dew and braved coming into work. Inside she was falling apart, but none of us guessed.

And then there's Jenna, who at eleven stone feels as uncomfortable as Nicky does with ten stone to lose. In life we should never assume or make comparisons.

We all have our struggles. Assumptions shouldn't be made based on a bubbly personality or a flattering haircut. Because that doesn't mean that they have any fewer issues than the next person.

I decide in that moment that my decision to lose weight has to be with a goal of improving my relationship with myself.

I am doing this for me. The rest will come after.

CHAPTER 11

Val chuckles at the sight of Jenna, who is waving her arms around like a loon as we make our way back inside. 'Oh my God! I've just had a thought!' Jenna shouts. 'Etta! Your ex is Robert Ward?'

Jenna resembles an overexcited performing seal now, bursting to get her words out. 'Well, I can't believe I didn't realise before, but I know Robert! He will be at our wedding! Jase's cousin went to school with him. They all play football together. This is just so brilliant! My wedding can be our target. We will diet, support each other and meet up to exercise and have weigh-ins. Then, at the wedding, you will feel a million dollars and, Etta, I can introduce you to Robert like I don't know you know each other, and we can watch him drool!' rambles Jenna, who then turns to the others.

'And you! You will look a million dollars as well! For your stepson's party!' she hiccups to Yana, then points at Val and Nic.

'And you two won't have to settle for nights in with your cats and chats with boring neighbours because you will be too busy being fabulous and buying dresses for our nights

73

out. All slinky numbers because you will both be back at your wedding day weights!'

When we had been talking about our ideal weights, Jenna said that hers was about nine stone. I'd said I didn't know what weight I was aiming for as I had never been less than eleven stone since I was fourteen. In a dream world I would be a size 8 to 10, though, in the real world where I could have the occasional KFC and still look in a mirror without having the urge to walk into oncoming traffic, I guessed a size 12 would be amazing.

Val and Nicky both agreed that their ideal weight would be the same as the day they got married. However, Nicky had added after that she would be happy 'just to see my toes again.'

I find myself channelling my inner nodding Churchill bulldog as Jenna gushes, 'Nearer the time I will start to get my Jason to mention to Rob how lovely looking and nice Jenna's friend is and how he will introduce you at the wedding. Imagine his face when he sees it's you!'

'It is important if we do this, we do it for ourselves, to make us feel better. Agreed?' Yana said when we are all back in her lounge.

'One hundred per cent. Not for anyone else; especially a man. We can get our revenge but that can't be our main driving force. That said, I would also love to see my ex's face if I get slim!' Nicky adds.

'I think now we make the plans,' Yana says, handing a notebook and pen that she has retrieved from the drawer in her coffee table to an eager Nicky.

Nic wears her glasses like my old schoolteacher, her big bulky tortoiseshell frames suspended from a metal chain around her neck. We watch as she unbuttons her black knitted cardi and uses her T-shirt hem to clean her lenses.

'I love Carole Baskin!' enthuses Jenna as she spots Nicky's

T-shirt. It's a shocking shade of orange, like men who dig up roads wear. 'Hey, all you cool cats and kittens' is printed in bold black writing with photos of baby tigers along the bottom.

Nicky looks at Jenna blankly.

'The T-shirt. It's from *Tiger King* on Netflix, isn't it?' Jenna says, noticing Nicky's confused expression.

'No idea, sweetheart. My son got me it as a gift because I love cats.'

We nod, giggling. Of course, he did.

Nicky then settles her glasses into place on the end of her nose, and scrawls across the front 'A MOMENT ON THE LIPS DIET CLUB' and announces, 'To remind us the two minutes scoffing isn't worth the lifetime of feeling how we do now.'

'Right,' I say, 'let's all think back to when we were slimmer. What did we do differently to now?'

No one can really remember because it's been so long. Eventually, we look towards Jenna.

'Come on, Jenna. Have a think. You're our best bet,' said Val.

'You were small before kids so how you stay so slim?' asks Yana hopefully.

Jenna has a little think. 'Well, it was the hokey-cokey really. I loved a bit at the weekends, so I basically fasted without meaning to but, after the boys came along, I stopped all that. So yeah, it was that for me to be honest.'

Nicky narrows her eyes at Jenna then at us over her glasses, clearly more than a bit confused. I then hear her mumble to Val, 'Is she talking about dancing or the drink?'

Val can't answer for laughing and Yana pulls an about to burst of laughter face, and says, 'I think that none of us will afford the drug habit, Jenna.'

Jenna nods and replies, 'Yeah, I know. Shit, ain't it?'

The penny finally drops for Nicky, who looks horrified as she puts her pen down and stutters, 'No, we can't do that! I read in the *Telegraph* that these drug cartels use rat poison now, to bulk out their class As. If my cats ever got hold of it I'd never forgive myself!'

I reassure Nicky that she doesn't need to panic as we definitely won't be staging *Trainspotting Three: the Care Assistants' Edition* anytime soon.

We spend a further hour googling ways to lose weight. There are so many diets – keto, fasting, blood group, shakes, soups – the list is endless. Between us, we have tried them all. And as we are all no further forward, they clearly are not for us.

It turns out, all we need to do is work out how many calories we need a day to maintain our weight as we are and then eat less than that amount to lose weight. You don't even have to exercise, although it is advised as it will help us to tone up, and the physical activity will also burn more calories; meaning you'll be in a bigger calorie deficit and lose weight faster.

And we can eat whatever we want as long as we count the calories! So, all these diets where you can only eat meat and steamed veg or drink juices are a waste of time, and are basically an expensive way of cutting calories.

'I don't believe this! If I'd known this before I would never have given up bread!' rants Jenna.

We come across an app where you can put in your current weight, age, activity level and your target weight. Then it tells you how many calories you can eat a day to achieve your goal. It also has a list of every food and drink going, so you can search and add what you have as you go. It keeps a tally and lets you know how many calories you have left so it's easy not to go over target. Even Val, who isn't great with technology, manages to work it under Jenna's supervision.

We agree that we're going to not get too caught up on the calories. Our priority has to be eating healthily. Jenna shows us some portion plates on Amazon. They are divided up to show the correct portion sizes for each food group. I know just from looking at them I eat far too many carbs. The plates say half the plate should be veggies or salad, one quarter should be protein – the lean meat, fish and eggs – and the other quarter should be carbs: the pastas, rice, potatoes and bread. We all order one. This will help us make sensible choices with our calories. Our diet cannot be just about restricting; we have to re-educate ourselves on portions, healthy choices, and self-control when we do have treats.

We also decide we are going to sign up for some fitness classes, and aim for ten thousand steps a day – the recommended daily amount for an adult. That sounds like some serious hard work, and fizzy drinks are going to make way for two litres of water a day instead. At least we are all in it together.

CHAPTER 12

In a moment of drunken madness, we all decide to have one last hurrah. Yana digs out a menu to the local late night kebab house and places an order. We decide on a fifteen-inch pizza to share before we start afresh tomorrow. I know, I know. Great start! But don't despair of us yet, as none of us even ended up with a slice of deep pan meaty max with extra pepperoni in the end – because it never arrived.

Well, technically that isn't true. It did arrive; it just never made it past the threshold. We had forgotten all about it, you see. Well, until the next day when Jenna forwarded us some voicemails. The voicemails, all four of them, were from an increasingly angry takeaway delivery man, who was trying to deliver our food. You can clearly hear him banging hard on the front door with us all in the background absolutely murdering songs on Yana's karaoke machine.

I giggle, hearing Nicky's version of 'Wild Women Do'. Then I cringe. There is something unspeakably awful about hearing your own voice back on a recording. 'That's my line. Stop! That's my line!' I hear myself shrieking.

By the time I have finished screeching out, Ace of Base

'All That She Wants', only breaking off to shout at the others again for joining in, I am wincing. I then close my eyes in mortification hearing myself bellow, 'She is me! This is my song! I live a lonely life. Robert Ward never loved me! But he will wish he had!' while the others whoop and laugh.

Good grief! I must have been absolutely shit-faced! Karaoke is my worst nightmare. But not yesterday, because, last night with the help of about twenty gallons of booze, I was Jenny Berggren, which is why we didn't hear the door. For us all to forget about a deep pan stuffed crust, we must have been having a really amazing time.

We are going to be good for each other.

CHAPTER 13

The following morning, the alarm hits like a hammer to the head. I take a big gulp of water from the glass at the side of my bed. Hangovers are so much worse in your thirties, which is unfair really. When you're twenty, you have all day to nurse yourself. Not that you appreciate it at the time, as you're lying on the sofa downing Monster Munch and full-fat Coke and thinking you're so hard done by. It's only when you have kids that you realise what a luxury being able to wallow all day was. I force myself to shower, dress, and make myself a coffee.

The rich earthy smell from the machine – the same one that usually makes my heart sing – makes me dry retch today. I pour my mugs contents down the sink. Despite brushing my teeth twice, and using mouthwash, I am sure I can still taste last night's apple sour shots, all six or seven of them. I lost count. Urgh! I resist the temptation of the chocolate drawer in the fridge, reaching for a banana instead, to eat later on when I can face it, and head off to collect Chloe from Grandad's for school.

Chloe greets me with her usual gappy-toothed beam. Her

hair has been lovingly plaited in pigtails, red ribbons to match her uniform tied in delicate bows at the ends. Pam is standing in a mint-green pencil skirt suit, her blonde tousled cropped do is freshly tonged, her favourite coral lippy glistens. Pam smiles as she pauses using a unicorn cookie cutter on ham sandwiches when I walk in.

'Morning,' I say with a yawn. 'Thanks again for this, Pamela,' I add.

Pam waves off my thanks. 'No problem, darling. We had a wonderful time. I got ready just in case you were late,' she adds, as she clocks me looking at her outfit.

'Ah, I thought you looked very smart. Is Grandad about?'

'Thank you. I found it on the internet. It's a Lady Di Chanel inspired recreation. All the way from America!' she replies proudly and then tilts her head towards the open back door. 'Your grandfather's probably in the garden – not smoking,' Pam says with a slight hint of humour.

Just as we are leaving, I hear the urgent clip-clop of her nude court shoes. 'Henrietta? Gosh, I nearly forgot! Are we still on for our power walk later?' Pam asks, her eyes meeting mine hopefully.

Christ! That is the last thing I feel like doing but I can hardly say no now, can I? Not with all the effort she puts in for Chloe. I'm going to have to, even if she trots out in her Penny from *Dirty Dancing* replica red leotard and gold belt. I nod enthusiastically and agree to see her later.

On the way back from the school, I catch up with my WhatsApp messages.

Jenna – 09:26

Christ, I feel like I've been hit with a shovel lol

· · ·

81

Val – 09:31

I don't feel too bad. I'm in Sainsbury's stocking up on healthy foods lol who knew that a slice of bread has 120 calories lol no more four rounds of toast for me in the mornings I've got myself some bran flakes and fruit ha-ha much better for me as well judging by the nutrition section on the app. I've also picked up some new scales I will bring them to work tomorrow so we can all do our weigh-in. There are tikka chicken breasts on special; does everyone like them in pittas? I'm making lunch for us all tomorrow! And I've set up my calorie tracker app (thanks Jenna). I'm on 1,300 a day. I would have had that before lunch usually lol

Nicky – 09:39

I have just grilled some bacon and am having it with tomatoes and poached eggs. Lean protein and veggies to start the day! Or is a tomato a fruit? I never did know. Either way, new beginnings, ladies! XX and I'd a love chicken pitta thanks Val x I am on 1,450 calories a day.

Yana – 09:40

I have 1400 calorie a day; I think this be okay. Today I make Simon sausages and fried egg, I have boiled egg and one bread roll with pepper. I eat everything, Val. I am not the fussy eater, thank you.

Jenna – 09:52

Just been in Argos and got myself a step tracker. Thanks for sorting lunch out, Val; I will do Wednesday. Home to paradise now. It looks like a bomb site. Jason thinks when he is looking after the kids that's all he can do: no toys picked up; no hoovering; no dishwasher loaded, or God forbid put on. He left wet washing in the machine last night as he didn't know 'how to get the door thingy open' – man-child! Xx I am on 1,200 a day. Going to make sure I hit my protein carbs and veg target – even if I go a little over calories. Make sure you all do the same. A few extra calories will be fine. Nutrition is the most important thing.

Etta – 09:54

Hello, I felt like I needed an ambulance this morning but feeling okay now. I am so tired though and I've only done 3,000 steps according to my phone. I'm waiting for Amazon to deliver my tracker, but I have to walk with my step-nan later so will hit the 10,000. I have had a banana so far. I've downloaded the app as well and I am also on 1,200 xx I usually eat that in crisps and snacks lol and one takeaway is probably way more so no more for me. I forgot to say I read on the app that we have to track everything even down to milk in drinks, ketchup etc. It said those little extras can easily add up to well over our daily allowance if we don't, and then we won't lose. Xx And agreed, Jenna – we must all hit our carb, protein and veg quota each day, especially now we are going to be so active!

Nicky – 10:45

I've been reading about fakeaways – it's all the foods like Burger King and Nando's, but lower calorie home recipe versions. Shall we have dinner at mine this Friday? I'll cook us a pretend Nando's. Ha-ha, it has heaps of lean protein chicken, and corn on the cob all grilled and can add some salad and make homemade wedges?...I have switched to red milk after seeing how many Cals are in blue. I drink too many teas to have blue lid any more! X

Yana – 11:01

I never go to the Nando's, so I am excited to eat this Nicky xx

Val – 11:21

Can't wait for that already lol although I haven't ever been to Nando's either. Agreed this diet has to be about us teaching ourselves to be healthy not to starve and deprive. If we feel hungry and we have had all our calories, we should have something anyway like fruit, cooked chicken, or yoghurt? Or we will just end up gorging on rubbish.

Jenna – 11:22

Will catch up later, the housework calls xx the extras are a killer if we don't log them, things like veg oil – watch that when you're cooking stuff, it's 45 cals a spoonful, I think! I have a George Foreman grill; I'm going to stop frying steak, bacon, sausages etc and start grilling. No oil needed and all the fat drains off. They are ace xx and agreed, Val, no starving ourselves. I am feeling so motivated. Having the support of the other women is going to make a real difference. We will keep each other on track. Very exciting times.

CHAPTER 14

Pamela greets me while hanging on the side of her Ford Galaxy, as she stretches out her calves. Shit, I think to myself. She's limbering up like people do at the start of the marathon. I hope to God that she isn't thinking we are going to jog, or worse, run. I get out of breath taking my ironing upstairs.

At least she is well covered though; not a thong leotard in sight. Today's outfit is actually quite demure: a light-purple top and a matching pair of yoga pants. Granted they are skin tight, and the top has fluorescent stripes running down each arm and around the bust area, but at least it is long sleeved, and she hasn't got her leg warmers on.

'Where are your lights, darling?' Pam asks me, as she places her hands on her hips and starts moving them round in an exaggerated circular motion like Chloe does when she is hula hooping.

I frown. 'My what?'

'Li-gh-ts, darling,' she repeats, slowly pointing to her upper arm and opposite thigh. 'To-Stop-You-Getting-Run-Over,' Pam says, talking to me like some of the Elm Lodge residents' families speak to them, as though they are two years old and English isn't their first language. The lights are then switched on to quick flash mode to emphasise her point.

'We'll be on the pavements, won't we?' I ask.

Inwardly I am panicked. Oh my God! She is taking me running on the roads, I think, as Pam flashes me a patronising smile and replies, 'Yes, Henrietta, but we have to think of short-visioned cyclists and the drunk drivers, darling!'

Oh great. 'Sorry, I didn't know I needed any. Shall I use my phone torch?' I ask half-heartedly, as Pam shakes her head and starts tugging at the Velcro strap on her upper arm.

'Here, for goodness' sake! You can have this one, although you'll probably have to wear it on your wrist, darling. It's a size extra small.'

I don't want to wear it, but I know it is going to happen so there is no point in me protesting. Pick your battles, as my grandad always says, and so, I just go with it.

'Thanks, Pam,' I say in my best upbeat voice.

Pam looks around quickly and then sharply scolds me. 'Henrietta! *The neighbours*! You know I tolerate Pam behind closed doors but not in public, darling!'

'Sorry, I forgot. Are we not taking the dogs?' I ask.

Pam gives me a brisk shake of her head. 'No, Charles has just eaten a jam roly-poly and custard, so he is digesting.'

I smirk at the thought of the barrel of a corgi in a stodge coma.

'Did Diana not fancy it?' I manage through giggles.

'She was offered but she hasn't really got a sweet tooth. I've left her with a diced pork pie, watching *Ice Road Truckers* with Chloe and your grandfather.'

I am about to say I meant did she not fancy a walk, not a jam dessert, when Pamela takes one look at her fit watch and says, 'Right. Anyway, come on, darling. Let's get going. I need to pass number twenty-four before she leaves for work. Sick Karen will be when she sees what I am wearing. It's from QVC's in-house French designer Coq au Vock.' Pam pronounces Coq au Vock like she is reading off a menu that she isn't familiar with. She then scans my face waiting for my reaction. Clearly, I should be hugely impressed. Then she lowers her voice, but even in her stage whisper you can hear the obvious glee.

'She's a size sixteen now, Karen at number twenty-four. I saw the tag of her cardigan at club last Tuesday. I couldn't believe it when I saw it. She tells everyone she's a twelve! And guess what else? It was unbranded! She'd tried to convince us all that it was from Wallis. I knew it wasn't at the time. I'd said to Lisa, "That isn't Wallis. No way, Jose", because Wallis is quality. I mean, you *know* Wallis when you see it, don't you?'

I nod and pull my best *definitely* face even though I wouldn't have a clue, never having been in Wallis apart from at Christmas when I pop in to buy gift cards for Pamela. I used to pick her out something from Dorothy Perkins or Marks and Spencer's, but she always used to open it and say, 'Oh, lovely. Thank you so much, darling,' – before casually enquiring – 'Have you got the receipt, darling, just in case it doesn't fit?' Nothing ever fit, so vouchers are easier.

'Anyway,' Pam continues as she speeds along, looking like she is playing charades and attempting to mime a champion skier – exaggerated arms, long strides, determined expression. I pant along next to her, 'Karen will love what I'm wearing because she adores lavender. I'm not really a lavender-coloured clothing person but I saw it when it was on as 'today's special value' and thought to myself, Pamela, Karen would love that. Then, when I saw she wouldn't be able to buy it because French couture doesn't believe in plus sizes, I thought, gosh, how marvellous, I have to have it just to see Karen's face.'

Turns out powerwalking wasn't too bad after all. Pamela felt her friend's reaction was acceptable. I personally thought Karen's so-called 'crestfallen face' was more one of bemusement, but I kept it to myself; not wanting to spoil Pam's jubilant mood. Even the 'walk like you mean it' playlist that was blasting out from her pocket speaker the whole way, so we could 'be motivated and energised!' wasn't that bad.

Admittedly I did get a bit embarrassed when Pam had started to do a one-woman Mexican wave on the spot as Rod Stewart 'Do Ya Think I'm Sexy?' belted out, while we waited for the build-up of cars who were indicating to go into the Morrisons petrol station and blocking our way to move.

'Keep moving, Henrietta!' she had encouraged at the top of her lungs. 'That's it! Keep the tempo, darling! You're burning fat!'

I know that people were laughing. They must have been. I mean, I would have been, but I just kept my eyes on the ground and focused on the thought of being at Jenna's wedding and feeling like a new woman, seeing Robert and him double-taking at me. Those thoughts give me massive motivation.

Plus, I did feel great after, and I burned 460 calories.

When I had stopped panting like a dog that had just been rescued from a hot car and was sitting at the table in the sun lounge, aka the conservatory, with my roasted chicken breast pieces, mashed potato and heaps of carrots, which I'd brought round in Tupperware for tea, my grandad had asked me, 'Did you enjoy your songs?'

Turns out Pam had spent all morning joining Spotify, and making a playlist that she thought I would like, in the hope that I would enjoy myself and agree to go with her again.

I felt really bad then for being so negative, even though I had only thought it all in my head and not actually said it to her face. I've agreed to walking twice a week from now on. To celebrate, Pam is ordering me my own flashing arm light, in 'size extra-large, possibly even double extra-large – just to be on the safe side, darling!'

CHAPTER 15

The first time I saw Elm Lodge residential home, despite it being a foggy, damp winter morning, it took my breath away. Tucked away on a quiet side street a few minutes' walk from St Ives high street, the imposing Edwardian building is nestled behind impenetrable conifers. There it stood in all its symmetrical glory, in the middle of its mature, pruned gardens.

The beautiful sash windows offer residents a ringside seat of the changing seasons, the comings and goings, and hours of entertainment watching the families of squirrels who raid the bird tables, from both their en suite bedrooms and the various day rooms at their disposal.

Residential homes, even the posh ones like Elm Lodge with its original varnished parquet flooring and the Laura Ashley drapes that frame the humongous bay windows, have a certain smell, which all the airing, carpet powders and air fresheners in the world cannot mask. Chloe was nine months old when I was offered the job over six years ago now. I was in my mid-twenties. As you already know Chloe's dad (bastard) and I had parted ways a few months before.

I will be honest with you; Elm Lodge wasn't my first choice but I was desperate to get out from under my grandad's and Pam's feet. Robert hadn't contributed a penny since she was born (double bastard) and I couldn't find anything else that could offer full-time hours, alongside the flexibility to fit around me caring for Chloe.

Saying taking a job as a care assistant wasn't my first choice is an understatement; it was more my only choice. I hated it for a good few months. Like properly dreaded it every day. The smell, the bodily fluids, the close intimate contacts. I felt permanently awkward and out of my depth. I remember Pam waving me off each day, my chubby rosy-cheeked cherub on her hip, my brave face crumbling as soon as I got out of sight.

I would plod the rest of the way there, biting my lip in an attempt to halt the tears burning my eyes while wishing I didn't need the money so much, so I could just go home to my baby. But life isn't always about what you want, so I stuck it out and, over time, it became easier as I became one of the team.

It was when I started to get to know the people I was caring for that I stopped dreading going in and began enjoying my shifts. The residents make the job, really. You grow to care about them as much as your own family. Like Mrs Platt, our retired school head teacher, who joined us after struggling to live alone; a gentle soul who has educated many people in this town, including Nicky, who often tells us what a lovely kind woman she was to her during her not-very-pleasant school years.

Then there is Alf, who believes he is here, not as a resident, but to observe and report back to Special Branch HQ. Alf was, until his disease took hold, a Royal Mail postie, and a lover of jokes. Even now he has the most sarcastic sense of humour going. I began to realise how much my help meant to not only the residents but also their families.

Rose, a quiet lady, joined us just before last Christmas and has a devoted daughter, who visits as often as she can. A month or so after we settled Rose in, her daughter pulled us aside to hand over a tin of home-baked cakes. 'Just a little thanks to you all,' she said, welling up as Jenna gave her a hug. 'My mum tells me how kind you all are to her. Every time we chat, she sings all your praises, and it means so much to our family. It has been so hard on all of us taking the decision for her to move into a home. We felt so much guilt, my husband and I, but we just couldn't manage having her with us, with the children and us both working full-time. Thanks to you all I can sleep at night, knowing she is well looked after and settled.'

Ageing isn't a choice; it comes to us all. It's hard on the residents, but often it is even harder for their loved ones, who feel powerless standing by watching it happen.

Val summed it up perfectly when I hadn't long started and she saw I was struggling. 'Sweetheart, just care for everyone with the same dignity and respect you would want the most precious person in your life to receive, and you will never go far wrong.'

Following that advice, it turned out, wasn't hard. In fact, it soon became second nature. They have a way, our oldies, as we affectionately call them out of earshot, of capturing a little piece of your heart. Each and every one of them – even the grumpy ones. And that is what makes the rubbish pay and feeling undervalued by the managers worth it. I love my job now. I stay for the residents and everyone I work with. All of them are brilliant. Well, apart from June. June's a bit of a dick.

June is the registered nurse and daytime manager, and doesn't she let us know it! Every morning she holds a staff meeting fifteen minutes BEFORE we are due to start work and expects us there promptly, so she can hold court. June speaks *at* us, not to us; much like a head teacher to a bunch of naughty ten-year-olds. 'Girls! Quieten down please!' is her usual greeting, as she puts her index finger to her lips.

Today was no different. 'Right, a few things on this lovely Tuesday morning. Firstly, on Friday, one of you didn't remove a tea tray from the day room before you left for the day,' said June, pausing briefly to pull her well-used 'I despair of you' face. 'You don't need me to remind you of our procedures. Just ensure that no tea trays are left in future. Tea trays are your responsibility.'

I hear someone mutter under their breath. 'Along with everything else.'

'What if the resident is still having their tea and I'm leaving then,' challenges Jenna with a smirk.

'Then you kindly pass this information on to the next shift and have them sign the handover comments, to confirm they have received this information to cover you should there be any backlash,' replied June whilst flashing a strained smile that didn't quite meet her eyes.

'Backlash! Are you winding me up? It's a tea tray, June, not someone laying on the floor with a broken hip. Chill out a bit will ya?' goads Jenna.

Yana catches my eye, holds up her step tracker and whispers, 'I do four thousand five hundred and ninety steps.'

I give her a thumbs up.

June gives us a purse-lipped look. 'Next item. There is some unrest regarding the new menu. The chef and Anika will not budge on the planned meals, but the residents are a little hesitant to try new things. So, it's your job to encourage them. And to get them to fill in the menu choice forms before two p.m. today for the week.'

June then scoops up a load of menu forms and dumps

them in front of poor Val. 'A lot are refusing to select their meals now, under the influence of a few of the usual suspects.

'Lastly, I'll be in a meeting most of the day so, Val, if you can hold the fort.' June heads towards the door and Val doesn't even bother to reply. We all know this is more of a statement than a question anyway. It's what happens every day. June tells us all the problems, then she disappears 'in a meeting' while Val does everything June is paid to do, and the rest of us run around like headless chickens as we are effectively a staff member down.

The most outrageous part of it all is that Val is a qualified nurse in her own right. She spent all her child-bearing years working part time in the local GP surgery then gave it up after pressure from her husband to concentrate on her boys. Tim had a fancy job in finance by then and they didn't need the money. About nine years ago now, Val decided she needed something to occupy her – a purpose – and, deciding she didn't fancy reapplying for her nursing pin, she started working here. Little did she know she would end up working full-time hours doing the job of someone no more qualified than her, for half the money.

'Meeting with Facebook and her kettle more like, the lazy cow,' sniggers Jenna as June opens the office door.

I think for a split second that June heard the sarky comment when she pauses and swings back round to face us.

'Oh, and one more thing, girls, there is a bit of a problem with the television room.' June drops this in casually, while not quite meeting any of our eyes. This is not a slight problem, as she well knows. She then blurts the rest out as quickly as possible. 'The remote has gone missing, and it needs to be found before *This Morning* starts. I am not sure if you've all remembered but it's Holly's fortieth birthday today and the residents are getting slightly agitated and uptight that they're going to miss it. Eve's granddaughter has provided some banners and a triple layer cake for them all to celebrate the big occasion and everyone's dressing up in their best. So, the remote needs to be found, like, now.'

When we ask how another remote has gone walkabout, June fills us in that the golden girls have accused Rose of taking it. 'They claim it is all part of a revenge plot in retaliation for them excluding her from the flower arranging.'

This isn't good.

'Fucking great day we're going to have if we don't find it,' moans Jenna.

'The remote we're using now is fourth replacement. There are no more,' Yana says to a shrugging June. The dismissive shrug translates to 'not my problem'. The remotes at Elm Lodge go walkabout more often than the complimentary toiletries in posh hotels.

'Why did they do that? Exclude her, I mean. They are so fucking nasty sometimes,' said Jenna disapprovingly.

'Rose accidentally spent a penny whilst sitting on the oasis bases,' said Nicky, who is still midway through explaining what florist oasis is to a confused Jenna, when June rudely speaks over her.

'Right. Anyway, I will leave all that with you. Okay, girls. You know where I am if you need me, but only if you really need me. I mean my door is always open but make sure you ask Val first as I am extremely busy. Any questions?'

Jenna raises her hand. 'Yes, mate, just a quick one.'

June's eyes narrow when she hears the word 'mate'. I cough to suppress my laughter. 'Did you say Holly Willoughby is forty today?'

June purses her lips and replies with an agitated, 'I did, Jenna, yes. Is that all?'

Jenna shakes her head in disbelief. 'Fuck me. She don't look a day over thirty. I bet she's had at least ten mils of filler to look that unhaggard with being a mum especially.'

We found the remote in the nick of time in the end and Rose's name was cleared in the process. Alf was a bit reluctant to hand over his 'satellite phone' but there is always a deal to be had with him. Jenna's tortoiseshell hair clip was the winning bargaining tool; aka a 'hidden spy cam'. Alf had promptly clipped it on to his pinstripe tie and returned to his leather chair and, when I checked back half an hour later, I found him settled back into his large print edition of *From Russia With Love*, tartan blanket over his knees, a hint of rainbow sponge cake in his bristly moustache.

Usually, us staff would all have a crafty slice each of the leftover cake. But not today. We all shared sliced apple pieces and Snack a Jacks. The caramel ones are lovely. I am going to get some for after dinner when I want something sweet.

'I've left two containers for you and Nicky in the fridge, hon,' said Val as we passed each other in the corridor. 'We've eaten ours already. Go grab your half hour now. Nicky's already in there. The calories are three hundred and seventy – including the mayo, the blush pear, and the Space Raider crisps. Fifty-nine calories a bag they are! What a bargain!'

When our shift finishes, we all crowd into the laundry room.

'Right, let's get this over with,' says Val, placing the new bathroom scales on the tiled floor and passing Jenna our A Moment on the Lips notebook. Nicky takes off her fleece, steps out of her Crocs and announces she will go first. 'I'll probably break them and save you all from your goes!' she jokes as she gulps, takes a big intake of breath and looks down. Twenty-two stone and two pounds appears on the display screen. Jenna logs it.

'Get a good look at that number, Nic, because it's the last time you'll be seeing it,' says Val supportively.

Nicky nods and steps off without further comment.

I go next. I'm expecting to see around fourteen and a half stone, which, when you're as short as me, is bad. I should be around eight and a half to just under ten stone. I blink and feel a stab to my stomach as the dial stops flicking through various digits, taking its time to make its mind up. Then I'm left staring at my weight. Fifteen stone eight pounds. 'I thought I was nowhere near that much! Fuck my life!' I say.

I feel like crying.

'You'll soon get that off. I thought you was going to be about thirteen, mate. You carry it well,' said Jenna.

She's lying, but I appreciate her trying to make me feel better.

Jenna then hands the book to me and has her turn. At eleven stone three, she has a lot less to lose than the rest of us. She tells us again that her aim is to be nine stone or just under before her wedding and seems quite upset that she's gone over eleven stone. I can't help thinking I wish I were her weight now.

Val weighs in at fifteen stone exactly; she wants to get down to twelve. She's incredibly positive, saying, 'We will all end up where we need to be. Let's just enjoy getting there together.'

At first, her positivity rubs off on Yana. 'I have no care of what it says because today we are the heaviest we ever will be again.'

It's short-lived though. As soon as the numbers settle, Yana is flabbergasted. 'This scale must not be working! I'm five feet six inch tall. How can this be? This much too much!'

We grimace, feeling upset for Yana. We watch helplessly as she steps off the scales, removes her watch and work lanyard, repositions the scales a few inches away and steps back on.

The reading is identical. Seventeen stone ten pounds.

Yana says nothing more. Nicky gives her a hug and I pass her jumper and shoes back to her. The only way to sum up Yana's expression is shell shock, like the people you see on TV shows when they have just been told someone they love has been in a serious accident.

'I just don't understand. I know I have been eating a lot of food but I'm over seventeen stone. I knew I'd got big, but I didn't think I'd got that big,' said Yana, wiping away her tears.

I know how she feels; I didn't think that I was this big either. 'Come on, let's not dwell on it,' I say, despite feeling much the same. 'We're all where we are. We just need to go forward now and get it off.'

I am force a smile.

Jenna tries to be helpful by adding, 'And we will have lost some already! Possibly a good few pounds. The first few days it always flies off!'

Probably not the best comfort telling someone who's having a breakdown about their current weight that they were probably even heavier a few days ago. Luckily Yana, who always manages to find the humour in any situation, starts to chuckle. 'Bloody hell, Jenna! Do not get the job manning phone lines at the Samaritan charity for suicidal people, will you? You would be very bad.' Yana is properly laughing now as she says, 'Ladies, I just realise this means I am nearly four stones heavier than my husband. For him this must be like doing the sex with dairy cow. I now think I know why Simon has very bad back. I squash him!'

So, now we have faced our reality, we all have our goals:

- Me: Current weight 15 stone 8 lbs; Goal weight 9 stone (we think I want to be a size 12).
- Yana: Current weight 17 stone 10 lbs; Goal weight 11 stone.

- Val: Current weight 15 stone; Goal weight 12 stone.
- Jenna: Current weight 11 stone 3 lbs; Goal weight 8 stone 10 lbs (but happy to get to 9).
- Nicky: Current weight 22 stone 2 lbs; Goal weight 14 stone (may change as she gets nearer her goal).

So, there we have it. We have the diet and exercise plan. We have weighed in.

Let the fun begin.

PART II
MAIN COURSE

CHAPTER 16

*Friday 3rd April, Evie Cottage, Farm Drove, Hemingford Gray,
Cambridgeshire*

I went to bed at seven-thirty last night, on the basis that, the
further from the kitchen I am, the less likely I am to binge.
Only because I am marginally lazier than greedy. Therefore I
can rarely be bothered to go back down to get snacks.

Yana hasn't had a good week either. 'I just can't stop
eating the secret food,' she'd despaired to us all on a WhatsApp voice note this evening. 'I know I'm very massive and
the delicious foods is why, but I just cannot stop it. Last
night I had this massive urge to eat a whole pack of Wagon
Wheels marshmallow flavour. I felt guilty for letting my
group ladies down. I just couldn't stop myself.'

As a group we decided that we are all culprits of this to
some degree. Night-time is the window where I really
struggle too. I went over calories yesterday. I inhaled a
Bakewell Slice almost on autopilot. At least it was just one,
though. Before it would have been the whole packet. I

managed to stop myself. I went upstairs and brushed my teeth and ran myself a bath, until the urge to binge passed.

Tonight we decided we are going to do a junk food amnesty. Give away what we have and stop buying our 'trigger foods', as Nicky calls them. They are basically anything in a packet or pastry: crisps, biscuits, sausage rolls, cakes, chocolate bars and – in Nicky's case – fresh tiger bread slathered in Kerrygold butter. We are just not going to buy them or, when we do, just enough for that day.

Jenna and I will find this harder because we have young kids and they expect a constant stream of snacks, but maybe having yoghurts and fruit in place of bags of Wotsits and handfuls of chocolate digestives will do the kids good as well. Later on me and Jenna ended up deciding we would still buy snacks in multipacks, after all, as it is cheaper to buy in bulk than individually, and neither of us exactly have money to burn. I am going to leave them at Grandad and Pam's, and Jenna is going to leave hers at her mum's. Then we will just collect what we need daily for the kids' lunch boxes and our (calorie-counted) treats. I am hoping this new plan will help us all, on the basis that we can't eat what we don't have.

Today I have had:

- One slice of wholemeal toast with Country Life (I can't stomach the ultra-low-fat spreads) with scrambled egg and a banana.
- Jenna made our lunch today of turkey salad wraps, a packet of Snack a Jacks and a Pink Lady apple.
- Two tangerines for a snack when I got in (I wanted to demolish a packet of chocolate Hobnobs).

- For supper, Pamela made lean lamb loin, grilled on my new George Foreman, together with steamed broccoli, new potatoes, carrots and three tablespoons of mint sauce lamb gravy (yep, measuring gravy is a thing now!).

I have been pleasantly surprised because I haven't felt hungry at all. Using the portion plate has helped me a lot, as I am filling half my plate with veg and also realising that I didn't need twenty new potatoes and four lamb chops in one sitting.

Pam gave me her old steamer today. It's great. You can have a lot of new potatoes in place of a small handful of chips; more filling and loads better for you. Plus, it's easy because you can bung it all in and then just grill the meat. I am going to try and steam fish in it this weekend. I cannot say I am enjoying eating breakfast, but it's better than shovelling a Twix in my gob mid-morning because I'm suddenly famished.

Val's knee is playing up, so she is going to do some gentle low-impact exercise that Jenna found for her on YouTube while we're at our new class on Thursday. Speaking of Jenna, we had to wrestle a KitKat Chunky out of her hand when she got to work this morning. She was stressed following a row with Jason. They are now not speaking because he has booked a four-day stag do to some Eastern European country where, if Jenna is to be believed, 'a ten year old can carry a firearm' and 'pints are thirty pence, and you'd have change from a quid for a blow job.'

Absolutely seething she is.

'Jase is trying to bullshit me that his dickhead best man has arranged it all without him knowing. I said I wasn't born yesterday, mate. *You knew. You fucking well knew!* And you don't need to be a rocket scientist to guess what he will get up to! There are more prostitutes there than in the red-light district. I mean, at least in Amsterdam they would all be too stoned to cheat. I might call the whole thing off now. That will show the tosser!'

Jenna raged all day, even asking a few of the residents what they would do in her shoes. The knitting group had all tutted in support as Jenna set about giving them previous real-life examples, to back up her belief that Jason simply can't be trusted, when he's with his 'wanker mates'.

When we finished for the day, Nicky tried to reassure Jenna that she has nothing to worry about, and how she was sure Jason won't do anything. Yana and I swapped knowing glances because we know better; men on stag dos are complete knobs. Then Val reminded us all that Jenna is also having a hen do in Ireland, Jenna, however, deemed that fact irrelevant.

'For woman is different,' agreed Yana as she made Jenna a cuppa to calm her nerves.

Jenna nodded sulkily. 'Exactly. You don't see women cheating on hen dos, do you? No, you don't, because women have so much more self-control and dignity than men.'

Val pondered this for a few moments then replied, 'That is very true.'

Nicky started nodding in agreement, then I said that women can be just as bad as men and told them all about the one and only hen do I had been on, before I had Chloe. How the bride-to-be had licked tequila shots off a naked stripper's chest, then snogged a stag (not her stag, for clarity, but someone's stag nonetheless) before being sick in one of her bridesmaid's handbags. Despite protests that it was time to call it a night, how we had then watched on in horror as she had scrambled on to a rodeo bull, right in the middle of the heaving bar, and started bucking all over the place; completely oblivious to the fact that her left boob had escaped her Ann Summers sexy bride costume, which, if I remember correctly, one of the bridesmaid's had told me was labelled as the 'take me up the aisle' on the website.

So, anyway, there she was riding like a cow girl on a cattle drive, with her left boob flopping about all over the place, as she hollered, 'I'm getting married next week! Woohoo, yeah, baby! And I love him even though he has no idea what a clit is! WOOHOO!'

Jenna, despite giggling at my story, she didn't appreciate my point of view. 'Etta, babes, I want solidarity and support at the minute, not the truth,' she said as she opened her phone notes page entitled 'Hen do to get list' and typed in 'supportive bra'.

CHAPTER 17

Body combat. Good grief! It's our own fault really. We should have taken more notice of the name; the key word being 'combat'. I was already exhausted before we started. The daily step targets are, quite frankly, a bloody nightmare most days. We are sticking with it, though, despite this class being the last thing any of us want to be doing on a Thursday evening. I can hardly believe that it's already mid-April. This is the longest I have ever stuck to a diet.

Five minutes into what is worryingly being referred to as 'warm-up', I feel like I've been dropped out of a plane and then run over. I had briefly questioned if it was a mistake when we were greeted with music that could only be described as aggressive nineties trance – on fast forward. Then I saw Louisa the trainer: a whippet of a woman in a headset – think Madonna in her 'Vogue' era. That was when it really sank in what a terrible mistake we had made.

Unlike Nicky, who took one look at the set-up in the leisure centre and declared she was going back to her car to get her inhaler and never came back, I didn't have the presence of mind to bail out before things took a turn for the worse.

All three of us suffered. No one came off worst, we were verbally abused and pushed to our breaking points, although Yana had an added stress due to her leggings being a bit loose, which is a good thing in a way as it means she's slimmer than the last time she wore them but not ideal when you're trying to keep a five foot, seven stone soaking wet tyrant – with a manic look in her eye – at bay by jumping around like a jack-in-the-box, and also trying to haul up your leggings that seem intent on hitting the deck every two seconds. Oh, and also not die from lack of oxygen and shock.

I took pity on Yana ten minutes in, took out my hair bobble and helped her use it as a tie to keep her leggings up. I quickly regretted it when I heard the robotic boom, 'You! What are you doing! Ten burpees now!'

I felt dizzy after three and just lay on the grubby wooden floor until Louisa marched over and poked me hard on the forehead with the toe of her trainer and shouted, 'Come on you skiver! Ten burpees now!' Everyone else was then ordered to do star jumps while waiting for me – their 'weak link' – then the absolute cow shouted mockingly, 'Clearly I'm going to have to keep an eye on these lazy newcomers!'

And that's when things really hit a new low. There was no escape. Because Louisa (probably for her own amusement) turned the class literally on its arse; the front became the back. So, there us three were now right at the front. That is when the she devil really went to town on us.

'What do you call that! You're pathetic! My nan can plank better than that!' Louisa shouted in Jenna's ear, while I debated just curling up in the foetal position and waiting for it all to be over.

'No! No! No!!!' she screeched in my face at my attempt at a mountain climber. 'Get back on your toes! Suck your belly in – and that's some belly! You need to spend more time here with me, and less in Burger King, chunky chops!'

Jenna caught my eye, her lip trembling, and panted, 'I'm so sorry. I didn't know it would be like this. I didn't know, mate. I honestly didn't know.'

Louisa really was relentless. Next, she was pointing at Yana. 'If you're talking, you're not working hard enough!'

Jenna mumbled in Yana's defence, 'I was just telling her that I feel sick.'

'You feel what!' came the incredulous response. 'Sick! I would do as well if I had a core as weak as yours! Sick from shame,' she scoffs, pointing over to the other side of the room. 'There's a bin there. We don't need to know all about it! Just be sick!' The whole hour was absolutely awful, but then something weird happened.

Just as I was debating faking a seizure or an asthma attack in a desperate attempt to be excused from the hell I was in, we began the cool down, then Luisa, who may well have a split personality disorder, came over and said, 'Good job, you lot. Great effort!' The three of us looked at her, awaiting the punchline, but it never came.

Sensing our bewilderment, Louisa said, 'Look, shedding fat isn't easy. I have to push you all to achieve your best. I wouldn't be doing my job if I didn't.'

After we lay on the mats for another few minutes and when my heart rate came back down to something that wouldn't be considered tachycardic, I felt like I was walking on air. Like completely amazing. Exhausted, shaky and sick, but amazing.

The only way I can think to explain it is to say it's a bit like having a child. Mother nature is twisted and cruel – it puts you through so much pain – hours upon hours of labour where you're wishing yourself dead just to escape the agony and you tell anyone that will listen, you're never doing it again and 'What the fuck was I thinking!' Then, just as you are about to break, like really lose your shit, it's over and your body pumps out a sneaky devious chemical to trick you into thinking it was actually all lovely and well worth doing again.

Which is the only reasoning I can offer in way of an explanation as to why, despite us nearly crying, being sick and publicly humiliated, we eagerly signed up for the full twice-weekly-for-twelve-weeks course. Apart from Nicky that is, who we found sitting sheepishly outside on the wall waiting for us.

'Sorry, ladies. I had a panic attack as soon as I saw the 'We do squats not excuses' written on the whiteboard.'

Admittedly the fact that Louisa had announced that we had all burned a minimum of five hundred calories – she had pointed in our direction straight after and bellowed 'and you whoppers even more!' as we left – may have also influenced our decision to commit to more of the same.

'We could go and have a bag of crisps, a KitKat, a can of red Coke, and half a tube of Smarties now guilt-free!' wheezed Jenna as we made our way home.

'That's worth it, isn't it?' I enthused, whilst dry heaving and gagging on my water.

Yana nodded and replied, 'I really enjoyed the lose the fat combat. Class was like binging backwards. Shame and self-loathing first, euphoria after!'

CHAPTER 18

I am buzzing. The five of us weighed in at Jenna's house the following Monday and this week we have all lost, as follows: Jenna – four pounds; Nicky – seven pounds!; Val – three pounds; Yana – two and a half pounds (she was so chuffed with this as she's had a few slip-ups. Goes to show how much exercise helps); and me…*drumroll* – six and a half pounds. That is nearly half a stone. I know I won't lose that amount every week, but I am over the moon. Seeing that loss made all the terrible sugar cold-turkey cravings that I've have this week worth it.

I didn't even eat my two-finger KitKat last night that I had saved as a bedtime treat, because I was too busy googling things like 'what does 6.5 lbs of fat look like' (you would be amazed!) and 'how many cubes of sugar weigh 6.5 lbs'. I feel re-motivated and proud of myself. That's not to say it hasn't been a hard slog. I didn't hit my steps twice this week. I was just too tired. On one of the days Chloe had announced that she had Victorian dress-up day the following morning (she forgot to give me the letter in her book bag, so I had literally a few hours' notice). I ended up making her an outfit out of her Christmas navy velvet ankle-length dress and made her a ropey-looking pinafore from one of my bed sheets. On the other day I was aching from all the exercise and just really couldn't be arsed. I needed a rest, so I had an early night with a bowl of grapes and watched *First Dates*.

CHAPTER 19

Pam has run me to the supermarket straight after work because I need some fresh salad and low-fat cheddar. The fakeaway night has turned into an every Friday evening occurrence, and it's my turn to host the next one, which is the first in May. The year is flying by.

'You have a rest. You must be exhausted!' said Pam when she caught sight of my step count as we pulled up. 'Eleven thousand and twenty! Well done, darling!' she added, praising me.

I was glad of the lift after getting up early this morning to do half an hour on my aerobics step before walking Chloe to school breakfast club, then to work and back. I am still finding the exercise and steps a lot harder than I expected it to be.

'Give me your list,' Pam commanded, gesturing to my crumpled Post-it note. 'I'll get these. You have a little five minutes to yourself. Now I am going to lock you in, darling, and I'll tell you why. A woman got mugged at the cash point at the big Tesco in St Neots last Monday. I read about it in the local weekly newspaper. Threatened with a sharp keyring, she was!'

Anyone who knows Pamela knows she loves to be busy, and I don't just mean with her gossiping. She always has a project in hand. She has a real zest for life. This year Pam has been insistent on having a koi carp pond to rival her frenemy Karen at number 24; her latest request being that it must be fully stocked with koi carp so large that they are able to 'suck your finger'. She also has a few long-term projects on the go: one being her weight; the other the corgis.

About two years ago, prompted by *The Crown*, Pamela decided she loved corgis so much that she was going to become not only an owner but an accredited Kennel Club Assured Breeder.

Out came the laminated business plan, which – long story short – was to source the best show-quality corgi puppies, breed them when they were old enough and then sell their offspring to the Queen and other people with titles or piles in the country and a flat in Knightsbridge – but mainly to the Queen. Pamela had fantasies of private audiences to discuss her upcoming matings, where she would of course promise Her Majesty the pick of the litter.

To be fair, there are hardly any UK breeders, so it was plausible that the pups may end up in royal laps. 'Imagine the ladies' faces at Slim With Us when they find out I am the royal corgi supplier! Gosh! I wonder if I'll get a Royal Warrant to use on my personal stationery like Waitrose has on their food packets!' Pam had marvelled over lunch one weekend.

Unfortunately, things haven't quite panned out. All started well. My grandad, true to character, showed willing by driving from Cambridgeshire to Wales and back, to collect a 'breeding bitch' – who was to be later named Diana – from a reputable, established breeder. Then, a few months later, they hot dashed to Stansted to pick up their stud boy, Charles, who had flown over from Germany on a pet passport. It became apparent when the pups came of age, however, that Charles just wasn't up to the job. Diana came into season and was gagging for it, waggling her bum in his face, but Charles just wasn't at all interested.

Pamela rang me a few evenings ago to commiserate. She now believes Charles to be homosexual. Diana is in season again and Charles is giving her the cold shoulder once more.

'There is no question about it. He must be. I mean Diana is show quality, and he knows what to do. I've seen him with next door's male poodle; humping frantically he was. Poor Pompy. He's twelve now and his eyesight isn't what it used to be. One moment they were sniffing each other, the next Charles had his lipstick out and was attempting to mount poor Mr Pompy quite frantically.'

I can't help but chuckle at this, but then Pam reminds me it is no laughing matter. 'Charles has always been a selfish dog, so I'm not surprised. Poor Diana. It has knocked her confidence; completely shattered her in fact. That's why I've rung actually, darling. I need your help.'

I was then told all about how Pam had been surfing the web on the computer and had found a website called Pedigree Studs Wanted. 'I need you to help me set up a profile on behalf of Diana, darling. She *needs* to be a mother; she is so maternal.'

There are lots of words to describe Diana but maternal isn't one I'd use. She is notoriously temperamental and snappy. She is also incredibly fat, largely due to Pam feeding the dogs the same food as she serves my grandad. Therefore, their diet consists mainly of smoked bacon, scrambled eggs and Sainsbury's rotisserie chickens with roast potatoes swimming in lashings of tar-like Bisto.

God, I would kill for a bowl of roast potatoes now! No

chance of that on twelve hundred calories a day. At least it's fakeaway night again tonight. I have a recipe for healthy Big Macs. I've struggled with the water this week; I haven't managed the whole two litres a day yet. Give me two litres of Coke and I would polish it off, so I know I'm just being pathetic. I've bought some sugar-free squash to add to the water from tomorrow at Val's suggestion. She said it's much easier when it has some taste to it.

～

'I wanna garden like this!' says Jenna, at my cottage later that evening, when I ask her between bursts of laughter what on earth she's doing balancing on top of the old creaky garden table on my patio. I think it's the fluffy pink onesie tucked into her silver Ugg boots that sets me off. 'I'm going to take a picture to show my Jason. This is exactly like the garden Miss Honey has in *Matilda*!'

'Jenna, you must get down before you fall down,' Yana calls, coming up the path. People are always blown away by the cottage and garden the first time they see it; not because it's fancy but because of its romantic charm.

The garden isn't even at its best yet. By the height of summer, the borders will be a riot of navel-height lupins and foxgloves, and the lavender that lines the path will spill on to the already limited walkway. Our little postage stamp-sized outside oasis also always attracts what seems like the whole county's butterfly and bee population. I love sitting on the patio in the late afternoons in the warmer months. I sit reading a book while Chloe plays on the tyre swing and our chickens peck away in their favourite shady spot between the delphiniums and rose bushes. Alice without fail will be found basking in the last of the day's sunshine, periodically springing into action, pawing the air, playfully shadow-boxing one of the many passing butterflies.

'The table and chairs were here when we moved in. They're quite rotten, so be careful,' I warn, giggling at the sight of Jenna, who is now attempting to make her way back down with the grace of a baby rhino. She turns for one last look before following me inside. 'I love this cottage! I can't believe you live here. It's the cutest place.'

I usually prefer to cook without an audience, not being the most confident chef, but when all four of them cram into my little kitchen I feel instantly relaxed. The ladies barely glance at what I'm doing and, other than when Val washes the lettuce and Yana helps toast the buns, they leave me to it, nattering happily.

'I've had a Müller Light yoghurt and strawberries for breakfast, and our salmon noodles for my delicious lunch. Thanks again for that, Nic, mate. I planned ahead, so didn't have my usual teatime snack. I saved enough calories so I can have a vodka and diet lemonade,' Jenna told us proudly.

My shabby kitchen table only seats two, so it's trays on laps. I feel a bit embarrassed telling them, but they don't flinch. My sitting room is mainly filled with two cream fabric sofas facing each other, one under the window against the wall, the other crammed opposite, with a table in the middle. Each settee can fit three people at a squeeze, or two comfortably. I opt to sit on the floor and eat on my knees at the coffee table.

I'd been fretting all day that I didn't have a proper seating area for us to sit at, and that my plates and cutlery are a mishmash of ones I've inherited from Pam and Grandad, mixed in with odd vintage find from charity shops and car boot sales over the years. No one was bothered, though. I have realised tonight that real friends couldn't care less about what plate they eat off, or that you don't have a fancy American fridge-freezer with an ice machine or, in my case, even an ice tray in the freezer that you got second-hand off of Gumtree for forty pounds when your old one packed up. 'No worries, mate. However it comes,' Jenna had said when I sheepishly apologised that I had no ice for her one and only vodka of the night.

'I need you to give the recipe for the burgers, and where you buy these micro chips? Never in my life I see chips come from the microwave,' said Yana, as she takes a massive bite of the double cheeseburger, the homemade low-fat version of burger sauce oozing out.

That's right. None of them even cut all ties with me when I served them micro chips; the easiest way for me to work out exact portions (164 calories!). I know what you might be thinking. That I sound calorie obsessed, but we have to be at the moment. When you have been overweight for a long time, sometimes as long as you can remember, you have no idea of what is too much. I have lived a life of excess where food is concerned. Think unattended child at a birthday party.

We have had many discussions, as a group though, about making sure that our main focus is a balanced diet, which it is. We aren't eating once a day and blowing our calories on a pizza and a can of Coke; we are spreading our allowance over breakfast, lunch and dinner, and using our portion plates in the evenings. Then having a little treat with the calories left. We are not cutting our carbs and fruit or only eating meat, we have shunned going down the route of anything faddy and unsustainable. Once we know what is enough, and we feel in control, we plan to phase out the logging of every-thing that passes our lips.

That said, being accountable for what we put in our bodies isn't a bad thing. Look where having free rein has got me! Not just mentally but the health risks are huge for someone of my size and weight. I have buried my head in the sand for too long. I feel empowered by taking responsibility for my own health. It's been a long time coming.

After we've finished eating, Val washes up while Yana dries, handing it all to me to put away while Jenna and Nicky fill us in on the plan they have come up with.

'So, we've thought of a way to find out what Tim's really up to, Val. Nicky thought of the first part, so you tell them, mate,' says Jenna, grinning at Nic.

'Well, when Theodore left, I was interested in knowing what his girlfriend looked like. So, I hired a car because he would have recognised mine, and then I waited outside his work and followed him. Then, when I found out his new address – her address – I just sat across the street and waited until I spotted her,' Nic says proudly.

Val grimaces. 'Bloody hell, Nic! I'm not sure. I don't think I can do that. Plus he's retired. Apart from the golf club, I don't even know where he goes all day when I'm at work. And I'd be too worried. He'd spot me a mile off – different car or not!'

Jenna, who was sitting cross-legged on the kitchen floor indulging Alice in cuddles, says, 'That's where we come in. He would spot you, but not us!'

Then she stands up and mimes swinging a club. 'Fancy some golf, girls!'

A small unsure grin forms across Val's face. 'I don't want any of you to get in any trouble, but that could work. The only problem is that the golf club is members only.'

Yana shakes her head and reassures Val we wouldn't get into any trouble, plus, members or not, we are not going to go inside or on the course. 'We wait at the car park and follow husband of Val when he leaves golf,' said Yana with a smile.

It's a good idea. I notice that Nicky seems a lot less

uptight this evening. She has only checked on her cats twice so far.

'Then you can either confront him, or we can use our new information to dig deeper and give all the information to your lawyer,' I encourage, knowing that we really do need to help Val get to the bottom of it, so she can move on.

Val, after we assure her again that we don't mind helping, finally relents and agrees it's a great idea and that following Tim from the club will be our best bet. 'Unless one of his legs is falling off, Tim won't miss his Sunday golf,' Val jokes, adding that he is lucky she hasn't thought of it herself as she would have been there already to give him a piece of her mind.

'Probably a good thing, Val. Now we can find out where he's going and who with. Confronting him might have made you feel better, but you can get answers this way. You could still confront him after if you still wanted to,' reasons Nicky.

It is decided we are going undercover next Sunday.

When Yana asks Jenna if she and Jason are talking again yet, she pulls a smug face and tells us they are fine now because she has put him under surveillance. 'So, you know I was well uptight. Well, I had this genius idea. He has this one friend called Pauly T, who never replies to messages. Like never. He is well known for it. What I have done is swap Pauly T's number for Porsha's old one on Jason's phone when he was in the shower, then I added Pauly T aka Porsha as a member of my Jason's stag do chat group. None of them will think anything of it. Now Porsha has real-time full access to what is being said and can screenshot it all and send it to me.'

Nicky whistles in amazement and we all give each other shocked, amused glances. 'Jenna, that is very devious. Devious, but also very brilliant!' says Yana to an incredibly-pleased-with-herself Jenna.

'You're wasted at Elm Lodge! You should be a detective! What's been said then?' I ask.

Jenna pulls a smug, satisfied 'I know I'm clever face' and replies, 'Nothing much. Mainly just how many drinks they can get for ten euros and something about quad biking.' Replies Jenna sounding almost disappointed.

'That's good, then. At least you have nothing to worry about,' Nicky says reassuringly.

'Umm, or he doesn't want any written evidence. Men are so sneaky. Who knows with them?' Jenna says rolling her eyes.

Oh, the irony!

CHAPTER 20

Met the others for lunch yesterday at the Waterside Coffee Shop to start off the working week. Val started listing all the positives of being single, like no listening to snoring, no more constant moaning, and being able to choose a holiday destination not based on how good the golf facilities are. Nicky says the best thing that came from her divorce is that she no longer has to host her mother-in-law for two weeks over Christmas and new year. Jenna says she has never got on with Gillian, Jason's mum, her soon-to-be mother-in-law, and that her overbearing nature has gone into overdrive since her and Jason got engaged. 'Gill thinks it's her bloody wedding!' Jenna grumbles. 'Bloody woman! She invited herself shopping for my dress a few weeks back. Not only did she invite herself, but she completely took over. Took us to this boutique shop. The type that practically asks for you to bathe in bleach before you enter.

'The shop assistants were French, and seriously stuck-up. Both of them had that pulled-back face look, where they could be any age between thirty-five and sixty with matching white-blonde hair in fancy updos. Their faces when Mum told them I was aiming to slim into a size twelve! You would have thought she had just said, "Don't mind us. We don't wanna buy anything. we'll just take a big shit here amongst the all-angle mirrors and tiaras and then we'll be on our way".'

Jenna's giggling now at the memory. 'They muttered something about not catering for plus sizes, while Gill whined back at them in a low strained voice, "I've tried to tell her this. Is there anything you can do with her? Anything at all?" The stupid cow honestly sounded like she had just been told her pet needed putting down. She was practically begging them.

'The shop assistants must look after their own because, like them, Gillian is no stranger to facial threads and a shit attitude. After a few more hushed conversations one of them handed us all pairs of white gloves and announced that she was "doubtful but would try one's best", and off they went to check their stock, not before reminding us to "refrain from touching anything" in their absence.

'I didn't put my gloves on, out of principle, but my mum did, just for a laugh. She climbed up on the counter and did a moonwalk and bellowed, "Oi, Gilly, who am I?" Gill just tutted and looked like she was about to have a stroke, then pleaded with Mum to get down and to "stop showing her up!"

'Mum did clamber down, but then she started picking up the knick-knacks from behind the glass cabinet, flashing them in our direction and bellowing things like "fuckin' hell! Four hundred and sixty quid for a hair clip! They're taking the piss!" and "I could get you one nicer from Claire's for a fiver. Couldn't we pick up a better one for a fiver, Clemmie?"

'Clemmie, my sister, was too engrossed in Instagram to even look up, but Mum had definitely gained Gill's attention, who, after gasping, rushed over to mum, who'd moved on to manhandling garter belts on display under a DELICATE DO NOT TOUCH sign.

'Here, Jenna, look at this load of shit! What is 1900s vintage virgin silk when it's at home!' Mum shouted over to me while Gill looked like she was about to self-combust. Her face as she frogmarched Mum back to the candyfloss-pink seating cubes. Miserable cow. Don't know how to have a giggle that one.

'Soon after, the Death-Becomes-Her duo returned like martyrs, carrying the "most substantial and pliable piece" they had found. Honestly, it looked like they had nicked one of my nana's doll loo roll covers. It was very 'when Katie married Peter'.

'I knew it was really shit when one of the assistants met the eye of the other as I waddled back into the viewing area and whispered, "It ees not our fault. Ve can only work with what ve 'ave!" Then Gillian shuddered at the sight of me. 'Good grief! No, definitely not!' she said in a high-pitched voice.

'When Mum saw me she started swearing and shouting at the shop assistants, "What the…! How dare you do this to my little girl! Are you taking the fuckin' piss or what?" Then she started screaming at my sister Clemmie to "stop taking fuckin' pictures" because "no one can ever see the state of her!"

'To be fair, it was pretty bad. The back fat was the worst. It looked like I had grown another pair of tits at the top and, in between the lace corseting, I had skin bulges. Mum said it reminded her of when my C-section scar got infected and started puckering. I started crying then, and Gillian said with a gloating smirk, "Can we get her out of it please, ladies, before someone deposits her to Waitrose, with the rest of the strung pork joints." Gill then honked with laughter at her own joke, but not for long, because my mum marched over and slapped her hard across the face.

'Then she growled at Gill that it was all her "fuckin' fault for bringing us to this shit hole". Gill held her face in shocked outrage and argued that the only person at fault was me because I had been aware of my wedding date for the last ten months and that she had, in fact, tried to support me by printing out an apple diet that Gwyneth Paltrow follows, and how she had even bought me a mini trampoline for my birthday. So, the fact that I was facing being a "plus-size bride" was due to my own laziness. She spat out the words "plus size" like they were dirty words.

'So, I have no dress still, and my mum keeps ranting that the next time she sees Gill aka "that C U next Tuesday" she's going to "fuck her up proper". So that's something to look forward to at least.'

'I'm glad your mum slapped her!' I said as the three other women nod in furious agreement.

'The shop can't get much custom with attitudes like that. The average size in the UK is a size sixteen, so they are excluding the majority of their market,' added Val.

'Least Gill speaks directly to you, though, Jenna. My ex-mother-in-law used to speak about me in front of me as the third person. "I must say I am shocked Nicola still hasn't started to address her obesity. I really think she should make a start pronto, before your managers' ball in July!" she would moan to Theodore while I sat at the table opposite her.'

We go for a walk afterwards, stopping at the fresh fruit stall at the market. We all stock up. The smell of fried onions from the burger stall opposite WH Smith's makes my mouth water. I'm not hungry, having just eaten chipotle lentil chilli in the café, but that doesn't stop me imagining biting into a jumbo hot dog slathered in ketchup and onions. From Yana's longing glances at the faded menu as we pass, I know I am not alone.

However, it is not just the constant temptations that are proving tricky; the daily steps are still a battle.

'I was walking from the kitchen to the lounge and back in a loop last night. Just to reach my steps. Bloody shattered I am!' said Jenna when I said how badly my legs ache today.

'Just think of how good you will feel when we get through this tough bit,' said Val.

We all know she's right. Every time I am tempted to revert back to old ways, I think to how I felt that night down by the river, after watching on as Robert went about his evening with the blonde goddess, and all the times I had wished he could be that way with me. I had always wanted him to feel proud of me before.

I have spent enough time daydreaming about how my life could be. Finally, I am doing something about it.

CHAPTER 21

'I can't believe we're doing this!' I laugh to Nicky and Jenna. It's Sunday and all three of us are parked up in Nicky's little Corsa outside Manor Tree Golf Club. Yana is keeping Val company because her IBS is playing up again, after a slip-up involving a can of squirty cream and half a chocolate brownie slab cake, so she didn't want to risk being away from a toilet.

'Show me the picture again,' Jenna says as she reaches for the plastic file on my lap. 'Right, that's his car. The black Volvo estate over there,' she declares, handing me back the folder.

'Yes, it is, so let's just sit here and wait. It can't be much longer. Val said he always finishes about three,' Nicky adds.

While we wait, we polish off the tubs of tuna pasta salad that I had made earlier for our lunches. Afterwards we share some crimson grapes that Jenna brought with her to snack on while we wait.

Just after half three, Tim appears, wheeling his golf clubs.

'That's him!' we all chorus excitedly as we compare the man in front of us with a photo from inside the file of Val and her husband together in happier times.

Jenna wastes no time in bringing Yana and Val up to date. She dials Yana's number, clicks it on to speakerphone and says quietly, 'This is Jenna. We have eyes on the target. I can confirm, eyes are on the target,' before ending the call without so much as a goodbye.

Then she starts videoing him as he places the leather golf bag in the boot then leans down to change his shoes. As he looks up, his eyes briefly settle on us.

'FUCK! He's spotted us,' Jenna screams.

My initial reaction is to knock Jenna's phone out of her hand frantically in case Tim realises we are filming him.

Nicky shushes us. 'Stop shouting. He'll hear you. He doesn't know us, remember, so just act cool.'

As Tim's Volvo pulls away and indicates right, Nicky is calmly on his tail. Jenna is worried about losing him and instructs Nic to just 'get a move on!' Nicky keeps to her speed while reassuring us she knows what she's doing. It's best to leave a one-car gap to not look obvious, she reasons.

We nearly lose him at a roundabout but manage to catch up with him on the dual carriageway. 'Gosh! I don't like to go above fifty-five miles per hour,' Nicky whines as her steering wheel vibrates.

Jenna and I shout in unison. 'Just put your foot down, mate!'

Finally, Tim's car halts at the wooden gate of a beautiful double-fronted farmhouse. Jenna adds more photos to her collection as the gates open. We decide that whoever lives there probably owns Labradors and does their big weekly shop at Waitrose.

Very fancy. At the end of the lane is a passing space. Nicky pulls up and turns off the engine. Jenna tells me to hop out and take a picture of the road sign — she is too close to the blackberry hedgerow to open her door — so we can check Rightmove later.

We decide to stay parked at the end of the lane, give it fifteen minutes or so, then drive back slowly to see if we can see anything else. Which we do, but all is quiet. Afterwards, we head straight back to Val's bungalow.

'I wonder if Val knows who lives there,' I say to Nicky as she flips her seat forward and offers me her hand to steady myself as I climb out. Two-door cars have never been my friend.

'I have no idea but we're about to find out,' says Nicky with a gulp.

CHAPTER 22

Val's bungalow reminds me of my grandad and Pam's house. Everything has its place. It feels warm and welcoming, and there is even the same yucca and spider plants in the conservatory. Jenna hands over her phone and Yana helps Val scroll through the camera roll.

Val gasps when she looks at the picture of the farmhouse. Not because she knows who lives there – having never seen or heard of the posh Stilton village address before – but because of the sheer size and beauty of the property. When we search the address on Rightmove the records show that it last sold eighteen months previously for a staggering amount – nine hundred and sixty thousand pounds.

'We could apply to the Land Registry and get the owner's name. That will give us something to go on,' Nic offers.

Val decides she wants us to do that.

Jenna helps herself to mugs and stands placing them in turn under the Neff built-in coffee machine. While she waits for the last beep to indicate that the final skinny latte is ready, she turns round to Val and says, 'We will get to the bottom of it, mate. Don't worry. Okay?' Val smiles appreciatively.

Nicky then connects her iPad to Val's Wi-Fi, and we use Jenna's PayPal for the fee and retrieve the information. A few minutes later we have a name. Adam Dolson.

'Maybe there is no one else involved after all,' said Nicky while squinting at her mobile. She is checking her pet cam screen.

'Could it be someone he worked with or a golf friend?' I suggest.

Val debates this. 'I've never heard Tim mention anyone called Adam, but, after what he's done to me, who knows what's been going on? So, yes, I suppose he could be,' she replies.

'What if he's seeing someone else, and she's married. That could be her husband's name,' suggests Jenna.

'Let us think of all options,' Yana said, agreeing with Jenna. We all sit sipping our posh coffees for a minute or two, digesting all the new information, each one of us running through the possible explanations in our heads.

'There's one way to find out, isn't there?' said Val as she calmly refills her mug. 'Next Sunday, when I know he'll be at golf, I'm going to go there, knock on the door and try and get some answers from whoever lives there.'

I feel panicked on her behalf. I know Val needs to get to the bottom of it but the thought of her walking into the unknown makes me anxious. I don't want her any more upset than she already is. 'We'll come with you,' I say.

'Yes, we'll go together. You cannot go there alone,' agrees Yana as Jenna waves away Val's half-hearted protests.

'Whatever he's playing at we are going to find out once and for all. We go together. Next Sunday. End of,' Jenna said authoritatively.

Val looks relieved and grateful.

So, the date is set.

This time next week, Tim, your game is up.

CHAPTER 23

Elm Lodge Care Home

Individuals who don't know a lot of elderly people may have a preconception of them all being sweet, mild-mannered and full of wisdom. Sometimes that is true. Sometimes, but not always. The male residents at Elm Lodge have their moments, but it is generally straightforward things: someone is sitting in someone else's favourite chair, someone feeling disgruntled because the resident next to him at dinner has a better pork chop...that kind of thing, nothing too complicated, and easily resolved.

At our care home, it's a small group of women – the golden girls – who are usually behind any major upsets. I can guarantee that in every residential care home there's a mean clique to some degree. Not always ladies – just a small group of residents who have a few more faculties than the others, and maybe extra luxuries, like a hairdresser who comes especially for them, a daughter who brings treats in for them to share and keeps them in premium cardigans...that kind of thing.

They will usually be the ones who try to control situations for their own benefit and to lord it over the others. The latest phase here is the golden girls' group holding private viewings in their rooms, sometimes with a small selection of chosen ones from outside their circle who they have deemed temporarily worthy to join them to watch a BBC or ITV series. *Last Tango in Halifax* is the current favourite.

All of the residents have their own televisions but something about feeling the need to be accepted means that the other residents compete for the places to join the club at their viewing; to all cram in together, to share the luxury tin of biscuits that one of their grandsons or daughters-in-law has brought in specially.

The space is never permanent. If they chew too loudly or don't follow the plot, or maybe threaten them in another way like showing too much wit or intelligence, they will be out on their ear. Our golden girls are as ruthless as a drug cartel. The members also try to charm us staff to get us on side. Should we not fall in line or dare to gently rein them in when their bullying or sniping comes to our attention, the group have no qualms extending their false smiles and underhand comments our way.

Much like a mean girls' club at secondary school, ours is led by their ringleader, Margaret. A retired actress, if you believe her stories. Although her son did write 'homemaker' on her application forms, which seems strange given her achievements and the very colourful life that she tells us all about at every opening possible.

Margaret has visited every country going and once kissed JFK at a dance hall in Bethnal Green. I cannot say either way if it's true or not. However the photographs of her when she was young prove just how stunning she was. Vixen-red hair, translucent porcelain skin and a pinched-in waist. To be fair to her, she may well have done and achieved all she says. Her son seems the type of man to not register his mum as anything other than a mother and a wife. I could see him deeming all Margaret's other achievements just as silly hobbies and not worthy of mentioning.

Margaret is a stern, formidable character. Her care is paid for by the aforementioned son, Edward Henderson. Mr Henderson, as we have been told to address him by June, works in a high-powered job. Margaret is enormously proud of him and can be constantly overheard boasting about her 'clever son, the City trader'. All us carers know from the endless insights from Margaret, that his salary is enough to make Yana gasp and say, 'In Russia you live for lifetime on this money you tell me!' He also has two children at boarding school in London. 'Thirty-three thousand a year. Each! Plus extras for trips and uniform. They went skiing last month!'

Bragging and belligerence clearly run in the family. Edward has this booming voice and clicks his fingers to announce his presence. He arrived today clutching a box of Godiva chocolates and a huge bouquet of peonies from Selfridge's food hall. 'VASE!' was his greeting demand as I buzzed him in the front door and said good morning. He held out the arrangement and gestured impatiently for me to take it from him. 'I'll keep hold of these, though!' he said, waving the box of chocolates close to my face. 'Mum said her last box went walkabout. She only got two!' he added accusingly.

I smile and say nothing, but debate letting him know that I remember clearly Margaret boasting all day about her 'premium luxury chocolates' from her 'utterly devoted son who lives in a six-bedroom three-storey, in central London.' And that I also remember seeing her scoff them one after another, as her disciples crowded round as she described the tastes and textures. And, how when she had polished them all off in one sitting, she had handed the wrappers to a nearly dribbling Olive, her second in command, to dispose of.

Instead, I force a concerned, 'Oh no! Poor her.'

He looks at me and narrows his eyes, probably trying to work out if I am being sarcastic or not. Which I obviously am.

I worry about Olive sometimes. She is quiet, easily led, and eager to please and fit in. The perfect sidekick for Margaret, who uses her as a puppet, basically getting Olive to say and do anything she dares not to herself. Margaret has got Olive in trouble with June so many times over the years, to the point that June thinks that Olive is the root of the problems and unrest between the residents when the real culprit is Margaret, or 'Marg' as Yana calls her.

Margaret is like Pam. She absolutely hates having her name shortened, and being called Marg makes her physically wince. Nicky often greets her with a friendly, 'Morning, Mrs H' and receives a tut for her trouble.

I try hard to always address her formally because that is her preference, although I can't help but chuckle each time Jenna forgets herself and utters the words 'Maggie, mate', knowing a haughty 'My name is Mrs Henderson to you, you stupid girl' will follow in response. I come off fairly unscathed as my formal, polite approach is usually well received, plus my watch scored some points with her early on.

I had been helping her with her bed socks and slippers when she noticed it and remarked that it was very ladylike and gave it an approving nod. On my twenty-first birthday, I got a delicate small-faced Cartier, with a deep-navy-blue leather strap. I have never taken it off before starting our A Moment on the Lips plan with the others, it's in my bedside table drawer for now. I had to remove it to make way for my fit watch.

When Margaret's son was rude to me today, it got me thinking: if I was slimmer, would he treat me as badly? Maybe he would. I am, after all, just a care assistant in his eyes. Which is so wrong. Anyone who treats someone badly because of how they look, or what job they have or their social status, isn't worth worrying about. There is no excuse in making people feel small or bad about themselves. It is nice to be nice.

CHAPTER 24

I've just realised I haven't told you much about my parents. My dad…well, least said about him the better. He got remarried to his perfect second wife when my sister Carly and I were still at primary school. They went on to have their perfect son. After that, Carly and I were surplus to requirements. The weekly visits soon became monthly, then we were demoted to two-minute phone calls and cards at Christmas and birthdays. Then they dried up. We haven't seen or spoken to him in many years now.

Then there is my mum. What can I tell you about Hilary? Well, she is a massive hypocrite for one. Mum also has a noticeably short memory. When we were growing up, she was the opposite of what would be deemed a good parent. Being a mum myself now means I do have more empathy for the younger her. Being left with two children, watching their father remarry and live the so-called dream life couldn't have been easy.

But that doesn't excuse the way she raised us. Mum regularly left us with my grandad and nan, and later Pam, for weeks on end, and, when they couldn't have us, we were dumped on babysitters who were usually still children themselves. Not so that she could go to work and make our lives better but because mum was always putting number one first, going out with her friends and doing as she pleased. She also went from man to man; each one more dysfunctional than the last. Most of them made her life hell, and by association also mine and my sister's.

I know she's my mum, and some of you who have had lovely childhoods and great relationships with your parents as adults probably won't relate to this and may find it extremely harsh and shocking, but I really cannot stand her, and I know the feeling is mutual.

We both pretend otherwise, of course. We play the game, as a lot of families do, because it's drummed into us that we all only have one family, blood is thicker than water, and all that jazz.

I pretend that I don't still harbour resentment for the crappy childhood I had because of her and her shit, and mum pretends that she doesn't resent me for not becoming her. I know she does – resent me I mean. My not failing as a mother just highlights how much she has.

I read somewhere that every single person becomes who they are as adults because of their parents. Either they replicate their behaviour or they make a conscious effort to be nothing like them. That is true. I am the latter. Whenever I'm unsure of something, I generally think what would mum do – then do the complete opposite.

Last year, my mum did try to have a heart-to-heart, mainly for Nigel's benefit. Nigel is her latest in a long line of men. He has lasted longer than most; it must be well over a year now. 'I'm sorry I haven't always been the best mother to you,' she had said in the tone of a petulant child. Understatement of the century. 'I'm in a good place now, though, and I want to make an effort and spend more time with you. But we can't talk about the past, especially in front of Nige. We need to live in the present, okay?' Which translated to 'Nigel mustn't know what I am really like. Consider yourself warned.'

From what my sister had told me, I knew Nigel was one of those hippy types who walk around telling everyone about their clogged auras, and claiming western medicine is poison. That said I was still a bit taken aback to see that he was barefoot when I met him. I would have probably just thought fair enough if we weren't in the Slug and Lettuce on a Monday lunchtime, in early November. Plus he had a scab on his knee that he was still picking at when he tried to engage me in conversation.

'So, Etta, Hilary tells me you have a daughter? Tell me about you guys.'

I began to politely tell him about Chloe, and he cut me short with a, 'Cool, cool. I notice your aura is aubergine like your mum's.'

I fucking hope not, I thought. You would have been forgiven in thinking that I had said it out loud from the warning looks my mum was firing at me from across the table. I'm not a cruel person, but I will admit seeing her squirm made my day.

Mum did look different since the last time I'd seen her; I'll give her that. It seems Nigel has led her down new paths. A bacon roll and a cup of coffee would have been her usual order, but the new Hilary selected a black bean burrito and a fresh carrot and ginger juice. Her hair was the same. She hadn't yet succumbed to the woman of a certain age cut. I can't ever see her chopping off her dark wavy locks. That said, never say never. I also didn't think that I would ever see the day that she would be wearing a baggy T-shirt with a wolf howling under a full moon while holding hands with a shower dodger who bites his toenails in public. Life is full of surprises.

'That's Chief Cherokee – your mum's spirit guide wolf. We picked it up at a spiritualist fair in Kent, didn't we, sweetheart?' Nigel said when he clocked me looking at my mum's top.

I could tell my mum was embarrassed, and it spurred me on. I know it sounds terrible, but I couldn't resist. 'I didn't know you were into all that New Age hippy stuff, Mum,' I said, attempting to flash my best 'I'm not taking the piss' smile.

'It's not New Age!' she replied quickly. A tight little laugh followed that didn't quite hide her irritation. 'Etta, you know I have always been spiritual. Don't be silly.'

'Do I?' I asked, innocently returning her smile. This earned me another one of her warning looks. Fuck it! In for a penny, I decided. 'That's not what you said at Uncle Ralph's funeral. You said there was no such thing as heaven. When you're dead you're dead, and what a waste of time it all was. No heaven, no hell, no afterlife. It's all bollocks, you said.'

Her first instinct was to turn to Nigel, who looks like a confused springer spaniel who can't quite work out where his ball has gone.

'Etta thinks she's funny. I told you, didn't I, Nige? How she's always like this? Now you can see all her spitefulness for yourself!'

Mum's exasperated expression turned to one of contempt when our eyes met.

Recognising this as a perfect opportunity to escape before I tell any more home truths, she busied herself gathering up her coat and bag, and flounced off. Just before she did, though, mainly for Nigel's benefit, but also because she has more front than Brighton Pier, she couldn't resist pitching her parting shot.

'Can't be happy for me, can you? Come on, Nigel, we're leaving. She's always been a spiteful little bitch. Well, not so little, actually,' she scoffed.

And there she is, ladies and gentlemen, my loving mother.

Nigel, in his defence, did look momentarily horrified and started to mumble something in my direction before following mum outside.

I watched on from the window in bemusement as the duo seemed to count to ten or possibly recite a prayer – I'm not sure which – while standing with their eyes shut right in the middle of a heaving Cambridge footpath. I was not the only one giggling as the pair of them take a slow deep bow and kiss the crystal pendants dangling around their necks, seemingly oblivious to the double-takes from confused members of the public.

I found myself involuntarily rolling my eyes as Nigel then sloped back inside and made his way towards me, his long honey-brown hair, all greasy at the roots, hanging like a near-end-of-use Vileda mop; the flyaway ends that graze his boyish shoulders severely split. If I were to imagine an ill-equipped man emerging after five heavy-going days at Glastonbury, Nigel would be it.

He hovered at the edge of the table until I looked up. 'She didn't mean to go personal, man. Your weight is your soul's cry for help. Your mum is a powerful healer, she could help with that if you just took down your walls.'

I felt the familiar burn of my cheeks; the way they always did when someone referenced my weight.

I took a bite out of my sandwich, trying to act indifferent, debating how long it would take him to piss off if I just ignored him. Soon after my sandwich was just a few crumbs on the plate. Nigel still hadn't budged.

'Help me! What a joke!' I replied incredulously. In return

I received a perplexed dog-lost-ball stare and head tilt. Clearly, he was waiting for me to elaborate. I decided to indulge him. 'Nigel, my mum will never solve any problem because she *is* the problem. You will find that out for yourself soon enough. Oh, and by the way, your perfect Hilary isn't a vegan and certainly hasn't been one since I was a child, like she claims. She's had more Big Macs than I have and, well, look at the size of me! On that note, I'll say goodbye and bid you good luck. You are going to need it. Nice to meet you. *Man.*'

Without another word, Nigel picked up his onion and courgette fritters and dropped them into his bumbag. He didn't even wrap them in a napkin. Absolute savage. Lastly, he slurped the rest of his detox juice, ignoring the bill next to it.

'You need a chakra cleanse, man!' Nigel called back at me as he turned on his very grubby heels. I picked up the bill. My cheese sandwich and coke came to five pounds fifty. Nigel's fritters and his large detox mud water together with my mum's carrot juice and her burrito, which was barely touched next to me, were listed underneath.

When I handed twenty-five pounds to the cashier, I told her to keep the one pound sixty-five pence change.

That was the last time I saw them. They cried off at Christmas in favour of a two-week tarot card workshop that they were co-hosting in Dundee.

Today the radio silence was broken by way of an invitation via email, for a wedding that isn't actually going to be legal as they 'refuse to abide by or recognise laws forced upon them by the corrupt English government'. The couple have instead opted to hold a 'love commitment ceremony' in Cornwall. The theme is 'positivity only', which gave me a good laugh given it was coming from the happiness vacuum that is my mum. There was also a gift registry attached that mum has set up in John Lewis. It seems nothing says spiritual like a climate protection super king mattress for the bargain price of £1,799.

My grandad nearly choked on his coffee when I read it all out to him this evening, especially when I got to the theme part. He sniggered then and said, 'I take it your mum won't actually in attendance then!' Grandad never says anything horrible about anyone, so for him to say that you know she really is a cow.

CHAPTER 25

Sunday was one of those drab, murky, typically British days, despite it being mid-May, with summer just around the corner – the ones when it looks like the heavens are about to open at any moment; dark low clouds, a heavy damp feel about the air. Despite each one of us being quite a bit slimmer than we had been, it was still a squeeze for all five of us to wedge into Nicky's Corsa. Yana, Jenna and I were in the back mimicking canned sardines, each of us hunching our shoulders in an attempt to give one another as much room as possible.

Val sat in the passenger seat, understandably much quieter than usual, no doubt speculating on what was to come.

'I don't think it's a time for the music,' said Yana, shaking her head at Jenna as she leant forward and plugged in her AUX cable.

'Yeah it is. Val needs to psych herself up. I've made her a playlist!'

When we arrived down the lane, Nicky drove slowly past the farmhouse to check that Tim wasn't there. The coast was clear. No sign of him or his Volvo; only the same muddy Land Rover tucked into the carport that was there last weekend.

It's a good job we're no longer undercover as we were about as far removed from inconspicuous as possible. Nicky did a three-point turn in the same passing space we'd stopped at last week and, as she did, the car fan belt started squealing in outrage.

A man putting a bag of rubbish in his wheelie bin double-took us as we passed. His expression said, 'What are you peasants doing near my middle-class home?'

Parked up directly opposite the house, I clock Val's hesitant expression. 'Are you sure about this?' I ask her.

'Yes, I'm sure. I just need a moment,' she replies.

We sit quietly for a few minutes as Val closes her eyes and takes a series of deep breaths. Nicky checks her cats via pet cam and speaks to Pinkie via the two-way speaker in her usual non-authoritative hushed tone, feebly ordering him to 'Get down off Mummy's curtains, you naughty boy!' Unsurprisingly, Pinkie, one of the two most pampered Siamese I know, neither answers his mummy nor climbs down. Jenna is typing frantically to Porsha, who has just sent her an update from the WhatsApp stag group. She then flashes the screen at Yana and leans into me and whispers, 'They're talking about strippers now. That's it! You wait till I get home! He's in big shit!'

During the week, we had discussed how we were going to approach today. If we were going to come in; what Val was going to say. Val had told us that, although she really wanted some moral support and someone to drive her back in case she took what she may find out badly, she was going to go in alone.

'I need to face this myself, but I'll be glad to know you four are waiting for me outside. It will give me the confidence to go through with it,' Val explained. She didn't need to, though. We understood completely. Sometimes, as hard as it is, you need to do things by yourself. A minute later, we watch on as Val takes a final deep breath and loops her handbag over her shoulder, then, without another word, she is off marching towards the farmhouse.

'Christ, she looks fuming!' said Jenna, as we watched Val stride towards the gates, which were thankfully open. 'I hope she doesn't attack anyone; not in that skirt. That wasn't a good choice. She should have worn trousers and flat shoes with some grip.'

'Of course she won't,' replied Nicky, 'and I suggested that skirt. There's a strong possibility Val's going to come face to face with the other woman. She needed to feel at her best. She's going in to talk maturely, not go five rounds.'

We watch as Val takes hold of the rope dangling at the bottom of the metal old school bell on the wall next to the entrance and gives it a good tug.

'No going back now,' I say when the sage-green door opens. Jenna and I shoot each other 'we were right' looks as two black Labs fly out, greeting Val like a long-lost friend, followed by a very yappy Jack Russell.

Despite our best efforts, we cannot see who has opened the door at first. One of the large olive trees either side of the porch is blocking our view, but then a tall willowy woman, who looks to be in her mid-twenties, dashes out to scoop up the Jack Russell, who having spotted the open gate had decided to make a bid for freedom. She reminds me a bit of Kate Middleton – casual but classy. The woman, I mean, not the dog. She is wearing a navy padded gilet over a fitted powder-blue shirt that's tucked stylishly into slim-fit inky jeans. Her glossy chocolate blow-dry is pulled back loosely in a claw clip.

'Doesn't seem like someone who has just been caught out

by the other woman, does she?' I remark as we watch the scene unfolding. From her hand gestures, it's clear that she's inviting Val to join her inside.

'She looks like daughter not girlfriend. If husband of Val left for her, it must be the mid of life crisis,' said Yana as the front door closes.

Jenna looks at her watch. 'Right, it's eleven twenty-six. If Val ain't out by twelve, we follow her in.'

Just as the clock is approaching midday and Jenna's starting to make noises about us all removing our earrings and tying our hair back in case things 'get heavy in there', the door opens.

'What the actual fuck?' Yana shouts in shock.

'What the hell is she hugging her for!' fumes Jenna.

'Let's see what Val says first. Remember the woman may not be involved,' Nicky reminds us all calmly.

Any thoughts that us seeing Tim go into the farmhouse the weekend before may just be a dead-end – perhaps lunch with a friend like Nicky has speculated – dissolve as soon as Val plonks back down into the passenger seat. She is visibly shaking.

Taking one look at Val's face, I lean into the front and pull the AUX cable out of the port. Now is not the time for Aretha Franklin. Jenna's choice was well-meaning. She was hoping – like we all were – for Val to reappear grinning and that she would strut back to the car feeling empowered. Jenna had leant forward and pressed play on what she called 'Val's victory number' as soon as we had spotted her. But for now, the song is on ice. It's clear things haven't gone how we anticipated.

Nicky squeezes Val's hand. 'Let's get back to mine, have a nice cup of coffee, then, when you're ready, you can tell us what on earth has just happened.'

Val forces a meek smile and says, 'Of all the things I was

149

expecting to find out, I never once dreamed of this. He really is a piece of work!'

Yana leans forward and puts her hand on Val's shoulder. 'Gather your thoughts. I think you have the big shock.'

The silence in the car feels too heavy, too expectant even, so I find myself telling them all about the koi carp delivery Grandad and Pam had received yesterday. How the fish were floating around on top of the pond in huge clear bags full of air and water, like when you win a goldfish at the fair.

And how Pam had made me hang over the side to grab hold of the bags one at a time so she could take pictures to show off to Karen, and how I had nearly gone in head first, tripping over one of the corgis the process. Val chuckles at the thought.

'They have to get used to the temperature or something,' I say when Jenna asks why Pam hadn't just plonked them straight in. I then explain how we had to follow all of the settling in instructions the fish came with because they cost so much. There are gasps all round when I tell them the heart stopping figure Pam and grandad parted with.

'Five grand on fish! You'd be giving them mouth to mouth, wouldn't ya, if they conked out!' laughs Jenna.

'You'll see them for yourself soon. You're all coming to the grand garden opening, remember.'

I'm looking forward to them coming. I've never had friends that I've been close enough with to invite to family gatherings before. As bad as it sounds, I've always been embarrassed of my mum and how she is, and Pam can be a little snobby and offensive sometimes without meaning to be, but, for some reason, I don't feel like I have to keep that part of my life separate with this lot. I've already told them all about my mum and her upcoming wedding – sorry, 'commitment ceremony'. They laughed when I told them about

Nigel, but also sympathised with me too, plus they think Pam is hilarious, having met her a few times.

Before, with friends, who I realise now were actually more acquaintances – people I was friendly with rather than real friends – I had always kept them at arm's length, only feeling comfortable showing them an edited version of myself, but now I can just say it how it is. It's a good feeling not to have to cherry-pick what you say, and constantly hold things back.

CHAPTER 26

Nicky is a posh shopper. The M&S and Waitrose Queen, our group playfully call her. Not that we ever complain. We love having food at hers, and when it's Nicky's turn to bring lunches at work, we're always in for a treat. Every one of us make an effort for each other, but Nicky always has the really special bits: the candyfloss grapes, the high-quality ham in brioche. Makes my mouth water just thinking about it.

Oh, I forgot to tell you about our little set-up, didn't I? So, we all work Tuesday through to Friday. Since this all started, we've been taking it in turns to make our lunches; one person each day makes everyone's lunch. That way we cook in bulk. It's cheaper and we aren't stuck with the same food for days on end. Plus, only having to do it one day a week lightens our load and makes it easier to stick to. We also try to have either lunch on Mondays together or Friday night dinner at one of our houses.

Today Nicky treats us to two Waitrose chicken tandoori kebabs grilled on her George Foreman (sixty-four calories each), a massive salad with balsamic vinegar (fifty calories), served with a Greek flat bread (one massive slice was a hundred and ninety calories) and a tablespoon of light mayo (forty calories). We tried the lighter than light mayo at the beginning but it's hideous. It made me gag. The few extra calories are well worth being able to have the middle-of-the-road one. The whole delicious lunch is so worth the four hundred and eight calories.

As we eat, Val tells us everything.

'Oh my God! When we saw her, Yana said she looked young enough to be his daughter, but I never in a million years would have guessed that!' Jenna exclaims, shooting her hands up to her open mouth in shock.

'Can you talk us through it again? I just can't take it in,' Nicky calls over to where we're all sitting, as she finishes loading her dishwasher.

Nicky's barn conversion has a huge open-plan kitchen and day room combined. It's slightly separated by a brick partition featuring a big iron wood burner in the middle that you can see from both sides. The seating area to the other side has a large flat screen TV on the wall and two deep-seated handmade sofas in a rustic orange and burnt-red pattern. They must seat at least six each, and are absolutely beautiful, despite the cats using the corners as a scratching post.

Val starts from the beginning, talking slower now, calmer after the meal and cigarette she has just had. 'I can barely remember it all. Some of it's a haze. I think I was in shock. I don't even remember hugging her when I left. God knows why I did that!' she says. 'She seemed to recognise me when the door opened, but I remember thinking that she didn't seem like a woman who had been caught out like what you all said. Far too friendly, relaxed even. When I said to her "I think you and I need a chat, don't you?", she just smiled serenely and replied, "Come in Valerie. I'll get you a drink".

'I'd forgotten that. She called me bloody Valerie! She

knew my name! Only Tim calls me Valerie. So, I followed her through and sat at a marble island in her swanky kitchen. I remember thinking, Christ, my whole bungalow would fit in that one room!

'Just as I was plucking up the courage to demand answers, Tiff – that's the girl's name by the way – said, "We'd all warned him this would happen one day".

'I asked her how long it had been going on. She avoided the question, but I just kept asking until Tiff sighed and said, "You know how Dad is. He's so stubborn. We honestly have been saying for years that he must tell you."

'I froze then when I registered her saying the words "dad" and "years". My face must have been a picture because she stopped and gasped. "You still don't know, do you? Blast it! I'm so sorry. I would have never said. Bugger! I'm so sorry, Valerie. I never should have invited you in. You really need to speak to Dad – I mean Tim".

'My heart was pounding at her saying dad again then correcting herself. Somehow, I managed to get it together enough to demand to know what was going on. But she'd clammed up, and just kept repeating like a robot how I needed to speak to Tim, and it wasn't her place to say any more.'

Val pauses briefly to accept a fruit polo from the crumpled packet Jenna had lent forward and offered her. Val took one, popped it in her mouth and continued filling us in.

'When I said I wasn't going until she told me everything, and also, while she was at it, she could fill me in on who Adam was and how he fits into all this mess, that was when her face really fell. She asked me politely to leave, assuring me that she wouldn't mention I had been there. I think she was probably worried she would have to tell Tim she had dropped him in it. I got up and made my way back through the hall. That was when I spotted it. The thing that really shook me up. There was a photo of Tiff, the woman who I had been speaking to, but as a girl. It was definitely her. Same wide smile, same mole on her cheek. She was sitting on a man's lap.'

I think Val could tell from our confused faces that we aren't following.

'The man was Tim,' she told us. 'A much younger Tim, but it was definitely him.'

Poor Val looks like she can hardly believe what she is saying, despite seeing it for herself.

A compilation of gasps, gulps, and 'oh shits!' follow.

'Sorry, I just need to check I have this right,' says Jenna, shaking her head in disbelief. 'So, Tim – your husband Tim – has a woman in her twenties who calls him dad, who you believe is his daughter, but you knew nothing about her before today, and you saw pictures of him in that posh house, and the picture was of him with a child who is a hundred per cent the woman who opened the door, but she is a kid in it?'

Val nods, slowly biting her lip. 'That's about the size of it.'

'What a complete wanker!' Jenna rages when it sinks in.

'So, which woman is husband of Val having an affair with?' asks Yana. 'Was there any photos of the other woman?'

Val shakes her head. 'I only saw the kitchen and the hallway, so no, nothing that gave me any idea. I wish I'd asked to use the loo now, so I could have had a snoop.'

By the end of the conversation, we are all more confused than when we set off to the farmhouse this morning; no one more so than Val. For a good hour or so afterwards, despite the poor weather, we sit in Nicky's courtyard garden, while the smokers of the group puff away on one B&H after another, I scoff strawberries, and Nicky dashes in and out checking on the cats.

'I mean, what if he was a surrogate or something? Maybe

he isn't having an affair,' Nicky says as we all throw possible scenarios out for discussion. Val discounts that idea straight-away. Tim is much too selfish to do anything like that.

When we've exhausted all possibilities, Yana finally calls it. 'So, are we thinking is affair then?' she asks.

Val tells us she is sure that's the case. 'There is no other explanation, the way the woman – his supposed daughter – said that they had told him it would all come out. The way me turning up there was no surprise to her. Knowing my name, the picture; it all only points to one explanation. I will never get the truth from Tim without a fight. He's proved what a liar and coward he is. I need to find out who the woman is. The one he's been seeing. Tiff's mother. If I can find her, I can get answers either from her directly, or, if she refuses, maybe if I have enough details and confront Tim, he will see the game is up, and I'll finally get the truth. But finding the woman will be how I get the answers I need.'

Nicky suggests we go back and wait for the woman to appear. Val says she thinks it would be a waste of time. 'When I asked Tiff if her mum would be home soon so I could talk to her, she said her mum didn't live there.'

When I say that she may well be lying to protect her mum, Val agrees it is possible, but that she didn't think she was. 'There was just something about how she answered,' said Val.

'Maybe Tim was just having a visit and does not live there either,' says Yana. 'That is so weird that she called him dad. If this was me, I would not be calm. I be manic woman.'

'And the name on the Land Registry could be Tiff's husband. Maybe it's her house that she lives in with her husband and Tim was just visiting. That would explain the man's name,' I offer.

Val says she thought the same.

156

'We need Tim's phone records. If we get the records, we get the number of the other woman and, if we get her, we can find out who she is, confront her and get the truth,' announces Jenna.

We all agree that Jenna is right, but that none of us knows how to get his records.

'Is Tim on contract?' Jenna asks Val, a few seconds later. Val confirms that he is. Jenna grins proudly and says, 'Let me think on it. I'll come up with a plan.'

CHAPTER 27

Jenna couldn't go to exercise class today because Jason had a mid-week football game (they had flipped for it – tails Jenna went to class, and he had the kids; heads Jason went to Thursday football and Jenna stayed home. It was heads). She was a bit down about it, so I offered to give it a miss as well and go round with one of Pam's Lorraine Kelly aerobic DVDs.

All started well but we gave up soon after. Roman kept clinging on to Jenna, whining and demanding, 'Pick me up. I want cuddle,' every two seconds, and Maxwell was screaming because he wanted to watch *Thomas the Tank Engine* 'on the big tele! Not my stupid bedroom one!'

We had a nice tea, though. Jenna grilled some Chinese-flavoured pork loin and sliced it into a noodle stir fry. After that, neither of us could resist a box of Heroes that Jenna's sister had dropped round for the boys, but we only had two each. Not through willpower, but because Jenna Sellotaped them up and threw them on the top of her American fridge so that we couldn't be tempted to eat any more.

With the boys finally in bed, Jenna filled me in on the

latest. She has been busy, having managed to obtain Tim's old phone bills. 'I was thinking yesterday evening, there must be a way around Tim being the only one able to request copies, then it came to me. My Jason. He wasn't keen at first. Whinging he was. "Jen, I am not pretending to be someone else to order copies of their phone bills." I was like, yeah, you actually are, Jase. You're going to come over to my mates with me now, my mum's on her way round to sit with the boys. My pal needs your help; don't be so self-centred. So, I took him round to Val's bungalow and basically got him to pretend to be Tim on the phone to the network.'

I purse my lips, swallowing my giggles. 'Weren't there loads of security questions?' I ask her.

'There were, mate, but we were prepared. Val had already written down Tim's full name, date of birth and their address along with his mother's maiden name and all that crap. Luckily, Tim had cancelled the contract the day he left, so the address hadn't changed. Then we put it on speakerphone and when the lady asked the questions, Jase made small talk asking how the weather was in her part of the world and did she enjoy her job, while Val quickly scribbled down the answers on a notepad in front of Jase so he could reply.

'It was a piece of piss really. Any day now she'll be getting the last nine months of his bills through the post, then we can get to work. I have an idea as well, that I used a few years ago when my Jase was a cheating little bastard. Any numbers on the bill that show up on the regular we will add to Whats-App, then we can see the profile photos. That will give us something to go on. We can also use the search bar on Face-book and Instagram. If the person has either account registered to her number, it will bring their profile up.'

I really do think Jenna has missed her vocation in life. MI6, she is here and ready for her first assignment!

CHAPTER 28

The second of June started eventfully: I got held hostage at work, and it was actually quite good fun.

At Elm Lodge, there are three main foundations of the residents' lives. Television, routine and food. The latter has become a massive issue of late. You probably remember it being mentioned that our chef had implemented a new menu, which has been met with a mixture of resistance, anger and sheer outrage.

It came to a head today after this week's menu options were given out. No one was happy and there were a lot of complaints, but it was Reg who decided enough was enough. 'I will not eat that muck!' he bellowed through the closed door as I perched on the commercial pack of toilet rolls, reading the *Daily Mail* on my phone. 'I want our old menu back. Until I see some steak and kidney pudding, fish and chips on a Friday and our Sunday roasts – and I mean beef, pork and chicken, not nut roast, whatever that is when it's at home! – we are staying put! And that includes the member of staff we have! That's right, we have a hostage! Etta is in here too!'

Joanie, Reg's last-minute accomplice, shuffles over next to him and shouts, 'That is all we have to say at this time! Oh, I nearly forgot. Lesley or Olive, if you can hear me, could you please go to my room and put *Corrie, Watchdog* and tomorrow lunchtime's *A Place in the Sun* on record, just in case?' Thank you, my dears.'

Joanie, I suspected had tagged along mainly for the status it will give her amongst the golden girls. A real-life account and all that. I was just collateral damage. I had been minding my own business, putting away the clean towels and stacking the skin ailment creams, when both of them bundled into the store cupboard, holding a bucket, a jug of juice, five packets of rich tea biscuits and a stack of newspapers.

'Sorry, Etta, but we need to make a stand,' Reg had apologised as he'd locked the door and wedged it shut with a piece of wood that looked suspiciously like a piece of skirting board from the dining room.

'What if we can agree to reinstate the Sunday lunch? Would that help, Reg?' called a disgruntled-sounding June through the crack in the door. Reg tells her to 'sod off' and that he wants to negotiate with 'someone in authority.' June shouts back indignantly that she is the 'daytime care manager!' After I hear some other residents chattering animatedly, no doubt revelling in the show unfolding.

Reg and Joanie then take a vow of silence, refusing to enter into further dialogue with June and, after her final attempt of 'stop being silly, open the door, and come for a chat in the office', all goes quiet.

'Etta?' calls Jenna through the door a few minutes later. 'It's me, mate. Jenna. Just to let you know June has put in a call to Anika. She was at a spa day at Henlow Grange. Halfway through a hot stone massage, she was, and now fuckin' furious to have been called in. Ain't that brilliant?'

Anika is the care home owner. She inherited the business

from her much older husband, who passed away before I joined the company. Anika has little to no input or interest in the home's day-to-day running. Every time I have seen her, which is maybe twice, all she seems to do is waltz from room to room remarking on the décor and why it all needs changing in her throaty Dutch accent. She has no idea who works for her. Val told me one time Anika had pointed at an empty plate on a table and barked, 'You! Get that moved now!' to a woman she thought was one of us staff, but who turned out to be a resident's daughter-in-law, who was not amused to say the least.

The news of the owner being on her way seems to perk up Joanie, who says in mock sympathy, 'Oh, how terrible for her!' while Reg, who has his head planted in the *Racing Post*, chuckles to himself.

About an hour later, Anika arrives.

'What is his name…Who…? Right, okay, Reg, this is the owner, Anika Willers. We cannot have a member of staff held against their will. If you do not send the hostage out, we will have no choice but to telephone the authorities – and your son!' she threatens through the door.

Moments later I hear Anika mutter something like, 'We must get them out. What if the staff member claims PTSD and sues?' Clearly not wanting witnesses to the spectacle, she then orders Val to disperse the crowd, and calls June and asks in a panicked voice, 'I mean, have you had proof of life? Good God, this is a nightmare! If the newspapers get hold of this, our exceptional rating will be out of the window. We will have to lower our prices!'

I laugh at the irony. Anika cares if I am alive only because it would harm her rating and in turn her bank balance. Nice.

'Can you confirm you're okay in there, Ella?' squawks Anika.

Yana corrects her, 'You get name wrong. Name is Etta,

not Ella,' before shouting, 'Etta, your good friend Yana here. I come to ask are you alive and well?'

There is no mistaking from her tone that she is trying not to laugh.

Despite June's demands for everyone to 'disperse with immediate effect!', Henry, one of Reg's friends, calls through the door, 'Don't back down, me old mucker. Remember we don't negotiate with terrorists!'

I try to snuff out my laughter as June can be heard practically begging Jenna to get out the After Eights to coax away the bystanders who are refusing to budge.

I shout back, 'All fine. No need to panic about losing our exceptional badge, and I think we can hold off a call to the emergency services and summoning Reg's son at the moment.'

The premium after-dinner mints obviously do the trick as all the busy chatter dulls, soon after June's shrill shriek of, 'Who wants an After Eight? Follow Jenna if you do!'

Then Anika's distinctive voice is back. 'Joanie, June tells me you're a sensible lady. Come on out and we can chat with Chef and see if there's a way to sort this out.'

Joanie looks to Reg for guidance. He finishes circling his afternoon runners and then asks if he can borrow my phone. I wonder if he's going to call the local gazette, but I reach into my fleece pocket and hand it over anyway.

I bite my lip as the chuckle – desperate to escape – burns my throat when I realise who he has phoned.

Reg switches his call to the local bookies on speaker phone. 'Reg here I have a hundred quid on account, so I'll have two quid each way on all of what I'm going to read out to you, apart from the sixteen-ten at Doncaster. Whack ten to win on that. I've heard great things about that filly.'

His insolent display pushes Anika over the edge.

'JUST OPEN THE DOOR NOW! I AM MISSING AN IMPORTANT MEETING FOR THIS!'

Anika is obviously unaware that June has already told everyone that her 'important meeting' is, in fact, a pampering day that she had to cut short to grace us with her presence.

Reg calmly continues to read out his chosen runners then when he is finished he closes his newspaper, places his spectacles back into his front shirt pocket, and then shouts back, 'While you are giving us sodding broccoli pasta bake and chilli con wotsit, there will be no sorting anything! I want my minced beef and potato pie today and that's final! And,' he adds, scratching his head, 'A LIE-IN ON SUNDAYS!'

With that, he turns to Joanie. 'What about you, luv? What do you want?' Reg whispers. It's like when a company gets an offer on *Dragons' Den* and they huddle at the back of the room for a quiet word to confer before accepting.

Joanie thinks about it for a few seconds. 'I want to be allowed a cat, or at least a budgie. I miss my poor old Sandy so much.'

'AND JOANNIE WANTS A PET. EITHER A CAT OR A BUDGIE. SHE WON'T BE FOBBED OFF WITH A GOLDFISH SO DON'T EVEN GO THERE!' Informs Reg before interrupting Joanie who's midway through telling me all about her beloved Pekinese who had to go to the Dog's Trust because Elm Lodge doesn't allow pets.

'Etta, what about you? What do you want, my love? You're not going to get another chance like this one,' he asks me, with a mischievous sparkle in his eye.

I um and ah for a few seconds then feebly reply, 'I don't know. Maybe have handovers in their time, not ours. That would be good.'

Reg rolls his eyes in response. 'Pathetic, Etta! I thought more of you! What you have to do is go big, then you get something. Go small like that and you get F-all. Watch and learn.'

Reg then marches over to the door and shouts, 'AND ETTA DEMANDS A COFFEE MACHINE AND SUPPLY OF CHOCOLATE BISCUITS FOR THE STAFFROOM, AND, MOST IMPORTANTLY, NO MORE HANDOVERS UNLESS THEY'RE PAID. YOU DON'T PAY ENOUGH TO EXPECT THEM TO ARRIVE EARLY AND LEAVE LATE EVERY POXY DAY! AND THAT GOES FOR EVERYONE WHO WORKS IN THIS HELLHOLE! NO MORE UNPAID WORKING!'

I gulp, imagining Anika's and June's outraged faces on the other side of the door. These are, after all, the same people who laminate signs like 'Only use the toilet roll you need by order of management' and 'All Johnson's talcum powder must be signed in and out by a witness.'

A very-pissed-off-sounding hushed discussion follows. June then calls back, 'Right, you're upsetting the other residents now. Anika usually would not give in to such underhand and outrageous blackmail but, for the good of the home, on this occasion, she is willing to speak to Chef and ensure that the old menu is back in place from tomorrow.'

Anika joins the conversation at this point, adding an indignant, 'You and anyone else who refuses today's dinner menu will have to make do with some crumpets or tea cakes. Although I don't personally know what is wrong with moussaka!'

Joanie high-fives Reg and then me.

'What about Joanie's pet, the coffee machine and an end to slave labour?' Reg barks back in response.

I hear Anika sigh dramatically.

'I cannot agree to animals in residents' rooms, due to health and safety, but the therapy dog is coming next week. What about if I ensure June gives Joanie an extra ten minutes with him? And every time thereafter?' Anika tentatively ventures.

The therapy dog is a star attraction; a huge fluffy Newfoundland with a dopey, bloodshot expression. The promise of extra time with him is a winner for Joanie, whose eyes are practically popping out of her head with excitement.

Reg takes her expression as a clear yes, so shouts a terse, 'Acceptable! Now what about the staff? What are they getting?'

Anika and June take turns to huff and puff before Anika finally responds with, 'I do not have the budget for fancy machines, but I am willing to have June stock a limited amount of Nescafé, supermarket-branded biscuits, and UHT milk in the staffroom. Say one coffee and two biscuits per four hours worked? And if it brings an end to this utter nonsense, I shall make clear that staff attendance out of working hours is not compulsory and should not be happening and that everyone should also be leaving on time.'

Reg pulls a what-do-we-think face. I shrug and laugh.

'Right, we will accept those terms, but I want it in writing. I know what you lot are like! But scrap the biscuits. Etta told me her and a lot of the staff are in the process of losing some pounds, so throw some fresh fruit into the mix and we have a deal.'

You can hear the relief in Anika's voice as she replies, 'June will have all this in writing to you by teatime. Now do come out of the cupboard. My staff member is very behind with her work, and the office lavatory is out of toilet paper. Again! Plus I have to get back to my business meeting.'

Reg stands firm. 'Pass it under the door or we are staying put, and make sure you sign it.'

I hear Anika splutter something that sounded very much like, 'For fuck's sake! He is really pissing me off now.'

A few minutes later, a handwritten note signed by Anika appears through the side slit in the door.

'Nice doing business with you,' announces Reg triumphantly. He carefully folds the note in four and places it into his pocket next to his glasses. 'And right on time to get the kettle on and settle down and watch my runners at Doncaster. Bonus!'

CHAPTER 29

That Friday, after we had all been home, seen our families and devoured our dinners – which in my case was chicken, leek and potato pie with heaps of peas and carrots coming in at four hundred and thirty calories homemade by Pam – the five of us meet outside the leisure centre at seven-thirty for our first yoga and meditation session.

We had all been reluctant when Nicky showed us the flyer a few days previously. She had won us round in the end, by reasoning that any class that will get us using our muscles and burning fat is worth a go.

Jenna put up the biggest resistance. Telling us that she thought any meditation was a waste of time and she would rather be catching up on *Ozark*. She had only relented when Nic promised that she would make some healthy version of carrot cake that she'd found on BBC food online – at only seventy calories and four grams of fat a slice – for after the class.

As we stood waiting, I couldn't help thinking that only a few months earlier I was in utter despair, pulling at my hair and lobbing fish and chips in public, just a few minutes away from where I am now queuing with four other women who I now class as close friends – in fact my only friends – for a Friday night yoga class. So much can change so fast.

Yoga is a stark contrast to the body combat class that is held in the same space. Mats spaced out, the harsh strip lights on the ceiling abandoned in favour of plug-in dim lamps that fade from moody greens to warm ambers right through to sky blues. The room, which usually smells of despair and sweat, tonight reeks of essential oils from the steam machine that is blasting out.

A serene man called Bear greets us. I was expecting the others to not take it seriously but, to my surprise, in the next hour Bear guides us gently through a selection of yoga poses and breathing exercises. He even takes the time to demonstrate some safe alternatives for Val when she apologetically explains about her knee.

Jenna, Miss 'I'm not into all that meditation; it's a load of wank', ended up liking it so much that she asked Bear what playlist he used so she could do a session herself at home in the week, when her kids were 'driving her fuckin' mental!'. Her face was a picture when Bear rummaged in his rucksack and pulled out a CD called *Pure Moods 1997*.

'I'll see if they have it on Spotify,' she says, taking a screenshot of the case.

Back outside, Nicky unclicks the lid of a baking tin and offers us all a piece of the promised cake.

'I couldn't believe it when he showed me that case! I thought people stopped playing CDs around the time Woolworths shut down,' said Jenna, laughing and taking a slice.

'I miss Woollies. I kitted out my whole first house between there and British Home Stores' reminisces Nicky.

Val polishes off her slice in three bites and says, 'I don't! Pick 'n' Mix and the cooked breakfasts from the Woolworths café in Huntingdon high street was the start of my troubles. Right, I've got no calories left now, so wine's out the window, but who wants to come back to mine for a glass of sugar-free squash?'

CHAPTER 30

Three days later, after a few weeks' wait the mobile phone statements finally arrive. I usually walk with Pam when I drop off Chloe on a Monday now, so, when I got back, I showered and then Grandad dropped me round to Nicky's. Jenna, Yana and Val are already at the table, armed with highlighter pens, when I join them.

'There's one number he rings multiple times a day, every day!' Jenna tells me excitedly.

'There's no others that show up like that one. It must be hers,' says Val, standing, hovering next to Jenna, who is still scanning the pages.

I help myself to skimmed milk from the fridge and start making myself a cup of tea. In a short time, us five have become so close. We all feel so comfortable with each other. Jenna had commented on this the other day. 'I have friends I've known since school who I don't even call round on without phoning first but, with us lot, we just treat each other's homes as our own. I mean I had a poo at Yana's the other day before body combat,' she'd said proudly.

Jenna beckoned me over to the papers strewn all over the

table. 'Get a look at this, mate. There are some numbers that show up a few times a week. Some Val has already crossed out cos they are her sons or Tim's family. There's just two numbers left. The one that he rings constantly, multiple times a day, that I've already told ya about, usually when Val would have been out of the house; and one more that shows up a few times a week at different times.'

Jenna directs Yana to read the two numbers aloud so she can key them into her own phone and save them.

'Right, first things first. Let's see if they have WhatsApp and, if so, what their profile pictures are. They may be set to friends only but it's worth a go.'

The first number she checks is the one that he rings less frequently, and a profile picture pops up.

'Right, well, that's the woman from the farmhouse,' says Jenna, turning the screen to us for confirmation.

Val nods in agreement. 'Yes, that's definitely Tiff.'

The other number is the one Tim has rung multiple times a day every day, but it has no profile picture.

'Shall I ring and see who answers?' offers Nic.

Jenna shakes her head and says, 'I have a few other ideas first. Let's try checking Facebook 'find friends' to see if the number is linked, and the same on Instagram.'

We watch as Jenna checks each one, but annoyingly both come up with nothing.

'What about if we just type the number into Google? Maybe it's linked to something else,' I say.

We give it a go and the first hit is for a property development company. Owned by a Mr Adam Dolson. The same man who owns the house on the Land Registry. The same farmhouse we saw Val's husband go into; the one where a woman claiming to be Tim's daughter spoke to Val. That same man is also the owner of a company and mobile number that the records prove Tim speaks to more often than his own sons.

Jenna is first to say what we are all thinking. 'So, who the fuck is this Adam Dolson?'

We try looking his name up on Facebook and find nothing. We do however manage to find the property development business page on Instagram. There is one picture of Adam Dolson. He looks in his late fifties and has that perma-tanned skin, gold Audemars Piguet watch dripping off his arm, and the general look of someone who wouldn't check the prices when he did his weekly shop.

'I wonder if he's the ex of the woman Tim is having the affair with?' said Nicky.

'That don't explain the phone calls, but he's definitely loaded,' Jenna decides, enlarging his profile picture. Val drains her coffee cup, takes one more look at the photo and tells us her plan. 'I am going to have a quick cigarette then I am going to come in and phone this Mr Dolson. Time to find out once and for all what on earth has been going on.'

CHAPTER 31

Ten minutes later, we are gathered round Jenna's phone, which is set to no caller ID, as Val dials the number, hitting speakerphone just before the call answers.

'Adam Dolson speaking,' said the assertive, posh voice.

'Good afternoon, Adam. I need to speak to you regarding my husband.'

I notice that his confident tone is replaced with a quieter, more hesitant version when he ventures, 'To whom am I speaking please?'

We all side-eye each other as Val responds. 'This is Val – Valerie – and my husband – well, soon-to-be ex-husband – is Tim.'

From his large intake of breath, there is no doubt that he knows exactly who he's speaking to.

Val strikes while the iron is hot. 'I need to know what's going on with my husband. Tim left me three months ago with no explanation. Since then, I've discovered that he has a woman in his mid-twenties calling him Dad, and I've seen pictures of him with the same woman as a child perched on his lap. I know this woman is called Tiff and she lives in a house that belongs to you. I also want to know why my husband has been phoning you multiple times a day for months before he left. Oh, and I also want to know who Tiff's mother is and everything else that has been going on behind my back for all these years. I think I deserve the truth, don't you?'

I was taken aback at how calm and eloquent Val was. She did amazingly. I would have been a stuttering mess.

There is a good ten-second pause before Adam speaks again. 'You know about Tiff? And you've been in my house? Does Tim know that you...' His words come out in a jumble

Val replies with, 'No, he doesn't know. He's had every opportunity to tell me the truth but hasn't, so I am asking you, and I would appreciate you cutting to the chase.'

Adam sighs defeatedly. 'Okay, but not over the phone. Can you meet for a coffee maybe? I'll tell you everything, but I'll be bringing Tim. He needs to face this. I agree, you deserve the truth. I've told him this for years.'

Jenna high-fives Nicky, and Val looks up at me and gives a thumbs up. 'I certainly can. When were you thinking?' Val replies coolly.

'No time like the present, I guess,' said Adam. 'Could you be at Café Nero in Ely High Street about one thirty? Would that work? I need to get Tim to meet first. I won't tell him you are meeting us until he arrives. He won't come otherwise.'

Val looks at her watch. About an hour's time. Easily doable.

'I'll be there, and thank you. I appreciate it.'

Nicky rubs her hands together. 'Right, I'll drive. Give me five minutes to put an audiobook on for the boys and spend a penny and I'll be with you. We may as well end the journey in the same car this started in!'

Val smiles and says, 'Thanks Nic. Finally, it looks like I'll soon know the truth.'

During the journey, Jenna asks Val if she's worried about what she might be told and about coming face to face with Tim after so long.

'Not really. I was in the beginning, but I've come to realise that the worst truth is better than the best lie and, at this point, it's the only thing holding me back from moving on completely,' said Val in response.

Val has a good point. Whatever she finds out, at least she'll have closure and will be able to start getting on with her own life. We know that Val has already decided that, even if Tim begs her, she wouldn't have him back now, but she just needs to know what's been going on. Who wouldn't in her position?

When we get to Ely, we drop Val off in the side streets by the cathedral.

'We'll park up and go and sit on the green, on the hill opposite the horses in the field, like where we sat last time we were here,' Nicky tells Val.

Café Nero is only a short walk, but we thought it would be better for Val to arrive early, get herself a drink, calm down and prepare for Adam's and Tim's arrival. Nicky manages to park up in a pay-per-hour car park on a steep hill. The four of us then make our way to the meeting point and sit down on the freshly cut grass. I'd already texted Pam and asked if she would mind picking up Chloe from school, in case we weren't back, and Jenna had done the same with her mum for her boys.

Ely is one of my favourite places. Summer days there can be whiled away having lunch in the many pretty tea shops, or bars near the river. Plus there are some great play parks for the children. It's a cheap day out. The five of us have been over there a few times on a Monday, doing our steps and having a picnic on the grass on a nice day, or enjoying a crispy oven-baked jacket potato with steaming baked beans or a chicken salad wrap in one of the little independent cafés on the more traditionally English drizzly ones.

Hopefully, today won't spoil the place for Val in the future. We are just discussing our upcoming garden party invites from Pam when Val's number flashes up on Jenna's phone. She answers, 'Yes, mate, of course we can. Are you still at Nero's? Okay, no bother. We'll be about ten minutes.'

'Val wants us to go and meet her at Café Nero.'

'Did she sound upset?' asks Nicky anxiously as she brushes the dried grass off her legs.

'Um, not really, I don't think. She sounded just how she normally does really,' said Jenna as we make our way back towards the high street.

When we walk into the coffee shop, Val is sitting collectedly, an empty glass latte cup in front of her, but no Adam or Tim in sight.

CHAPTER 32

'Did they turn up?' I ask.

Val nods. 'They did, yes. It was very enlightening. I wonder if we could have a walk back to the car. There isn't much space in here for us all, is there?'

Val has a point. I glance around the heaving space, which is mainly full of mums with pushchairs that are invading the small gaps between the cramped tables. Not that I'm complaining, having been one of those very mums not long ago, with a buggy in tow, getting tutted at left, right and centre in practically every shop I went in.

We start walking down the hill towards the car. It's surprisingly steep for fenland – which Ely technically is – and the path is so narrow we have to walk in single file. Our unusually fast gait is a give-away at how eager we are to hear what Tim has confessed to Val, who is strolling along, seemingly without a care in the world.

'So, what did he say?' I ask, not being able to take the suspense any longer as soon as we pull out of the car park. A minute later Nic nearly drove through a red light from the shock of what Val had divulged to us.

'Hold that thought!' Nicky announces as she indicates into a petrol station and pulls the car to a standstill near a tyre pressure checking machine. 'Right, I can't drive and take this in. So just to confirm I followed that. To be clear, Tim came into the coffee shop, sat down in front of you, with that Adam, and said I'm so sorry that you have to find out like this but there is no other woman, and Tiff is not my biological child.

'Then Adam said that he was telling the truth and that she was his daughter from his previous marriage but that she does think of Tim as another dad. And that was because for the last two decades Tim and Adam have been in love after meeting by chance. Then you looked down and they were holding hands!' says Nicky.

Which was indeed a shortened version of what Val had just told us.

Val sighs and nods her head. 'Yes, you got it all right. That is exactly what happened.'

Jenna leans forward and says, 'That is fucking unbelievable! Is Tim gay then?'

'It appears so,' said Val. 'When I asked him how can you have been having a relationship with a man, when we have two boys and a thirty-year marriage, he just shrugged and said he did love me, he *does* still love me, just not in *that* way, and that he hadn't meant for it to happen. Then he started crying and said that he was so sorry but he just couldn't live a lie any longer.'

'He is fucking coward! This is no excuse for how he treat you!' rants Yana.

'I mean, Yana is right. I have no issues Tim being bisexual or gay or whatever he identifies as, but in my eyes, gay affair or straight, it is still a major deceit,' Nicky agrees.

I have to say I agree too. 'So why did he leave like he

did?' I ask. 'Why leave when he did after carrying on behind your back for so long?'

'He got seen. By one of the couples we used to socialise with. They were more his friends than mine really, or so I thought. They – Adam and Tim – were on a romantic day trip to Castle Rising in King's Lynn. I was at work apparently! According to Adam, they were mid romantic pub lunch when they were stumbled upon. They had been kissing so Tim couldn't deny it. Apparently, our friends gave him an ultimatum: Tim was told if he didn't tell me, that they would. That was what prompted him to finally leave me.

'When I asked him why he left with no explanation, he said he just couldn't face telling me, and that he planned to say it was a new relationship after we got divorced. So, there was a plan to tell people he left because he liked men, and he couldn't suppress that side of him any longer. Just not the decades-long-affair part!'

We all sit gobsmacked.

'What are you going to do now mate?' Jenna asks Val.

'I am going to go home, have a nice bubble bath and my baked cod and roasted veg with a brandy, and an early night. In the morning, I will update my divorce lawyer and ring up that couple who saved me from potentially many more years of living a lie and thank them. Then I will come to work and see my four best friends, like I do every Tuesday, and start to get on with my life.'

Nicky turns to Val. 'Are you not livid? How can you not be?'

Val smiles. 'I am angry that he has allowed me to live in a dream world, and for my sons, of course, but they're adults; they'll be fine. I do feel sad for Tim, though. Sad that he didn't feel he could tell me the truth. I mean, if it had been a woman, I think he would have told me. For anyone to feel that they couldn't be themselves for so long I can't not have sympathy for. And, truth be told, as selfish as it sounds, it makes it easier to accept in a way. None of it was personal.

'After speaking to him, I do believe he wouldn't have dragged things out if he had felt able to be open. It is a lot to get my head around, but I will, and then I can start moving on. I have forgiven him and one day maybe we will even be friends. Not any time soon, but one day. At least now he can live his life openly and I can start rebuilding mine. You have to remember I've had nearly three months to mourn him leaving me. Knowing why was the final piece of the jigsaw for my healing.'

'Right, well, we'd best start getting some good headshots of you, Val, ready for Tinder, because you're back on the market!' announces Jenna.

'Jenna!' we all shout in unison, apart from Val, who is too busy laughing.

Finally, when she composes herself, Val says, 'I am not sure about Tinder, but I do have something you can help me with. I want to reconnect with old friends on Facebook.'

'Yeah, I can do that, mate,' replies Jenna as she sings away to Aretha Franklin 'Respect' the song she'd waited to play for Val for so long.

'While we are on the subject,' Nicky ventures casually, as she indicates out of the garage, 'I want you all to help me with a dating profile. I'm ready to find a new gentleman.'

Nicky's little Vauxhall erupts with claps and cheers. Then she says before we can, 'I know, I know. About fudging time!'

CHAPTER 33

Friday 26ᵗʰ June, Evie Cottage

I have been thinking about how I have been ruled by my size. I have let it dictate every part of me. I was always delaying things until I lost weight; like that was the gatekeeper to a fulfilled life. In reality, I just used to use it as an excuse: can't go swimming because I will look awful in a costume; I will find a boyfriend when I'm thin enough to attract one; can't go horse riding with Chloe because my bum would be too big for the saddle, and I would be mortified if I were told I was too heavy.

But also in reality, there is no reason why I can't do any of those things. I'm no heavier than the average man, so I could go riding. There is no weight limit to swim, and plenty of overweight women are in happy, healthy relationships.

I am trying to get into the mindset of I *have* fat not I *am* fat. That is such an important way to think. Having excess weight doesn't define you as a person. There is so much more to everyone than the number that appears when they stand on the scales.

My plans, mental health and life activities have centred around food and my weight. I used food as an emotional crutch – and an excuse not to live how I really want to. I have been my own worst enemy. Being heavier makes you lazy because it is hard work carrying around stones of excess weight. It is easier and more comfortable to just stay at home, which then just makes you fall deeper into the habit of avoiding people and social situations until all you have left is food.

So tomorrow I'm taking a big step into my uncomfortable zone. I am taking Chloe riding. I am, of course, worried that I will humiliate myself, but the look of joy on my daughter's face when I told her makes the anxiety bubbling inside me worthwhile.

Although I did have one boost today. I fitted into a pair of size 16 jodhpurs, and they were only a tiny bit stretchy! That would probably sound horrifying to most people, but remember I was barely squeezing into a size 20, so it's a massive deal to me.

I did a little happy dance as they zipped up. I had been battling with myself all day because I really fancied some Krispy Kreme doughnuts. The jodhpurs fitting helped me past the craving. Them fitting me felt better than any take-away ever could. I just need to keep reminding myself of that in the weak moments.

When I rang up the riding school to book, the woman on the line asked in a gruff no-nonsense manner, 'How much do you weigh, and what's your height so I can match you with a suitable mount?'

I gulped feebly and replied, 'I'm five foot three and thirteen stone four pounds. I'm getting lighter every week – I'm on a diet – so I hope that's okay.'

I don't even know why I said the last part. Maybe to acknowledge that I know I'm heavy but doing something about it. Anyway, I sounded as pathetic as it reads.

Lynn, the riding school owner – as the gruff voice introduced herself – didn't gasp or scold me. In fact, it seemed like no big deal after all. 'Don't fret, luvvie. We have riders up to sixteen stone so no bother there. Just make sure you wear a boot with a slight heel, no wellies. Hats can be hired for three pounds. We'll see you on Saturday at nine a.m. Prompt.'

With that, the line went dead, and I found myself having this weird feeling in my stomach. Not the anxiety that had been swirling around and making my ears fuzzy when I plucked up the courage to dial the number. This was different. Good butterflies. Excitement.

Friday evening, for the first time in months, Chloe didn't stay at Grandad's because she wanted to stay with me, ready for riding the next morning.

So, after I finished my shift at work, we all ate jacket potatoes that Pam had made us. Grandad and Chloe had grated cheese and beans while Pam and I had tuna salad with low fat mayo and no butter, then I went to yoga with the ladies.

After I got back, we lit the candles in the lounge and watched *International Velvet* while Chloe chattered the whole way through, excitedly talking about how she had told her friends that she and her mummy were going riding, what her horse may look like, how I had to take my phone so we could take photos.

At the end of the evening, I realised I hadn't even thought about food since dinner. My Time Out bar that I had been saving all day was on my bedside table, but I decided I didn't even want it. I was happy as I was, so I did something I rarely do: I left it for another day.

CHAPTER 34

The riding school wasn't what I expected, although I don't really know what that was. I guess the years of reading *Jill's Gymkhana* and imagining being married to Jilly Cooper's Rupert Campbell-Black had given me grand expectations of an immaculate courtyard of brick stable blocks and a sea of horses lined up waiting for us to admire them, their coats glistening like conkers as they happily munched away at their hay.

Fen Equestrian Centre is the opposite of that: a mish-mash of wooden stables; the peeling paint and rotting doors a testament to how long they have been sheltering the muddy horses and ponies that greet us with a variety of neighs, high-spirited head shaking and door kicking as we pass. There are several open-sided metal shelters piled high with a mixture of square bales of straw and round rolls of hay. Various terriers, mainly of the scruffy variety, are roaming around, happily wagging their tails.

Chloe and I pass an American barn that looks to be home to at least thirty more horses. A teenage girl with the most beautiful auburn hair plaited in pigtails flashes us a genuine smile as she works diligently on stable stains that are splattered all over a dappled grey pony's withers. I smile to myself as I notice the sign on his door. 'Graham The Great'. That's one hell of a name for a pony, I think, as Chloe looks on in awe.

The girl with pigtails clocks this, stops what she's doing, leans down into her plastic grooming tray and holds out a purple dandy brush in our direction.

'Would you like to help?' she asks as she offers the brush to my delighted daughter. The girl introduces herself as Fran, raves non-stop about the yard, and is just telling us how she has worked for rides at the weekends since her thirteenth birthday when a bulky woman strides through the yard wearing a battered wax Barbour and filthy navy jodhpurs. From the way everyone suddenly becomes remarkably busy – brooms move faster, the chatter dies down, a squeaky wheelbarrow is heaved on to the heap with new vigour and diligence – I decide that she must be the riding school owner, Lynn.

Chloe clutches my hand as we walk towards the mobile home next to the sand school, which, judging by the stream of people coming and going, seems to be the nerve centre of the yard.

'Who do we have here then?' the woman asks as she pushes a chicken off her desk and takes a massive bite out of a Greggs Steak Bake.

'Hello. I think we spoke on the phone. This is Chloe and I'm Etta.'

The woman nods without looking up from her scruffy, tea-stained bookings diary.

'Let's put Chloe with Dora. Lisa, you can lead and get her tacked up. Etta, you have Charlie today. He isn't a plod, but he's sensible. You said you've ridden before?' said the woman who is definitely Lynn, and who still hasn't glanced in my direction.

'Not for ages,' I squeak.

I'd mentioned I used to ride before I had my daughter when Lynn had asked on the phone if I was a beginner, but missed out the fact that I used to have my own horse until I became a mum. I lost confidence when I had Chloe, with the weight I'd gained, so I gave up and sold him to the family who'd had him on loan while I'd been pregnant.

I used the money to pay the first month's rent and deposit on the cottage. I try not to think back to that time in my life. I feel so sad when I do. Selling my horse was the final nail in the coffin. Giving up riding was a symbol of losing the old me. I think a lot of new mums struggle with keeping their identities as a woman. I know I did. My twenties were not a good time in my life. I have decided that I'm going to make sure my thirties make up for them.

I'm nervous about getting back in the saddle, and I think it shows in my face. As Lynn finally looks up, she takes one look at me and says, 'You'll be fine. It's like riding a bike! Go with Zoe. She'll look after you.'

I wave at an ecstatic-looking Chloe as she heads off with her helper Lisa to locate Dora. I hear Chloe giggle when Lisa says, 'Dora is everyone's favourite. She's amazing. You're going to have a fab ride on her today.'

Content that Chloe is in good hands, I start to look around the Portakabin for someone who may go by the name of Zoe. A woman balancing a saddle over her forearm appears by the door and gives me a small wave, gesturing for me to follow. She leads me down to the end of the American barn where I later learn all the riding school horses are kept.

Zoe stops outside the stable door of a sturdy bay Shire cross Irish draft gelding. At sixteen hands and built like a tank, Charlie is quite a sight. His mane is hogged, which makes him look a bit like a punk rocker, as he nudges me playfully from over the door.

My mount stands patiently as I give him a quick groom, lifting his feet without fuss for me to pick his dish-sized hooves. Charlie is an ex-police horse and Zoe said he is bombproof – as much as any living animal can be anyway.

From the moment I tacked him up to when I gave him a big thank you pat at the end, I wasn't just a mum, care assistant, granddaughter or fat bird to be sniggered at. I was Etta.

Anyone who loves to ride, even if they have had a long break, will know what I mean when I say it was the smell, the sound of the hooves clip-clopping on the concrete and the feel of the reins back in my hands that made me feel alive again.

Time went so quickly. I could see Chloe in front of me and every so often, she would turn around and Lisa would point me out to her. She would then wave and flash me a massive grin. I do feel a bit sad and cross with myself that I have allowed so many years to pass, depriving myself of something I love so much because of my weight. The good news is with what I am saving on not buying takeaways and junk food, even with the exercise class costs, I can afford for both me and Chloe to hack once a week.

I make a promise to myself as I climb into Grandad's people carrier afterwards. I promise I will never stop riding and deprive myself of something that makes me so happy again.

From the way Chloe chatters away non-stop to Grandad all the way home, telling him how brilliant Dora is, it's clear that she has caught the pony bug too. I'm pleased. It's something we can enjoy together, and I can't get over how welcoming the other riders were as well. They kind of have their little group like me and my ladies have. All different personalities, but brought together by the horses.

I had told them about our A Moment on the Lips diet club when, during our hack, Lynn asked me about my weight loss that I'd mentioned on the phone. I didn't go into detail – just how we were calorie counting and exercising – and she'd said I should try and rope the others into coming with me next time.

When Nicky hits sixteen stone, I am going to ask them. It would be fun to ride together. I won't mention it before because Nicky loves animals, so she would be disappointed to not be able to come just yet. With how well she is doing though the day won't be far away.

CHAPTER 35

Friday 10th July, Evie Cottage

Had a difficult week. I went to body combat twice but didn't manage my ten thousand steps every day. I am so tired. Today I found myself walking on the spot before bed. My new pleasure comes from hearing the little buzz and beep when I hit my target steps on my watch. I've been craving my favourite Marmite crisps every day this week. I had one packet yesterday, thinking it would curb my urge for them, but it just made it worse. Last night I dreamt I biked to Lidl in my nightie to get a multipack.

I walked with Pam two evenings this week, both times getting beeped at by men in white vans. Pam said she felt it was proof of me being a 'butterfly emerging from my cocoon'. I said I felt it was more proof that her white all-in-one workout playsuit was slightly on the more sheer side than she thought. At least I have stuck to my calories and used them sensibly. Full disclosure though: I did have a moment of weakness and had half a sausage sandwich and two chocolate biscuits with my grandad on Wednesday evening. But, in his words, 'No one ever got fat on half a sausage butty and two bloomin' hobnobs!'

I've been having extra chicken breast and a yoghurt in the evenings when I come back from my exercise classes. I'm always so famished. I thought that it's better to have something sensible using some of the extra calories I've burned off in class than end up scoffing the Skips and Breakaway bar earmarked for Chloe's lunch box that are always in the kitchen giving me the side-eye.

Tonight, the five of us went to yoga and weighed ourselves afterwards in the changing rooms. We all had losses. Yana was a bit disappointed with her two pounds, although she did say she didn't expect much else as she went over her calories this week – once when Simon came home with Greggs sausage rolls and pink doughnuts; the other when she made a huge midweek roast when Simon's family came over and she didn't want to have to explain her own healthy meal so ended up having a plateful of roast and a 'small slither' of toffee cheesecake for dessert.

Yana has now decided to be honest with her husband Simon about her eating issues; how we are trying to lose weight together; that she is calorie counting. He is somewhat oblivious at the moment. Obviously he knows that we all go exercising together and she does her steps each day but not how Yana struggles to control her eating and the bingeing, or the extent of the effort she is making.

Yana had explained to us that she felt too embarrassed to even mention anything about her size to him initially and wanted to diet privately, but now she feels uncomfortable keeping him out of the loop and, realistically, long term, Simon needs to be on board for it to work. So tonight she is going back to sit him down and tell him it all – even about the bingeing. It's the right thing to do. He can't support her if he doesn't know.

Nicky is doing brilliantly. She has struggled with portions so has upped her calories and is filling up on protein, fruit and veg. It must be working because she lost another five pounds this week. To date she has lost over three stone!

Val was happy with her loss of one and a half pounds, having had to cut her steps down to six thousand a day, and to working days only, and her exercise regime to only yoga on a Friday. I say 'only'. Even what Val is doing now is still a massive undertaking and commitment when her knee is bothering her like it has been. She is waiting for a hospital appointment about it. Hopefully, it will get sorted out for her. Even at work she's been struggling.

I am finding the steps the hardest to achieve. I can only describe them as a noose around my neck each day. A little dramatic, but they fill me with a sense of dread. Especially on the exercise class days. Speaking of which, body combat must be helping because Jenna lost four pounds this week despite her having an evening off for Jason's birthday and going out for, in her words, 'a massive fuck off Chinese'.

I have decided that I'm not going to do my steps on Sunday anymore; I need a rest day. I am also going to have a few extra calories on a Sunday, taking me to one thousand five hundred.

I was worried that it would hinder my weight loss, but, after speaking to Louisa, our body combat instructor – who, by the way, has turned out to be so supportive of us – I came away with a different opinion. 'One hot day doesn't make a summer. Take one day a week to recover and have a small treat if you feel you need it,' she told me.

So, I am going to do just that.

Louisa also advised me on the odd day when I have really hit a wall with my steps to do twenty minutes with my low-weight dumbbells that I got from Argos instead, even taking the time to email over a sheet to show me what exercises to do with them, to target toning my arms, stomach and thighs.

Louisa is another example of 'never judge a book by its cover'.

Despite this week being hard going, I lost five and a half pounds, which reinforces that, when you make kinder choices, your body will respond. I am starting to really notice the change in my figure now. Not so many rolls. Seriously looking forward to relaxing on Sunday though.

I have a busy Saturday planned. Riding in the morning and then takeaway at Grandad's in the evening. Another thing learned from Louisa – we can still participate in family meals as long as we make sensible choices. I am going to have tandoori lamb starter as a main with the huge salad it comes with, a few spoons of my grandad's saag aloo, and half of Chloe's keema naan. Should be no more than seven hundred calories.

I will have a Lidl cereal bar and a small apple before riding in the morning for about one hundred and twenty calories, then a boiled egg for a one hundred calorie snack. At lunch I will aim for two hundred calories, so probably cod, new potatoes, with loads of carrots and peas in the steamer, because it's so filling and will see me through to our takeaway in the evening. I will even have enough calories left for a little sweet treat at bedtime.

Not that I have been thinking about that Indian all week! I know it sounds a bit obsessive, but I plan ahead so there is no room for me slipping up or going well over my calorie allowance, which is easily done, and I am doing so well. I owe it to myself to keep going. In time I will get used to what is enough and will be able to judge what I choose to fuel my body without tracking. For now, though, I need to keep control and count the calorie contents and monitor my portion sizes.

On Sunday, Chloe has a fun surprise in store too. Pam has booked her in with Lynn for a private lesson – and I was shocked to hear that Pam is also joining her! 'Just for moral support darling,' Pam reasoned unconvincingly. If Pam enjoys herself, I'm going to ask her if she wants to start coming on Saturdays with us. We shall see.

CHAPTER 36

Saturday 7th August, Hunstanton, Norfolk

Jenna rang me at eight this morning. 'Hiya! Get ready cos me and the boys will be round in half an hour to pick you and Chloe up. We're going to the seaside!'

By 9 a.m. we were on our way to Hunstanton. Chloe is in the back, happily playing on her iPad with Jenna's eldest, while Roman, her toddler, kicks the back of Jenna's seat, screaming demands for her to put the *Dora the Explorer* soundtrack on.

'It's broken, mate. We can't,' she lied. 'I've put this on for you now, so stop screaming and show the Kings Of Leon the respect they deserve.'

The full-to-capacity electric sign above the seafront car park barrier, together with the lines of bumper-to-nose parked cars on every piece of non-double-yellowed road, was proof that we weren't the only ones who had woken up on what was turning out to be the hottest day of the year so far and decided that a day at the beach was just what the doctor ordered.

After driving around all the other parking sites, the only one that had any spaces was a hotel charging twenty-five pounds a day. 'Fuck that!' Jenna fumed. 'We'll park at Tesco and walk. It ain't that far!'

The kids were not impressed about having to walk 'miles and miles' or with being slathered in factor 50. Maxwell, who is surprisingly robust for a five year old, put up a pretty impressive fight and Jenna spent a solid five minutes wrestling with him, shrieking things like, 'Just pack it in, Max! Do ya wanna end up like the man we see on *Brits Abroad* on Channel Five? The one with them blisters the size of his head! Don't pull that face with me! If a grown man on morphine was sobbing, imagine what you'd be like on Calpol' – much to the amusement of several shoppers returning to their cars, pushing their trolleys full of bags of classic barbecue bits: bottles of Fanta, burgers, hot dog rolls, Pringles and bumper packs of Stella.

In the end it wasn't the threats of ending up with third-degree burns but a promise of a Mr Whippy when we got to the seafront that got things moving.

We had a lovely few hours on the beach, and at the fair. At lunchtime, we treated the kids to fishcakes and chips.

'We've done our steps, so sod it,' I reasoned as me and Jenna tucked into a tray of chips between us, together with the ham rolls and water that we'd been pushing around in a cool box under Roman's buggy since we arrived. Jenna said she really fancied a battered sausage when we were in the queue, but decided it wasn't worth half an hour of body combat.

We do that a lot now. If we fancy something, we ask ourselves would we do body combat for it? The answer is usually no. Usually, but not always. Sometimes we decide that whatever we are craving would be well worth it.

Before we all headed back to the car, we changed some coins into two-pence pieces for the kids to play the arcade slot machines. Anyone who has spent time around children will know that things can be blissful one moment and the next a full-on tantrum can erupt. Throw the sun and three ice creams into the mix, and them missing their usual midday sleep, and you may well have yourselves a problem.

Roman was becoming overtired and grumpy, so with his whingeing older brother Maxwell standing on the buggy board and Chloe sulking because she wanted one more go on the carousel, Jenna and I decided to walk back along the front, in the hope that Roman would fall asleep in his buggy, but there was too much to look at so he wouldn't give in. The lights from the amusements gave him a second wind for a while, but it was short lived. Jenna refusing to put two pounds in the crab grabber to win him a knock-off version of a Mickey Mouse cuddly toy, was what really pushed him over the edge.

Roman, in usual toddler fashion, had thrown himself dramatically on to the floor while screaming, 'I wanna Mick Mouse! Hate you, Mummy! Why you not get me Mick Mouse?' throwing in some windmill arms and legs and launching his Fruit Shoot bottle for full effect.

As Jenna tried to peel him off the floor and comfort him – 'Come on, mate, you're tired. Have a cuddle with Mummy and then we'll get back to the car' – a man who looked like the Fat Controller's shorter, sterner brother stopped eating a pickled egg on a white plastic fork, frowned at us, and tutted disapprovingly. 'Single mothers need to learn how to control their kids! Should be working, not here spending benefit money that my taxes pay for!' he raged in our direction.

Jenna, who had managed to get Roman back into his

pushchair, shot a glare at the man in response as she thrusted the buggy towards me. 'Etta, babes, take the kids. I'll meet ya outside in a minute. I am not having that prick talk about us like that!'

As I stood counting seagulls with Chloe and Maxwell, I overheard some of Jenna's wrath – not all of it but enough keywords ('disgusting'; 'stereotyping'; 'full-time workers'; 'ashamed of yourself'; 'if my Jason was here') to get the gist of the conversation.

I then pushed the buggy back to the car, while Chloe and Maxwell hung on to each side, so that Jenna could hang back and have a much needed stress fag. During which she rang Jason and had a massive go at him, she informed him that it was in fact all his fault that the man 'had a pop at her'. 'He wouldn't have dared if you were here, Jase!'

By the time we'd got back to the car, Jenna was still in full flow. Jason was a failure as a fiancé and a father. 'What kind of man are you, not to be here to defend the mother of your kids?' she'd asked him dramatically as I struggled to collapse the buggy and shove it in the boot.

I couldn't help but giggle when Jason let Jenna rant on until she ran out of steam and then coolly reminded her that the kind of man he was, is a knackered one up a roof, on overtime, on a weekend after a fifty-hour working week, earning money to pay for his fiancée's dream honeymoon to Barbados, and not just for her, but also for their kids and his mother-in-law. The mother-in-law that had to come so that the bride, aka Jenna, had help with the boys, so that she could sunbathe all day, drink all night and have lie-ins each morning – as per Jenna's request. But, by all means, he would happily scrap the idea and take her to Hunstanton instead so that he could confront pickled egg man and defend her honour. Kill two birds with one stone.

Jenna shut up then.

I heard Jason laugh. 'Would you like me to do that, Jen? How does two weeks in Searles caravan park sound to ya, love? Bit of bingo at Billy Nuns, romantic strolls to the Sea Life Centre?' he teased.

Jenna rolled her eyes at me and pulled a 'never happening' face. 'Nah, babe. I think we should stick to the Sugar Bay Resort now because we have the deposit down. Will you be home when we get back?' she asks, changing the subject.

Jenna huffs when Jason says, no, he won't be back until after seven.

'God's sake, you left at six this morning! I suppose I'll be doing bloody bath and bed tonight then. Oh, and, Jase, don't forget to stop at Aldi on ya way home. We need nappy pants size five and I want some of those ninety calorie mini chocolate bars that you got me last time. Bring me one home, but drop the others at Mum's. I'd go myself, babe, but I've been on my feet all day,' said Jenna, with no hint of irony whatsoever.

As we pass the Golden Lion Hotel on the way out of Hunstanton, Jenna shouts, 'Oh my God! There's a tiger loose somewhere between here and our house! That sign said anyone who spots the escaped big cat gets a quid, so keep your eyes peeled kids!'

I look at her confused.

'We can't let them sleep on the way back now mate; not now I'm lumbered doing bedtime. I need some me time,' Jenna tells me in hushed tones. 'Bloody Jason! He takes the piss out of me.'

During the drive back we chat about how lucky she is to be going to the Caribbean, and more about my history with Robert.

Jenna also tells me how Jason had casually mentioned to Rob, under her insistence, that Jenna has a new 'really hot' mate, and how we need to shop for my wedding outfit soon.

I told her not to big me up too much. After all, we can't perform miracles.

Jenna admits she knows how lucky she is to have Jason. 'I know I give him shit but he loves it.' she giggled.

Jenna must be doing something right. She has Jason wrapped around her little finger and I can't even get a man to speak to me. Last time I was approached was when I was out with Pamela and the Slim With Us crew (yes tragic, I know). I had agreed to join them on their monthly night out, based on the promise that we were going to a quiet village pub for dinner. For reasons unknown, I decided that wearing a jumpsuit from the ASOS Curve range in candyfloss pink was both flattering and a terrific idea. I feel I need to go on record at this point to make it clear that a size 20 jumpsuit in any colour is in fact always going to be a completely fucking dreadful idea.

Anyway, I was lied to, both by ASOS who marketed the zip up piece as 'versatile and slimming' and also by Pam re venue. So, to say – when the minibus pulled up outside the River View – that I was not best pleased, would be putting it mildly.

'I thought we were going to a country pub?' I questioned Pam, while glaring at her accusingly.

She flashed me her best sorry but not really sorry smile and replied, 'It's for your own good. You won't find a man on the sofa watching *Location, Location, Location* with a meal for four from the Chinese Dragon, darling!'

I let out an outraged gasp. Meal for four! How dare she? I mean, Pam knows how big the portions are from our local Chinese. I couldn't ever eat more than a meal for two.

'Plus, its two-for-one on main courses here on Saturdays.

We needed an extra person to take full advantage of the deal!'
She'd replied as if that answered everything.

As much as I love food, I hate eating in public. I am
slowly getting better with it now, but at that point I would
avoid restaurants because I felt that everyone was scrutinising
me and sniggering at what I was eating. If I really had to go
out for family occasions, I would try to book places out of
town; not that I know many people here anyway, but faces
become familiar, don't they? If I really had to, I would go to
quiet pubs and order things I'd never usually choose, like
chicken breast salad with no dressing, or grilled fish, and I
would never order pudding. I would then go home and make
myself a sandwich and have a few packets of crisps and some
chocolate or a dessert.

I once even ordered a kebab an hour after I had returned
from a fifteen quid a head all-you-can-eat carvery. My mum
and one of her boyfriends were there. I forget which one.
Possibly the car salesman from Brighton, or maybe the
trainee youth worker from Bedford. My sister was also there,
alongside Grandad and Pam. While everyone else piled their
plates high with potatoes, Yorkshires and three types of meat,
I had chomped on dried-up looking turkey, over-boiled veg
and one potato, then sat there claiming, quite unconvincingly, that I was full while everyone else went up for seconds
and thirds.

Anyway, back to the Slim With Us night out. So there I
was feeling seriously pissed off that I had been hoodwinked
into coming to the River View on a packed weekend evening.
I sat picking at my limp plaice, garden peas (substitute for
onion rings) and still-rock-hard new potatoes, listening to
Pam and her friends gossiping in-between gobbling down
their triple-cooked chips and biting into juicy steaks.

When all the food was finished and cleared away, the
music was turned up. Cue the makeshift nightclub. By ten

o'clock, the disco lights are flashing, and the place is so rammed the door staff start manning the lines that snake right up the high street.

Pam and the others are quite a few Cinzanos deep by this point, so it is no surprise when they all stand up glassy-eyed and sway towards the dance floor to answer Beyoncé's call. As someone who would rather staple something to one or even both of my nipples than dance publicly, I offer to watch the coats and bags.

After about ten minutes I start to get a bit bored. Don't get me wrong. Listening to Pam and the others drone on about if they think Karen from number 24 has had a secret tummy tuck or not is not exactly riveting stuff, but it is better than sitting on your own in silence.

I catch a glimpse of myself in the mirrored background of the booth opposite. That can't be right, I think, double-taking and staring back at someone who looks like Bob the Builder's inflated female apprentice. Her body appears to be much larger than her head. Fuck! It really is me! I am hideous. So, I do what anyone would in my situation. I down the drinks – all the drinks. Even the half bottle of Cinzano.

Afterwards, I stagger to the bar and order a double of whatever. Fuck the bags! I no longer care.

'Hello, sexy,' he murmured in my ear. Not my usual type. Deep laughter lines, not very muscular, a bit lanky really, plus he was wearing muddy trainers with a crumpled shirt and jeans.

But I was bored, and drunk, and I was pathetically grateful for any attention. It had been so long. So, I let him make chit-chat and join me back at the table for novelty's sake.

A short while later, a group of his friends came over and

introduced themselves. It is all a little hazy I must admit because, well…all the drinks.

I remember them referring to me as Percy, and me chuckling along, obliviously out of the loop. Eventually it became a bit tiresome, so I corrected them. 'My name isn't Percy,' I said, to which one of the group replied, 'Well, it should be. You know. Percy Pig!'

I stared at him blankly as he let out an almighty laugh as his friends all pat him on the back in an 'Oh, you're so funny! Well done!' manner. I didn't get the reference at the time. If Nicky had been there, she would have, her spending a lot more time in the M&S food hall than I do.

Anyway, there I am, standing there while some loser who should had been at an emergency dentist not a pub – judging by the numerous black open cavities that I saw as he threw his head back, in order to let his amusement ring out at my expense. Hideous.

I stand up to leave, my cheeks flushed, and, as I do, the man who approached me in the first place clutches my arm, frowns at his mates, who are all still howling of laughter at me and says, 'Guys, that's enough. How dare you? I mean, look at her! She's a babe!'

I smile pathetically at him, but the smile dissolves as fast as it formed when he follows up with, 'Have you seen the film?'

With that, the whole group falls about hooting.

I walk home alone in tears. When I get there, I rip up the jumpsuit and throw it in the outside bin. I then take a multi-pack of Wotsits and a family bag of Jelly Tots out of the larder, get into bed and binge eat them all.

But that was then. I am not that person any more. Luckily, you can always lose weight, but, unfortunately for people like them knobs, you cannot have a personality transplant.

CHAPTER 37

Tuesday 10th August, Evie Cottage

With everything that has been going on, I forgot to tell you about how things went with Yana telling Simon. It was definitely the right thing to do. He's vowed to help his wife in any way he can. Even offered to join her preparing and sharing healthier meals, not bring home high-calorie temptations, and to start walking together to hit her steps.

Yana was so happy when she told us. 'Simon has applied to come off the nights, which means he will be on Monday to Thursday day shift, so, I still have my Mondays free, but he will be home in the evenings to keep me busy and my hands out of the fridge! He also say we will start walking together, and he will buy me the dog – a Bichon Frise, like my family dog in Russia!' she had enthused. 'This morning when Simon got home, I walk down the stairs and he had for me scrambled eggs, the grilled tomato and the bacon. He is very nice man. I think now I should have told him sooner. The weight has been lifted from my shoulder!'

Yana's face was one of pure relief and happiness. I am so pleased for her.

In other news, Jason is off the hook. If you remember, Jenna saw a screenshot of some of the stag party discussing strip clubs when we went with Val that Sunday, but it turned out to be a false alarm. Jenna was all going back home and reading Jason the riot act, but then he saved himself by replying to the chat and saying no way was he having anything to do with strippers. So Jenna had decided it wasn't worth blowing her cover by bringing it up. Surveillance, however, continues.

CHAPTER 38

Pam has kept on having her riding lessons with Chloe on Sundays.

'Lynn said I had a natural seat,' she'd boasted proudly the Monday following her first lesson in-between bites of pitta bread pizzas that she'd made us for tea.

I have to say I was quite surprised by her enthusiasm.

As I mentioned before, Lynn's yard isn't exactly the National Stud in Newmarket and I thought Pam may have turned her nose up at the set-up, but she didn't even mention it. She was actually really excited. 'I need to know where to go to buy equestrian outfits. The really good kit. I'd like a ruby-red jacket with gold buttons, white breeches and black shiny boots – like this,' she'd said, flashing a screenshot of international showjumper Ellen Whitaker at the Horse of The Year Show under my nose. 'Where would I get that, darling?'

I took a second or two to think of a diplomatic response. 'I don't think the local tack shop stocks showjumping jackets. To be honest, Pam, you would be better off in just a T-shirt or a light jumper and jodhpurs — especially now the weather is changing. You'd be awfully hot in all that.'

Pam wasn't convinced. 'You can't do these things half-heartedly, darling. I intend to compete. I'm considering getting my own stallion. Maybe a thoroughbred.

I think I'd look fabulous on a grey, or possibly a black one like the Black Beauty on the Lloyd's Bank advert!'

My grandad looked round from his television programme and rolled his eyes at me in amusement.

I asked Pam if she wanted to join us hacking on Saturday now that the garden party had been postponed again due to the 'disaster' that being her water lilies, which she has commissioned to be imported from Malaysia, being further delayed. Without them, the floating candles wouldn't be as effective, she had decided. This resulted in her sending out a second lot of panic-stricken date change cards.

'I'll be sticking to my private lesson with Chloe on a Sunday. I appreciate the thought darling, but I like to be in the sand school.'

I asked why, reasoning that it was so much nicer to be out in the fields and on the bridal paths. Pam had then shaken her head solemnly and said, 'Not for me, darling. I'm happier knowing that I'm near the first aid kit, and that the rapid response helicopter could land in the car park, should the worst happen and I needed to be airlifted to Addenbrooke's intensive care unit or rushed to theatre for spinal surgery.'

My grandad started chuckling then and said, 'That's the spirit, Pamela. Positive thinking!'

CHAPTER 39

'Etta, come here,' Jenna says, two days later, while practically dragging me into the staffroom by my arm.

'We think Minnie has the rat in her room!' announces Yana, shuddering at her own words.

'What! Oh God! Have you seen it?' I ask, grimacing.

At that moment Val joins us and closes the door. 'Right, this isn't good. I've just been back in there, and I can definitely hear something scratching and squeaking.'

This makes Jenna and me shriek like schoolgirls.

Val borrows June's favourite finger-to-lips gesture and shushes us. 'You two quieten down or the residents will hear you. You know the hysteria it will cause if any of them get wind of this. Right, here's the plan,' Val says in a low, calm voice. 'You're going to get the puzzles out and coax the residents away from their bedrooms, and somehow keep them all busy. Meanwhile, I'll get on to Roger.'

Roger is our well-past-retirement-age resident gardener and odd-job man. He must be at least seventy. Bless him. I'll never forget the time he was held against his will by an overzealous agency staff member, who was covering when several of our weekend staff went sick with seasonal flu. The agency care assistant hadn't believed that Roger was there to fix a leaky radiator; her view being that he was in fact a resident with dementia. Despite Roger's pleas and protests, the lack of identification meant that he was guarded in the television room, until one of the permanent staff came on for their night shift nearly half an hour later and could verify that Rodger was in fact who he said he was. Funny, but not. We all have had to wear name badges since that incident.

'When Roger arrives, we'll search Minnie's room, then we better check all the rest of them while we're at it. Not a word of this out there, remember,' reminds Val, pointing to the door. 'If the golden girls hear about this, Marg will be on to her son and encouraging Olive to alert the media, and that's the last thing we need.'

'What are you and Roger going to do when you find it?' I ask Val; the thought alone making me shudder.

'Just get everyone out into the day room and leave it to me. Get out the fancy boxes of biscuits from the kitchen – the ones put aside for visitors' day if it comes to it – even wheel out the music player – anything. Just try your best to keep them in the day room,' pleads Val.

We assure her we will do our best and start trying to coax everyone out of their rooms, which is no easy feat – rather like herding cats. Our residents all have their own routines: afternoon naps; home makeover and gardening television programmes that they watch without fail every day; radio shows they tune into on the dot, and they do not appreciate us encouraging them to deviate away from their schedules.

'What's the meaning of this! This wasn't in the week-to-come round-up newsletter! I'm sure it wasn't. It can't have been. It would be on my calendar,' moaned Joanie as she made her way down the hallway.

Olive could also be heard complaining in front of us.

'Margaret and I had just settled down to *Loose Woman* and opened a packet of Marks and Spencer's Viennese Whirls. A bit more notice would have been appreciated.'

We somehow managed it though, Jenna set up a manicure and pedicure station, and I started offering myself up as a human hair curl and set conveyor belt.

Yana darts round with the Tesco Finest Belgium biscuit tins as though they are offerings from God. 'Take three each! Many more where these came from! You like tea, coffee or hot chocolate to enjoy also?' was her well-rehearsed speech. Although our oldies are never ones to pass up an extra few biscuits and a cup of something hot, they are no one's fools, I notice a lot of them eyeing us suspiciously.

It's our Reg who unsurprisingly pipes up first, while watching the scene unfolding around him with great amusement. 'What's all this in aid of then, Etta?' he questions me.

'Nothing, Reg. Just thought you all might like a bit of a change. We decided to go mad and crack open the good biscuits in your honour!' I reply playfully.

He rolls his eyes, a mischievous grin forming as he looks at me over his spectacles. 'Is that so? The thing is, Etta, the key to running a successful con is not to overdo it,' replied Reg as he gives a pointed glance at Nicky, who has a feather boa draped around her neck and is dancing about to an old Supremes number.

Reg glances back at me, raising a wispy eyebrow in my direction before turning round and clocking Jenna, who has four ladies in a row; two of whom have their feet submersed in foot spas; the other two with cucumber slices from the kitchen over their eyes.

'Ten out of ten for effort though,' Reg chuckles as he gets up from his chair, helping himself to a handful of foil-wrapped biscuits from the tin on the table. 'When in Rome, Etta. Cheers!'

～

An hour or so later, Val walks past wearing a pair of yellow Marigolds and gives us a thumbs up. 'Yana, can I borrow you please?' Val asks casually.

Off Yana trots to join Val in the office, only to reappear a few minutes later. I can tell by the way she's biting her lip that she's fighting back tears of laughter. I watch her lean into Nicky as I remove curlers from one of the golden girls' pearly locks. After a few seconds of whispering, Nicky starts to roar with laughter. Then, like Chinese whispers, Nicky repeats the process to Jenna, who shoots her hand over her mouth as loud belly hoots escapes. Jenna then trots over and sidles up to me, her hand covering her mouth in an attempt to be discreet.

'It's not a rat, mate!' Jenna manages to tell me between gasps of giggles. 'Minnie has stashed a hamster under her bath, in a pink plastic cage! The squeaking was the little wheel it was running around on. It's got its own name badge on its door. Guess what it's called! Its name is Channing Tatum!'

'He must be God's gift of the rodent world!' I said, joining in the giggling.

After a hushed conversation with a tearful Minnie, it comes to light that she was looking after him on behalf of her granddaughter, who was very upset about leaving the rodent while the family went on holiday to Rhodes, so Minnie had agreed to look after Mr Tatum.

We should have filled in the incident book, issued Minnie with a warning and informed June. Instead, we turned a blind eye, bar suggesting that the bath panel should be left off and the bathroom window left open to give the room some fresh air. Val also removed the wheel, just to be on the safe side, ensuring that no one else would notice the noise and investigate. Five days later he was collected by Minnie's daughter-in-law, who was, judging by the blanket the cage was draped in when she departed, well aware of the no animal policy. Val had a word and explained that we had made an exception, but please could she not bring Channing Tatum back.

On the plus side, if it weren't for Minnie's granddaughter's hamster, we may not have discovered that Nicky had never seen or heard of Magic Mike, and we then wouldn't have spent the next few glorious weekends watching the real Mr Tatum in action while shouting 'phwoar!' and 'oh my God!' at regular intervals. Nicky had needed her blue asthma puffer a few times during both of the films; that's how much she loved them.

'Gosh, this is better than Poldark! I thought he was a sexy so-and-so, but this, well, this is something else! My glasses are all steamed up!' Nicky had panted as we all roared with laughter.

CHAPTER 40

A sweltering hot, late August weekend, Port Isaac, Cornwall

Mum's 'love commitment ceremony' was this weekend. It was as I expected – completely ridiculous. We had to leave at five in the morning to travel to Port Isaac down in Cornwall, which Val had excitedly told me is where *Doc Martin,* one of her favourite programmes, is filmed.

It was a really long way, about five hours, nearly six including our stops. Chloe was soon back fast asleep, only waking up briefly when we stopped at the Tesco Extra for petrol as we joined the M5. When Chloe woke up again around nine-thirty, we'd just under two hours to go and decided to stop for a McDonald's breakfast, so it wasn't too bad for her.

I had already decided that I wasn't going to stress about calories too much while down there, but, trying to stay within my limits, I declined the chocolates from the service station and stuck to my homemade sandwiches and fruit. I did have a Sausage McMuffin and a coffee, though. Pamela didn't eat a thing; she was too carsick to eat. Luckily, though, she'd had the foresight to come in a travel outfit – a lemon velour tracksuit that had 'Juicy' spelt in diamante across the bottom, and a pair of replica Gucci sliders that she got from a market in Bodrum, during our family holiday to Turkey last year – so at least she wasn't sick on the sky-blue dress suit and matching hat that she'd purchased from Wallis for the ceremony.

Port Isaac was beautiful, with rows of whitewashed cottages and Cornish slate roofs, a shingle beach, and the water was sparkling aqua blue. We had booked into a little B&B in a nearby town called Camelford.

I'm embarrassed to say that I had never been to Cornwall before this weekend, but it is the nicest place I have been in England. I fell in love with it. Not just its beauty, but the whole way of life. It's so friendly, and the flora is amazing. With its palm trees and huge displays of wild flowers, it feels like somewhere far away.

The ceremony was held in an overgrown field on the land of one of Nigel's reflexologist friends, inside a very wedding-ish marquee, which my mum and Nigel kept referring to as their 'spiritual tepee hut', but it was a marquee. When we walked in, we were met by a shaggy-haired man, who urged us to remove our shoes to 'recharge and connect with God's earth'. Pam took one look at the grubby man in front of us – his feet hidden by the churned-up grass – and replied, 'I would rather not, thank you so much.'

It was a warm day, and the sides of the tent were tied up in an effort to circulate some air. Pretty jam jars of wild daisies and heather were placed on wooden picnic benches, extra seating was provided in the way of hay bales, and a woman in a peacock dress with an army of bangles down each arm stood in the centre with a wooden guitar slung over her shoulder. She sang songs, some of which I recognised from my Friday night yoga sessions, into a wonky microphone.

As I took in my surroundings, I spotted my nan and sister perched on a bale by the opening at the other side of the tent.

'I'd better go and say hello,' I said to Pam, gesturing in their direction. Pam nodded as she reached into her bag. 'Okay, we'll be over here, darling,' she replied before turning to my grandad. 'Could you possibly go back to the car and get the hand sanitiser? I must have left it behind. And I am going to need a carrier bag to sit on, darling.'

My sister Carly looked out of place. To be fair she looks out of place in most situations unless it's a beach or a night-club. Her usual poker-straight ice-blonde hair has a slight wave, set off by a daisy chain headband placed around her crown like a halo.

She had tried, though. No miniskirts or plunging neck-lines is really unusual for her. At my uncle Ralph's funeral, she had a black dress on – that she had later told me was from Forever Unique – which had so much side boob the pallbearers nearly dropped the coffin gawping at the flash of nipple as she bent down to place a rose on the lid. Granted, the white Grecian maxi dress she was wearing today had slits up both sides, and was translucent enough to spot more than a hint of her racy lace purple bra and thong underneath. Very Sienna Miller, if arguably a tiny bit sluttier.

I always thought that wearing white to a wedding that isn't your own was a massive no-no but maybe that's just me because next to Carly was my nan, who was wearing a creased, milky-white shift dress. Nan was sitting puffing away on a cigarette, seemingly oblivious to the fact that she was sitting on a flammable hay bale.

Life has not been kind to her. I always read in glossy magazines that unhappy people age faster, and that seems to be the case with nan. She, like my mum, hasn't followed the usual trend of women who get to a certain age and start chopping off their hair in favour of easy-to-manage styles like Judi Dench. Nan has a long, frizzy waist-length mane. It's a custard yellowy blonde with a good four inches of ashy grey roots. I had wondered if Carly's love of lip filler and Botox would have rubbed off on my nan by now. But judging by her sagging jawline and the clusters of wrinkles that would rival a Shar Pei that formed across her forehead as soon as she set eyes on me, clearly not.

Nan must have also (probably not so politely) refused to remove her shoes when accosted by the man on the door because a pair of scuffed matt nude flats with tassels finished off her look.

My sister held out her sylph-like arms and pulled me in. 'Etta! I thought you weren't coming!'

Carly reeked of Avon Far Away perfume and strong liquor. I looked at the glass in her hand. Most people would have mistaken it for blackcurrant cordial to quench her thirst on the scorcher that the day was already turning out to be. I mean, it was barely lunchtime, but I knew better. My money was on Pernod and black. This won't end well, I thought to myself.

'Hello, Carly. We've just got here. We had to check into our B&B and get changed,' I explained, guiding her back down to the hay bale. The jury's out on whether it was the five-inch wedge sandals or drink making her sway. Although I know which one my money would be on.

'Hello, Nan. Probably shouldn't smoke while you're sitting on that hay. How was your journey down?' I asked her politely. She looked me up and down like I was something the cat had just dragged in.

Isn't it weird how someone you were once so close to, can become so distant and hostile towards you? To the point that it's like you don't even know one another any more. Worse, you actually do know each other and have a strong dislike. If we weren't family, my nan would be someone I would avoid at all costs, to be frank.

'You look a bit less fat,' said Nan finally, after looking me up and down again and totally ignoring my question. Before I could say anything else, she flicked her fag end on to the grass, stood up and stomped on it. 'I mean you're still very fat, but an improvement on what you did look like.'

'Thanks, Nan. Yes, still fat but less fat,' I said.

Carly narrowed her eyes at me. 'You have lost weight. How has that happened? You're not ill, are you?' she asked, eyeing me suspiciously.

'No, I'm not ill. I've just been dieting and exercising with my friends, for a few months now. I've lost about three stone so far.'

Carly seemed happy for me and went to say something, but before she got a chance my nan piped up again.

'Friends? What friends?' she scoffed.

My nan has a way of dropping insults and then changing the subject before you can respond. This was a prime example of that as I was just about to fill her in on the fact that I did have friends – thank you very much! – when she spat, 'Look at the state of her! Anyone would think it's her wedding!'

She nudges Carly to get involved. Carly very much reminds me of Olive at Elm Lodge. On her own she's lovely but under the influence of someone else she is vastly different. My sister around my nan is not my sister.

'Who?' asked Carly, scouting the room for suspects.

'The Queen of Sheba over there in the Hyacinth Bouquet hat – Mrs Stir It Una! I see he's still running around after her like a lost sheep. Never had a backbone that man, and never will.'

This pushed me over the edge. My nan has no reason to be nasty to Pam or my grandad. Pam has never been anything but friendly in their infrequent meetings. But that hasn't stopped my nan being nasty at every opportunity. She finds it hilarious to call Pam 'Stir It Una' – a reference to Pam reminding her of Bridget Jones' mum.

'Nan, don't start, not today. Just try and be nice. Break a habit of a lifetime, will you?' I snapped sharply. She looked at me like I was from another planet for daring to answer back.

'What do you mean? I'm always nice,' replied Nan with a smirk.

'No, you're not. Calling Pamela 'Stir It Una' isn't nice, is it?'

As my nan chuckled away, I shot Carly a look that said don't encourage her.

'It's funny, though. Plus I never say it to her face. Everyone knows the best nicknames are the ones people don't know they have,' wheezed my nan.

She always needs to have the last word, but today I decided I was going to have it. When she'd finished sniggering, I replied 'That's true. I suppose ignorance is bliss. I mean imagine if you knew what people said and called you behind your back. But you're right, what you don't know doesn't hurt you, hey? Anyway, I'm off to get a drink now. Catch up later' I said with the biggest smile I could muster.

As I strode off, I could hear my nan questioning Carly furiously. 'What is she talking about? Who says what about me? What am I called behind my back?'

Not long after rejoining Chloe, Grandad and Pam, I heard my mum's voice beckoning me. 'ETTA!'

Oh great! She's signalling for me to join her next to a row of mats. They remind me of the sacks you sat on when you went down a helter-skelter as a kid. I spotted a sign next to them that read 'Past life regression therapy. Donations for fuel home welcome. Suggested donation £35'. For a horrible second, I thought she wanted me to lie down, so one of her amethyst-wand-waving mates could tell me that I am a fat disappointment in *this* life because I was a soldier who starved at war a thousand years ago in a past life or something along those lines.

Therefore I was relieved when she launched in with, 'Have you seen her, then? Carly, your sister? She's ruined my ceremony. She's wearing the same fucking dress as me!' said Mum through gritted teeth.

'You glow different in yours. This is *your* day, Hilary,' says a pink-haired lady sporting a 'Mother Earth is our only God' T-shirt, whilst eyeing me up like it was me who bought the dress for my sister just to fuck up Mum's day.

'Etta, tell Carly she has to put a coat on during the ceremony,' Mum said, her hazel eyes locking with mine.

'I don't think Carly will have brought a coat with her, Mum. I doubt she even owns a coat. Plus, it is very hot.'

Mum tuts loudly at me. 'Well, fucking well find one!'

My mum's pink-haired friend looked a little unsettled at the stern outburst, rummaged in her jean skirt pocket and pulled out a vegan chocolate bar wrapper and a golden orange stone. 'You're picking up on other people's emotions again, goddess. That aggression isn't yours! Do not let it take you! Centre yourself. Use this,' she instructed, as she dropped the stone into my mum's hand.

I watched on with amusement as Mum then starts humming with her eyes shut. The things you do to bag your man!

Speaking of which, Jenna has some more news on the Robert front. He's confirmed that for the wedding he won't be bringing a plus-one, so, whoever that blonde was, he either isn't seeing her any more or it isn't serious. Plus, he is keen to be introduced to Jenna's new 'fit' mate, aka me.

Oh Christ! I wonder how he will react when he sees me after so long.

We're going shopping in a few weeks to look at outfits that I will hopefully fit into by the time Jenna's day comes around. I still want him to notice me, obviously, but only so that I can give him a taste of his own medicine, then tell him I'm not interested.

I'm wearing a size 14 today; a knee-length blue dress. It is both stretchy and floaty, alongside it being from New Look—well known for always being generous in their sizes – but nonetheless, a size 14!

Once the ceremony got going, my grandad sighed with relief that he didn't have to give my mum away. He wasn't sure if it was expected or not. I'd known it was a worry hanging over him; not because he longed to keep his daughter – God, he would probably pay someone to take her – but because he hates to be the centre of attention.

I know I've said it before, but he really is a lovely man. My nan may mock him for opening doors for Pamela and pandering to her whims, but he is what a man should be – a dying breed of gentleman. He wears a pressed shirt, tie and trousers every day, he's polite, and has time and respect for everyone. Whether you're a cleaner or a millionaire, I can say without a doubt, he would treat you with the same high level of respect.

Grandad is also more tolerant than anyone I know, and you can always depend on him. I'm proud of him and I'm glad he has someone like Pamela who appreciates him. Yes, she can be demanding at times and makes him smoke at the bottom of the garden, out of sight of the neighbours, and douses him in Febreze when he comes back in, but she looks after him, makes sure that he never runs out of his prescriptions, is kind to his friends – even Arnie, who comes around and always overstays his welcome, talking about motor bikes and the strength of the euro, which I know she finds annoying – but she never shows it because she wouldn't want to embarrass Grandad. They're a partnership. Always laughing, joking and simply happy in each other's company, and that's what life is about. If I can find that in someone for myself one day, I will be happy.

Later, my mum's (not legal) husband number four came over to us after the hour-long rather eventful ceremony of poems, and angel spirit card prayers – no, I have no idea either; I zoned out and planned my food for tomorrow, so I cannot explain even if I wanted to, apart from to say that there was a bit of annoying chanting and burning of some herb that stank.

Mum and Nigel didn't exchange rings, opting to exchange bracelets that Nigel had made out of their own entwined hair instead. Rank.

'Thanks for coming, guys. Carly and the MIL are meeting for a late lunch tomorrow with us. It's not far from your digs – a little vegan converted bus on the beach, no plastic waste. They do an amazing beetroot juice! Can you make it?' he asks us all but looks at my grandad expectantly.

I know from an earlier conversation that my grandad wants to take Chloe to a little rock pool in a cove that the owner of the B&B had told him about, then grab some fish and chips to eat on the beach and leave by midday at the latest.

Grandad is in his early seventies now and it's a long way to drive. I'd offered to share the time behind the wheel, but he is not a good passenger. I know the last thing he wants to be doing tomorrow is leave later so that he can sit eating smashed avocado in a bamboo bowl and sip on gritty vegetable juice while listening to my nan's sarcastic digs.

I decide to step in. 'It's a shame, but we won't be able to join you, Nigel because we car shared, and I need to get back for work. Thanks for inviting us, though. It's been great,' I lie, as Pam starts nodding in solidarity and flashes her best grin in Nigel's direction. 'It really has been wonderful. We can all have a proper catch-up next time you visit,' she adds.

Nigel is unperturbed. 'Ah, never mind. Car share. Can't argue with that. Save on pollution. Yeah, man!'

He went to high five me and I, of course, pretended that I didn't understand the gesture. I know it was extremely rude but I just couldn't bring myself to go palm to palm with him. I mean, I've seen him. He picks his nose and toenails with his hands in public. I can only imagine what he gets up to with them in private.

'And thanks for suppressing your negativity, man. Shame about your sister's outburst but I understand. It's cool. Your nan explained that Carly had a bad reaction to antibiotics. I keep trying to tell everyone that you're being poisoned by prescription drugs but none of you listen. We're planning on driving up in Commer for a week in December so we can all do some bonding and energy swapping then!' said Nigel.

It's clear from Pam's face that she simply cannot wait for Commer, aka Nigel's ancient VW campervan, to be parked up on her drive for all the neighbours to see. At least the painted man-size cannabis leaves that cover the whole of the bodywork will blend in with her hanging baskets.

I think it would be fair to say that the 'outburst' Nigel was referring to wasn't a result of antibiotics chemically altering my sister's brain, but in fact more of a reaction to her being more than a bit put out at me asking her to wear Grandad's suit jacket over her dress, as per Mum's request, combined with several litres of various alcoholic beverages.

Still it wasn't my sister's best moment. As the ceremony was drawing to a close, Carly, for reasons known only to herself, had decided that when Nigel and Mum's 'high priest-ess', who was leading the ceremony, asked if any of the one hundred and ten people present had any special words of support or anecdotes for the couple, was the perfect time for her to stagger to her feet, using the bald head of the man sitting to her right as a leaning post.

'I have some words, actually it's more of a question really for all you vegans out there!' Carly had announced at the top of her voice. From the way Grandad and Pam had side-eyed me and gulped they knew something was coming, which it was. I have to say she really surpassed herself this time, though.

'So!' Continued a slurring Carly, 'I've been thinking about this a lot!' Hiccup, hiccup. 'So my question is, and this is a very serious question! Are you truly a vegan if you swallow cum? I only ask because if you're not, then there's no way that mummy Hilary is one if you know what I mean!'

A chorus of outraged gasps confirmed that everyone did indeed know exactly what she meant. Surprisingly though not even one of the guests found it remotely funny. Well, that's not completely true actually, because I was a guest and I nearly wet myself.

It was my mum's face that did it. Disbelief, anger and horror all rolled into one. I knew I shouldn't have been laughing but I just couldn't stop; mostly because I couldn't believe that Carly had said it.

In my defence, I did get up and snatch the microphone off her before she said anything else, and I did attempt to apologise on her behalf but I just couldn't get my words out due to hyperventilating.

Which, in retrospect, was probably why I was asked to vacate the 'spiritual tepee hut' along with my paralytic sister.

'It's a fucking marquee, you weirdo! Stop calling it a tepee like you're something special!' Carly had slurred at Nigel as she was manhandled in the direction of the exit.

Shortly after, my nan and Carly were instructed to leave

the site. Not because of 'the outburst' but because the two of them did something apparently much more unforgivable. They had disappeared in my nan's rusty maroon Sierra, nan at the wheel puffing away on one of her beloved Peter Stuyvesants, as usual, the same Lionel Richie cassette tape blasting out of the windows as the one she played when I was a girl, only to return a short while later with a bulging, golden arched brown paper bag resting on the dusty dashboard. Apparently, when you're invited to a vegan wedding, eating a Big Mac meal, even in your own car, isn't acceptable.

But the buffet was awful, to be fair. By teatime we were famished.

'Let's get back to the hotel and get some food,' I said to Grandad when my stomach graduated from small grumbles to loud growls.

Back at the B&B, we were happily scoffing Dominos and chuckling while reminiscing on my nan's deadpan expression as she sat munching on her cheeseburger while a small angry mob had gathered around her car and had started banging on the windows, chanting, 'flesh-eaters be gone!'

Pam said she didn't blame Nan and Carly for getting fast food. 'It was a long day, and it was all seeds, lentils and tofu. No one appreciates aggressive veganism. As I told Hilary I buy free range eggs. I do my bit.'

My grandad agreed. 'It wouldn't have hurt them to put on a small spread of sausage rolls or some ham sandwiches,' he said between bites of a slice of mighty meaty.

'Exactly Darling I don't like marmalade but I still offer it as a breakfast condiment. It's just good manners,' said Pam as she dunked a potato wedge into a garlic dip.

'Why Hilary is even pretending she is a vegan, I do not know,' said Grandad. 'Anyway, I hope that it lasts this time around and that she's happy. That said, alongside hopeful, I am realistic, so I won't hold my breath. Time will tell.'

CHAPTER 41

Monday 14th September, Evie Cottage

I haven't updated you about our losses lately. Jenna is well on the way to her goal; she's now nine stone ten pounds and looks amazing. Val's weight loss has been slow and steady; she's lost just under two stone. Her knee has also improved. Val isn't sure if it's coincidence or because of less weight on her joints but either way she's chuffed.

Nicky has done amazingly well; she has so much grit and determination. This week she joined Jenna, Yana and me at body combat. I can't believe that she's now seventeen stone five; that's over five stone lighter than when we started nearly six months ago. Nicky's GP has raved about how much healthier she is. Her cholesterol and blood pressure are back within normal levels and even her asthma has improved.

But it's also mentally that Nicky has changed for the better. Losing weight has helped her outlook on herself – something that goes for all of us – but it is most noticeable with Nic. Not only has she started getting her hair dyed, eyebrows waxed and treating herself to nice clothes because she feels worthy but she also no longer feels the need to check up on what her ex-husband is doing because she no longer cares.

A few weeks back, he had sidled up to her at her son's birthday lunch and murmured into her ear, 'You're looking better. You'll have to look me up when you're back to the size you wore when we first met. For old times' sake.'

Before, Nicky would have jumped at this. The old Nicky that is. The new Nicky turned to him, smiled sweetly and whispered back, 'More chance of hell freezing over. Now kindly piss off.'

We were so proud of her when she told us.

Yana has had a few blips along the way, as have we all. She has taken the approach of each day as it comes, and, if she slips up, she carries on without beating herself up afterwards. Before, Yana and I would have gone over calories or binged and thought, sod it, may as well just give up. But it is important to remember that one hot day doesn't make a summer. As long as we have more good days than bad, we will see results.

When you have been a binge eater for so long, it is really hard to just switch it off. In fact, it is impossible. Bingeing is more than learnt behaviour – a habit – it is a compulsion. Often one that individuals battle with for many years. It would be silly to think that we could just completely change our ways in just under six months, but I have come a long way. My binges are controlled and fewer and further between now.

Food addiction is underplayed in society. It's as troublesome and difficult to break away from as drugs or alcohol. Sufferers need support not ridicule.

I think exercise and having so much more to do with my time has helped me a lot because I have been busy and now lead a more fulfilled life. That in turn has improved my mental health.

My decision to continue to not have the food I would binge on in the house in large quantities has also helped. But having the other four women to support me has made the biggest difference. That said there is only so much others can do to help you, and these last few months I have realised that I have to be accountable for myself.

The first month was the hardest, then I started seeing the results and the high I feel now in beginning to feel confident in my own skin is better than any junk food binge I could have.

Having friends to speak to openly about my issues has made me realise that I was eating to comfort and console myself, though strangely I didn't realise that I was at the time. You don't always realise how unhappy and empty your life is until it gets better.

We are all in the habit of sending messages or voice notes whenever we feel like bingeing or going over calories, and, between us, we talk each other out of it.

I know that I wouldn't have got this far without our group being there to motivate me. From when I didn't feel like going to our exercise classes to them listing the reasons the takeaway I fancied wasn't going to help me reach my goal, we have an all-in-it-together mentality, so we want to do our best for both ourselves and each other, and that makes all the difference. Support is the most important thing with losing weight.

That is why Yana has come on in leaps and bounds. As much as we were rooting for her, she needed that little bit of extra support from the person who loved her most to tackle her bingeing, and Simon has really stepped up. He has been amazing. It has only been a short time since he has switched his shifts, but so much has changed for Yana. They have been planning their meals and cooking together, and taking evening walks to get their steps in.

At our last weigh-in, Yana was fifteen stone four and was so chuffed. She had set a mini target for her and Simon's anniversary, which is coming up soon. A few weeks back she'd ordered a special dress for the occasion. A size 18. Two sizes smaller than when we started this.

'It's really tight but it's on! I can't believe I did it!' She'd updated us on a voice note when she tried it on a few days ago.

We were all over the moon for her. It's been tough physically and emotionally draining for all of us at times, and Yana has had some really bad days over the months, with a lot of tears, especially during the weeks that she had put weight back on. We have all had times where we gained or didn't lose, but Yana more than the rest of us. She has struggled, but she did it anyway, so I couldn't have been happier that she made her mini target. No one could deserve it more.

I feel like a different person. I know people who lose weight always say that, but I really do. I am eleven stone two pounds now and am writing this wearing a size 14 pair of jeans! Actual denim jeans! I never thought I would see the day.

I still have a few stones to go, and I have far from the perfect body, but I am proud of how far I have come. When you lose a large amount of weight what you don't hear about is the loose skin. And after speaking to the others about it, I know I am not alone. I don't have masses of it but, I do have a little bit on my belly and some stretch marks.

The five of us were discussing the topic after yoga last Friday. Jenna thinks that every woman, whether they have had a baby or lost weight or not, will have some stretch marks and/or loose skin to some degree. I think this must be true as well.

Even my mum, who has taken great pleasure in rubbing my nose in the fact over the years that she has never been bigger than a size 10, and snapped back into her tiny size 8 trousers days after having both myself and my sister, has some loose skin on her belly and the silver telltale lines of stretch marks.

I'd thought previously that maybe it was more an inherited thing made worse by being bigger. To some degree, this may be true, but Jenna has never been massively overweight, and she has them and so do all her other friends – even the ones who haven't had kids. Nicky said that it was the same for her. That since the age of fifteen she has had them; first on her hips, they then crept around her belly button and later during pregnancy they spread, only to appear all over her as she gained weight over the years – the insides of her thighs, over her boobs and the backs of her calves. Upon hearing this, Yana had nodded and said, 'I have these on the tops of my arms and all over me. I think everyone has these too. I do not worry about them.'

Jenna told me about some MAC body make-up that she uses when she's wearing outfits that show her stretch marks. 'I cover them for me,' she said, 'just because I feel more confident, but don't ever feel embarrassed about them. Seriously, we all have them!'

I am going to get some of that body make-up for the wedding, not because I'm ashamed of my marks but because I want to feel as confident as I can. Isn't it funny that for years I've looked at celebs and women on Instagram who look seemingly perfect and it's all just filters and airbrushing! Real women have cellulite, scars, stretch marks and a bit of a tummy, even when they diet and are active.

We as a society have put so much extra pressure on

ourselves with the perfect Instagram culture. It is a dangerous thing in a way. People see the photos and they don't realise that they contain hours of make-up, hair extensions, facial fillers and Photoshop. In doing all that, they have raised the bar to an unachievable level. We are all striving for something that isn't even possible for the people we're trying to be like! As a mother of a young girl, it makes me sad to know that she is growing up in a world where individuals feel the need to smooth their skin and digitally pull in their waist and alter their faces on a computer before posting it to the world.

That's not what I want for Chloe. I will make sure that she knows that what you see online is not always real and achievable, even for the people who are in the photos. It's all smoke and mirrors.

CHAPTER 42

Thursday 17ʰ September, Evie Cottage

Yana sent me a text this evening asking me if I was able to come to the River View 'very urgently'. My heart sank for a moment. I knew she was out this evening for her anniversary and had this horrible irrational anxiety-driven thought that she may have got drunk and bumped into Robert, and blurted out my plan to make him desire me, and he now wants to see his stalker, and have a good laugh at my expense.

I know Yana wouldn't do that. I just have this tendency to concoct awful scenarios in my head. Thank you, crippling anxiety.

I have just texted her back, saying, yes, of course. Why what's wrong?

She sent me a hushed voice note in response. 'I'm in the toilets. Please come very quickly, bring talc and the carrier bag.'

I reply, 'Oh God, has it happened again?'

She replies instantly. 'No, is much worse. Please come quick.'

I fill Chloe in. 'Right, we need to go and help Auntie Yana. Can you run upstairs and grab your bath talc and then get your shoes on for me?'

Chloe nods eagerly and gallops up the stairs into action. Aren't children the most wonderful creatures? So accepting of unexpected situations without question, a chameleon like adaptability.

I debate getting changed but remember the focus was for me to be quick, so I let my hair down from its topknot. Then I drop the talc that Chloe has handed me into a Waitrose bag (obviously Pam's, not mine – I'm an Aldi and Lidl woman and think Sainsbury's is a treat. Pam got me some pears from Waitrose last Wednesday – £3.99 for four! Delicious but outrageous). Anyway, five minutes later Chloe and I head off up the track towards town.

When we arrive, I wave at Simon and divert over to his table.

'She's been in there ages,' he tells me anxiously. 'She said it's nothing I can help with. I did ring her and see if she needed anything.'

'Okay, I'll go and see what's happening. I'm sure she'll be back out soon.'

As I walk through the booths towards the toilets, I catch sight of myself in a mirror and cannot help but double take. I am completely different. Apart from at the changing rooms in the leisure centre where I try to avoid gawping at myself because I'm usually in a state of undress or tomato red, I haven't really seen myself in a full length mirror since I started my diet.

It's definitely me in my bootleg jeans, and crisp white T-shirt. I am in no way skinny, but my hourglass figure, thanks to the daily walking, along with our exercise classes and my weekly horse riding, is looking toned and healthy. My waist and upper arms look much smaller compared to a few months ago.

As I push open the door of the toilets, I call out, 'Yana, it's me. Which one are you in?'

The end cubicle door, which has a disabled and baby changing only sign, opens a crack.

'I'm here,' Yana calls back.

A quick glance is all I need to know that it is no sight for a child. So, I open the Netflix app on my phone.

'Right, Mummy is going to help Yana. You stay here. I'm the other side of the door and I can see your legs from the gap at the bottom, okay?'

Chloe nods happily, clicking on a horse series she loves.

I lock the door behind me and ask what on earth has happened.

'There was no toilet hole in the slim knickers. I had to take them off. I had to. I had no choice,' said Yana like a victim with PTSD.

When Yana had found her ideal bandage dress, she'd ordered it in a size 18 as her target dress for her anniversary dinner, as you know. What I forgot to mention is that a week before the big try-on, Yana was worried the dress wouldn't fit her and was concerned about the bulges it would show underneath even if she did wedge into it, so, on Jenna's recommendation, she got herself some slinky slimming pants. The pants are made of a material that clings to you tightly and compresses your flab back in, which is how they make your silhouette look a dress size smaller. That fact isn't advertised, though. I suppose the fact that you're a dress size smaller when you're wearing them because your fat and organs are compressed so tightly you feel like you're being turned inside out wouldn't be the best advert. They are awful, and I'm speaking from experience. No good comes from them. I have my own story about these little devils, but for now back to Yana.

When I close the cubicle door, Yana's dress is slung on top of the toilet seat along with her heels. She is standing barefoot in a bra, and her slimming pants look more like she's borrowed beige cycling shorts from Chloe. They are all bunched up. She's managed to get them up to her hips, but, instead of reaching under her armpits like they should be, they are rolled up like an Arctic roll and her belly has burst over the top. Her face is red, and she has beads of sweat on her forehead and mascara streaks down her cheeks.

'You've got to help me. I can't get into the dress without them! You need to talc me!' she pleads, the desperation in her voice clear.

I have horrible flashbacks to the *Friends* episode with Ross and the leather trousers.

'I think we need to unroll them first,' I reply.

Yana looks panic-stricken. 'No, Etta, I am claustropho-bic. I am very panicking! We must just get them up. Now!'

I say, 'Okay, don't panic. It will be fine,' and take the talc out of the carrier bag. I start dousing her all over her belly and back until she resembles a snowman.

'Etta, you must talc the inside of the knickers,' Yana says.

I frown. 'I can't. They're too rolled up. I'm going to try and tug them up a bit then I will.'

Yana is a good three inches taller than me so I'm strug-gling to yank them up, as much as I try.

I stop for a few seconds to think and come up with a plan. 'Right, I'll stand on the toilet and yank the back, while you tug on the front, okay?' I say, as I drop her dress into the bag and climb up on the toilet. I tower over her now.

Yana nods and takes a deep breath.

'Right!' I say, 'On three. One, two, three!'

We both start tugging and heaving with all our might.

'Errgghhhhhh!'

'ARRGGHH FFUUCCKK! THIS NOT WORK!' screams Yana.

It's no good. We got them just past her belly button before they pinged back down. The sides need tugging as well, but we just don't have enough pull power. I'm just about to suggest that she lies on the floor, and we try again, or maybe ring Jenna for an extra pair of hands, when a woman outside the cubicle clears her throat and calls in to us.

'Erm, excuse me, are you okay in there?'

Yana rolls her eyes at me, and I call back unconvincingly. 'Yes, thank you. My friend is just having a bit of a problem getting back into a dress, but all under control.'

A few seconds silence.

'Are you sure? I mean, I could help if you like?'

I'm about to say no thank you when Yana mutters 'fuck it' and clicks the lock open. 'Thank you. I need help. I have big problem. My husband is waiting for me and I cannot get back dressed.'

A stunning woman with shiny blonde hair – the sort of perfect girl who I would never dare even say hello to as I would feel too inferior – squeezes in to join us.

'Oh, shit!' she says with a small not unkind laugh. 'Don't worry, we've all been there,' she adds, as she puts her bag down on the floor. I'm fairly sure that she has never been there, but I appreciate the comment on Yana's behalf. In the end, we decide the best course of action is for Yana to lift her hands above her head to 'elongate her body' as the blonde woman, who has since introduced herself as Clara, suggests, and that we should basically heave the pants with all our might, side to side rather than back to front.

After a few failed attempts, we manage it. Ten minutes later, we have patched up Yana's make-up and wiped away the talc from her legs with wet pieces of tissue, and she is back in her dress. After a lot of sincere thanks, Clara leaves to rejoin her friends, promising to never breathe a word to anyone.

Yana and I are still gushing about how lovely Clara is and how that's what real womanhood is as we are walking back through the bar when I notice her at a table, her dazzling white smile beaming in recognition as she spots us. How did it not register before, I think. I knew she was somehow familiar but I couldn't place where from. It was when I saw him sitting next to her. That's when it all clicked into place.

Clara, the woman who has just helped us in the toilets, is 'her' – the girl in the red dress who was with Robert the day I had a meltdown by the river. I somehow manage to shoot her a smile back with a little wave.

Yana also clocks Robert straight away. She had after all seen pictures of him courtesy of Jenna's Facebook snooping many times. I watch as her mouth drops into an 'O' shape. She turns to say something to me. I shake my head and save her the trouble, 'I know I've seen him. I need to leave now.'

I say my hurried goodbyes and head towards the exit. Chloe picks this moment to stop and tie her shoelace.

Feeling a great urgency to vacate the pub, I lean down to speed things up. I'm still kneeling on the carpet when I hear a deep rich voice that I used to know so well.

'Alright babe! You look great. The best I've seen you look!'

I glance up, and, as I do, Robert winks at me. The same wolfish grin that used to make my heart race spreads across his face.

Even though I was fairly sure from the direct eye contact that it was me he was speaking to, my mind is still sometimes back inside size 20 Etta. When you lose a lot of weight, it takes a while for your head to catch up with your new body. I look behind me to check that it was definitely me he was speaking to, and there is no one else there.

I surprise myself with my response. I glare at him nonchalantly and reply, 'Please move away from me. I wouldn't want people to think I am in any way associated with you.'

Robert rolls his eyes; the arrogant expression ever present. Then his eyes scroll over to Chloe.

'Well, they would be thinking right, wouldn't they? You are very much associated with me.' His eyes challenge me. Smug fucker.

This gets me flustered. The thought of Robert's next words possibly being, 'Hi, Chloe. By the way I'm your dad,' start swirling around in my brain. As much as I wanted this reaction from him, I didn't want Chloe to be part of it.

I take Chloe's hand and attempt to stride away, but in my panic I manage to drop my bag in the process.

I scoop it up and hurry towards the exit.

Now I'm home I don't know how I feel. Half of me is thrilled; the other half is anxious. I am not sure what to do next. I am going to ring Jenna and update her. She is always good for advice.

CHAPTER 43

Right, so I'm back, following a chat with Jenna. Her view is that Robert is one thousand per cent going to try and pursue me now. She even asked Jason for a second opinion. 'Jase, come here! I need to ask you something!' she'd shouted at the top of her voice.

'Hang on, babes. He's downstairs loading the dishwasher. Right, he's here. So, Etta was in the River View kneeling on the floor and Rob, your Rob, well, actually he is more Etta's Rob, really, anyway he said that she looked better than ever and winked at her. Then Etta said, "Go away from me" and that she didn't want people to think she was associated with him. And Rob said, "Well, you are very much associated with me" and then looked at Chloe all cocky. So, what do you think he will do now?'

I heard Jason in the background asking why I was on the floor.

'It doesn't matter why, Jase. What? No, of course she wasn't pissed! Fuck's sake! She was doing up a shoelace. That's not the point. We need to know what you think!'

I heard muffled conversation and then Jenna shrieks,

'Right, you're on speaker phone! Jase, tell Etta what you just told me.'

I notice I'm shaking and I'm not sure why.

'All right, Etta? It's Jase. I just said to Jen that Rob will no doubt chase after you now. You're his type. Well, we already know that because of before. I mean must have fancied you before and I know he likes the exotic look – the olive skin, petite, long dark hair – so you're right up his street, especially now you are, you know, really petite after losing weight. He will probably try and get back with you.'

I can hardly take his words in. Mainly because I'm still swimming in Jason calling me petite. I cannot help but laugh as I hear Jenna say to Jason, 'Thanks, babe. Can you start running Maxwell's bath now, and just have a tidy round upstairs while it's running? I won't be long.'

Now that Jason has served his purpose, he has been reassigned to another task.

'Right, Etta, mate, you're off speaker. See, I fucking knew it! I knew Rob would be begging for another chance. God I can't wait to see him face when you tell him to fuck off!'

I explained about the girl in the toilet; her being the same one that I saw him with that day when I was walking home months ago; how she was really kind.

'Fuck her, mate! He isn't seeing her. She's just someone he's passing the time with. She's in her early twenties, you said? Well, she's far too young for him for a start, plus you said she was blonde and tall. Well, you heard Jase. He likes the opposite of that. Plus, you will be doing her a favour. He's a shitbag. Plus let's not forget that you ain't actually gonna get back with him! As long as you keep Chloe out of it, what harm will it do?'

So I have decided I still want to go ahead with making him feel a snippet of how I did. Maybe then in the future he will be kinder to women.

PART III
DESSERT

CHAPTER 44

Saturday 26ᵗʰ September

Grandad and Pam's garden party finally went ahead. Nicky had arranged a local taxi service to pick up all five of us, just after two in the afternoon. When we pulled up outside, we were greeted by Pam, who was standing at the end of a red carpet that was rolled all the way from the back garden gate to the end of the driveway.

Pam always makes a massive effort. There she stood, dazzling in a replica of the black full-length, off-the-shoulder gown that Princess Diana famously wore on the evening that she danced with John Travolta, also known in the media as 'the revenge dress'.

I smiled fondly as I noticed her faux sapphire and pearl choker glistening away at her throat. I had bought it for her as a Mother's Day gift from Chloe and me this year, from an Etsy seller who specialises in making costume jewellery based on items that members of English royalty have worn.

It is clear that Pam is in her element, seemingly unperturbed by the fact that it is a Saturday afternoon in our quiet little Cambridgeshire town and all of her guests are wearing clothing that I would place under the 'smart casual' bracket whilst she was fit for a ball.

'Wow! You look stunning! Like, amazing! You're such a glamour puss, Pamela!' said Jenna, planting a kiss on her cheek. From the first time Jenna and Pam met, they just clicked. They can't get enough of each other. Pam loves Jenna as she floods her in compliments and Jenna finds Pam hilarious, whether she is trying to be or not.

'Oh, thank you, darling! I was worried it was too much,' Pam replies, coyly returning the cheek kisses.

'Pamela, you look like the film star!' Yana enthuses kindly.

'Thank you, darling. You also look just superb, Yana. In fact, you all do. You've all done so well. Now, be sure to help yourself to bubbles, and I'm going to start circulating the Marks and Spencer's canapés shortly. Look out for the mini hot dogs; they are only a hundred and forty-three calories each! I thought of you all when I purchased them!'

We thank Pam and then leave her to welcome her next attendees, who have stopped mid red carpet walk to admire the fountain in the middle of the front lawn, which was one of my grandad's earlier projects.

Speaking of my grandad, he has done an amazing job with the pond. It has the wow factor. The lilies, reeds, and various aquatic plants look like they have been in situ years, not a matter of days, and the thick bamboo screen covering their oil tank looks very on-brand, or so Jenna says. I don't know what that means, but it does look nice.

However, it is the koi carp that are the real stars of the show, bobbing up greedily to the surface, opening their mouths wide to hoover up the food pellets, and in doing so displaying themselves in all their beauty.

Pam decided against a colour scheme with the fish in the end, deciding that silvers, golds, reds and oranges – even mottled and spotted, in all different sizes – would be the most eye-catching. 'Variety is the spice of life!' she had joked when they'd arrived, and she was right. I could watch them for hours; they are beautiful.

'So, which one is the famous Karen from number twenty-four then?' Nicky asks as The Four Tops 'Loco in Acapulco' blares out from the outdoor sound system.

'Erm,' I say, trying to spot Karen in the heaving garden. 'Ah, there. The lady sitting next to the giant Buddha on the decking, with the perm,' I say, finally spotting her.

'That's some outfit! I haven't seen double denim like that since I was in my twenties,' giggles Val as she glances over to take a peek.

'She's a nice woman from what I know of her, but she and Pam just get a little competitive,' I say, catching Karen's eye and swapping polite waves with her and her husband. It is during this exchange that I notice a crowd making their way towards us.

'Brace yourselves,' I warn. 'Don't look now, but Pam's slimming club friends are en route. They can be a little full-on.'

As soon as they pitch up next to us, wearing much the same outfits and hairdos as each other, albeit in different colour combinations, a few of them start manhandling me, squeezing my waist, wrapping their hands round my fore-arms and wrists. Hysterectomy Sally wasn't far off frisking me in the manner I would imagine you'd be subjected to if you walked past a drug sniffer dog at an airport and it sat down next to you and started barking.

'Oh, Etta! You look a-maz-ing!' one exclaims.

'Yes, you really do. You must have lost, what? Eight, nine stone?' said another between bites of battered cod on a stick, to which Jenna sniggers an amused 'charming' under her breath.

Yana, knowing this would have probably got my back up, protectively answers for me. 'If Etta lost that much, there would be no more Etta!'

The Slim With Us members all take turns in looking me up and down, remarking how much better I look compared to when I was a 'shapeless ball of blubber', as one so tactfully put it. Then came the usual hushed whispers of 'How did you manage it? Was it a gastric sleeve?'; to which I patiently tell them that I did it naturally with the support of my friends, that we all restricted our calories; in my case down to about twelve hundred a day. I also explained that we had aimed for ten thousand steps each day and attended exercise classes a few times a week.

This was met with unconvinced narrowing of the eyes; one of them even calling over their club leader Mandy to witness my claims.

'Etta said she's lost weight exercising daily and counting calories. She eats whatever she wants; just doesn't eat or drink more than twelve hundred per day! Apart from Sundays when she has fifteen hundred!' said Tracey, who looks to be the same size as when I met her when I went to their club that time, when I'd just had Chloe.

Everyone looks at Mandy expectantly. I'm then asked even more questions about my 'after body'. At one point a pair of hands comes towards me without warning and lifts up my top in order to see my belly, seemingly wanting to view for themselves any evidence of tell-tale surgery scars or a saggy loose-skinned stomach.

'It's surprisingly firm! Are you sure you haven't had a gastric band and tummy tuck?' Mandy jokes, but her words have a serious undertone; like she wants to place some doubt into her members' heads to ensure that they don't follow my path. I understand it's a natural reaction to ask someone you know questions when there is such a drastic change in their appearance but I can never understand the close-to-the-bone comments and the physical touching.

It's a bit like when you're heavily pregnant and people, including complete strangers, find it acceptable to place their hands on your stomach and say things like 'God, you're like a sumo wrestler! Are they sure it isn't twins?' or 'You're hardly showing! Is it growing properly?'

It's like the result of being a childbearing woman is having to be subjected to being touched and withstand extremely personal and sometimes hurtful comments about your body. At a time when you are already quite possibly feeling anxious and low in self-confidence – who wouldn't with all the physical and emotional changes that you go through during pregnancy? – so the last thing you need is the woman behind you in the queue in Boots patting your belly and announcing, 'Blimey! That must be a ten-pounder! You'll need a C-section, or you'll be in agony for months after with all the stitches you'll end up with *down there*!'

However well-meaning people may be, I wish everyone would think before they speak because words can be extremely damaging. I probably did look like a 'waddling walrus' but that doesn't mean that I want people I barely know to tell me.

For that reason, when Charles and Diana – the corgis – made an appearance, I was relieved. It meant that all attention was diverted towards them, giving me the opportunity to excuse myself, declaring to my friends that it was time for us to 'Help my grandad with that thing', who all then enthusiastically bobbed their heads and said, 'Oh yeah, we better had.'

Well, all of them apart from Jenna, who just looked blankly at me, squinting and muttering, 'Huh! What thing?' which was met with a sharp look from Val that prompted Jenna to back-pedal a little too enthusiastically. 'Oh, yeah! *That* thing! Let's go and do that *thing*!'

When we headed over to my grandad, I had to laugh. We had barely got half a metre away when I heard Mandy utter sourly, 'One thing losing it, ladies; quite another keeping it off. She'll pile it all back on, plus more by the end of the year.'

Mandy was clearly more than a little put out that her club had seen real-life proof that you can lose weight without buying six qui packets of branded powdered soups and ready meals. Even Pam has seen sense and stopped buying it. She eats much the same as me now and keeps an eye on her calories and copies the half a plate of salad or veggies, quarter plate of fish or lean meat and quarter plate of carbs; claiming only to be still attending the weekly club meetings 'out of habit and commitment'.

Although it was probably Jenna who pushed Mandy to snap. I had cringed when she'd turned around and said, 'I'd quit that processed shit you all buy off Mandy and just calorie count. If I could have a meal replacement bar with more E-numbers than a packet of Smarties from that shit range your slim club flogs you, or a crispy jacket potato with chicken and bacon with low-fat coleslaw and loads of fresh salad for the same calories and half the money, I know what I would choose. It's a con! Sorry, Mandy, mate. I know you're trying to earn a living but Pam showed me the meals she got off ya, and what a load of shit!'

I also saw Mandy's pursed lips when Val then told one of the Slim With Us ladies about the app we use, adding, 'It's free and if I can work it, anyone can!'

Never mind. Telling the truth isn't a crime.

I had a lovely rest of the afternoon, chatting to a few of the neighbours; some of whom I have known since a child, while the ladies got stuck into the mini burgers, hot dogs and fillet steak bites and had a chat with my grandad and his friends.

It was a really good party. At about six o clock, we decided to walk round to Jenna's, so we could all freshen up, and then go into town. Chloe, having already asked to stay at Grandad's for the evening, was happily playing in her Wendy house with one of the children who lives a few doors down. They're in the same class at school so often play together at the weekends.

I was a free woman.

CHAPTER 45

'I think I'd better go home and get changed. I can't go into town wearing these jeans, I've just noticed that I've got ketchup on them. I should have thought to have brought some fresh clothes with me like you lot have,' I said as we got to Jenna's.

'Just shower here. I'll find you something to wear of mine and I'll do your make-up as well,' replied Jenna, pulling her 'don't be thick' face and handing me an Asda own-brand vodka and lemonade in a can.

'I doubt anything you have would fit me,' I said hesitantly.

'You could always borrow my suckie in knickers!' chuckles Yana.

We go upstairs so we can start getting ready. Jenna hands me a towel with Velcro on the side to hold it up and a matching microfibre hair towel. I do as I'm told and shower and wash my hair. When I come out, Jenna's dressing table is covered in products.

'Right, face first,' she commands, gesturing for me to sit

on the stool. Jenna is really good at make-up, so I'm actually excited to see what she does with me.

Yana showers next, dries and plaits her hair and then slips into her Spanish floaty flamenco-style dress. It looks flattering, and, better yet, there is no need for uncomfortable underwear; it's loose and ruffled, so plenty of breathing room. Nicky reappears, wearing a sleeveless khaki-green maxi dress.

'This is a size twenty. I feel so good, I haven't even had to use my chafing cream in weeks! And look, body combat has done wonders on my bingo wings!' Nic tells us, waggling her arms proudly. She looks good, and you can tell she feels it.

Val reappears from the shower not long after. Her short, platinum Victoria Hamilton inspired hair is dry within a few minutes of it being blasted with a hairdryer and her telephone-box red cropped trousers and black Betty Jackson V-neck top make her look both smart and expensive. Two gold bracelets, various rings and a chunky belcher necklace finish off the look along with a generous squirt of Youth Dew. Val then pops outside for a cigarette, declaring she will 'put her face on' when she gets back.

Jason is still at football drinks and Jenna's boys are with her nana for the night, so the house is unusually quiet. Only the UK garage anthems from the Amazon Echo can be heard between Jenna's running commentary.

'Your skin is a lot more olive than mine,' she says, holding out the products like she is on a YouTube tutorial, 'but luckily I have this darker, really dewy iconic foundation from when I came back from Cyprus. I was the colour of a tree trunk! Looked like one 'n' all, I did. Put on half a stone in a fortnight. Bloody all-inclusive!'

Nicky pulls an impressed face as she watches Jenna apply the foundation carefully, using a brush then dabbing concealer under my eyes and each side of my nose.

'I am now applying coats of YSL black mascara and this Charlotte Trilby eyeshadow.' She holds up a bronze shimmery tub. 'Then I'll use this black gel liner and this applicator to give you a fox eye. All that together with some MAC silk individual lashes to the outside of your lash line is the best way to make aqua green eyes like yours really pop.'

Judging by the 'oohs and aahs' Val makes when she comes back up, Jenna is doing a good job.

'Right, I've decided on this NARS lipstick in colour orgasm because it will give that delicate pink lip, plus I have the matching liner. Babes, this is going to be banging!' Jenna enthuses. 'Then to finish, I'm using this liquid highlighter by NARS on your cheekbones, and a touch on your brow bone and Cupid's bow.'

Val has already done her face by the time Jenna says, 'Lastly, I'm opening my new liquid blush, which is also from NARS – bloody gorgeous it is! – and guess what it's called? Deep Throat!'

Nicky starts coughing on her drink. 'Where are all these make-up products from? They sound very risqué!' she remarks.

Jenna grins as she starts sponging on the highlighter. 'My Jase has been buying me them. For every three pounds I've lost, he's treated me to a new cosmetic.'

Val says how thoughtful that is of him.

Jenna makes uncommitted 'um' noises before adding, 'Just don't mention anything about it to him, because he doesn't actually know he has yet. I've used the emergency credit card.'

After I've been sprayed in the face with what smells like hairspray, but was assured was actually make-up setting spray, Jenna pulls the towel off my head and lets my ebony curls cascade down my back.

'Right. Head upside down,' Jenna says as she starts

squirting and spraying various products, then starts scrunching it with a hair diffuser.

Yana gasps when I put my head back up.

'You'll do,' Jenna says to me, like a proud mum.

'Etta, you look like the Kardashian!' says Yana.

I smile, never one to take compliments, and thank Jenna.

'Right, no peeking yet! I'm going to find you some clothes,' said Jenna as she opens her built-in wardrobes. She browses several heaving rails, pulling out a few things to consider before returning them. The last dress she pulls out is a vibrant, warm, flimsy burnt orange material with long sleeves and a deep neckline, delicate bronze buttons run down the front, finishing at an elastic ruched waist. I have read that ruched waists are good for my type of figure: hourglass, big bum, big boobs, small(er) waist. It looks extremely short but will probably be just below knee-length on me. Jenna holds it up and declares it 'perfect!'

The other three women also give their approval.

'Right, try these with it,' Jenna says, holding out a pair of nude gladiator crisscross stilettos. They are the type that lace right up your calves. Jenna sees my dubious face.

'They'll fit you babes. I bought them because they were on sale and I love them, even though they only had a size four – far too small for me – I thought I'd wedge my feet in, but no luck! I also have some new seamless knickers so you can have a pair of those. They're still in their packets.'

I thank her again.

'Oh! What bra do you have?' Jenna asks me in a panic. 'That's one area I can't help you with, Mrs Big Jugs!'

I rummage through my folded clothes pile and show her my sensible white padded T-shirt bra. Not that I need padding; the only place I haven't lost weight is my boobs. In fact, they look bigger now than before because they no longer rest on my belly. My back size has gone down eight inches though. The bra I've been wearing today is a 34DD.

'Right. Perfect. That will work,' said Jenna.

'Let's spray it with Febreze and pop it in the dryer with Lenor sheets for ten minutes to freshen it up,' said Nicky, already heading for the door with it.

I look at the dress laid out on the bed.

'It's gorgeous but that will never fit me, Jen,' I say in horror.

'Yes, it will; it's the twelve,' says Yana, checking the label.

'Just try it. If it doesn't then Jenna will find something else,' Val urges.

I nod, not wanting to come over ungrateful. When Nic returns with my now fresh bra, I try it all on. Amazingly, the dress does go on and Jenna zips it up at the back without any struggle. I step back so that they can all have a proper look. I look nervously at them for their verdicts.

'Fuck! You look insane!' Jenna shouts, and all four of them spend the next five minutes hyping me up; genuinely encouraging me and giving me confidence. Yana and Jenna then cover my legs, and chest in body make-up mixed with body shimmer. I can tell by their faces they are being truly honest when they say I look good.

I trust that they wouldn't let me go out looking like an idiot. I've never really had any friends who were genuinely happy if I tried to improve myself. In fact, as I've said before, I haven't really had any genuine friends as an adult at all.

I've already explained that when I had Chloe, I drifted apart from my school friends because we no longer really had much in common, and making friends as an adult is bloody hard work. The problem I had was finding anyone on my wavelength, though I did try. I went to all the baby groups, but there is nowhere harder to infiltrate than an already established mums' clique. I really think it would be easier to be accepted into an organised crime group. Being young didn't help. I had nothing in common with the other woman, and I felt they openly turned their noses up at me.

That said, I thought that at the time, but us five are all different ages and that has never been an issue. I just think the woman at the mum and baby clubs thought they were all too superior to include a twenty-two-year-old single mum, who lived with her grandparents, but maybe it was me who just felt that way about myself. Either way, the last seven years have been very lonely ones.

I sit on the bed as Yana helps me wind the stiletto strings around my legs. Then I stand up in front of the mirror.

I'm stunned when I see myself. I look slim, my hair is shiny and my skin glowing. The make-up is enough but not too much. I still look like myself, but the polished best I can be version. And most importantly I am happy. I feel more comfortable and confident than I ever have before.

'Thank you so much!' I say, hugging Jenna.

'All right, calm down, babes! You'll be smudging your face!'.

CHAPTER 46

We had a brilliant time in town yesterday. The best night out I've ever had. All five of us spent the whole evening drinking, laughing and dancing. That's right. I, Etta, even danced! In public! Jenna took loads of photos, and I didn't shy away from the camera, because I no longer get a sense of dread about the thought of seeing images of myself.

The night flew by and, before we knew it, it was a quarter past one in the morning and we were sitting on a wall in a line, swinging our legs, enjoying small doner kebabs while we waited for Simon to come and pick us up.

And guess what else! I ate half my kebab, felt full and threw the rest away. That's when I knew I had really cracked it. Sod what people like Mandy the Slim With Us diet club leader thinks! I am in control. I fancied a treat, so I had one. Today I will have a normal healthy eating day, do my steps, and not dwell on going over my calories, because I now have the hang of what I'm doing, and I know what's best for me. It's a good feeling.

I nearly forgot to tell you the funniest part, which happened this lunchtime. We all had a video call, and Yana said, 'Which lady left their black clutch bag in the car of Simon?'

Val replied that she thought that Jenna was the only one who took a black bag out with them. Jenna then said she had, but that she was sure that she'd had it when she'd got back in. 'Hang on, I'll check,' says Jenna, walking down the stairs. Then Jenna said, 'Yeah, that will be mine, Yana mate, and we'll need to do a swap because I picked up your car log book by mistake.'

She then waved a black folder with Citroen service stickers all over the front of it at the screen.

'What are you going to blame? Your eyesight or the vodkas?' I ask her through fits of giggles.

When Jenna says it must have been her eyes because she wasn't even that drunk, Jason appears and starts to laugh and shouts out, 'Not that drunk! Jenna, you came in the bedroom, stripped off, got in bed, and started snoring like a bear. Then when I nudged you and said go on your side, you sat bolt upright and said, "Oh God, no! Who's died! Actually, I'm too knackered. Just tell me tomorrow"!'

Jenna rolls her eyes and shouts indignantly as we all howl with laughter, 'Who asked you, gobby? Least I managed to find my own way home, unlike you, Jase, mate, the complete dipstick who ended up in the wrong house. Shall I tell them about when you were woken up on next door but one's sofa by the screams of a very frightened child? So pissed on Jäger-bombs he was that he'd let himself in the wrong back door.'

Jason could then be heard pleading his case in the background. 'These houses all look the same! It could have happened to anyone. Stop keep telling people about it. It wasn't even a big deal!'

Jenna's still belly laughing as she replies with, 'Jase, babes, you were stark bollock naked and spread-eagled on our neighbours three-piece suite, with half a packet of Pom-Bears from their kitchen on your stomach. The poor little girl dropped her Frosties in shock. Eight years old she is. You're lucky you aren't on a register, mate!'

We all start howling with laughter then, only for Jason to bellow, 'I WAS ON ANTIBIOTICS. IT WASN'T MY FAULT! EVEN THE POLICE AGREED – IN THE END!'

Jenna shouts back, 'All right! Calm down, Nigel!'

That's what finished us all off. Anything that brings back memories of my stories from my mum's wedding aka 'vegan gate' as it's now referred to by us all, makes us all snort with laughter until we cry.

Just as we'd calmed down, Jase comes back into view and sulkily tells Jenna not to 'forget to tell Etta she left all her make-up here'.

I look at the screen and Jenna pulls her 'trying not to laugh' face. 'Oh yeah, Etta babes, you left all your new make-up on my dressing table. Jase couldn't believe you spend so much on cosmetics! He saw it all on my dressing table and thought it was mine, so he looked up the prices online. About to have a massive go at me he was!' Jenna somehow manages to say with a straight face.

When Jason disappeared, Jenna leaned into the camera and said in a low voice, 'I must have been well pissed before we even left mine. I can't believe I left all them bits out. I had to tell Jase you had a bingo win, Etta. If he offers to drop it all round, just go with it and then bring it into work on Tuesday.'

I whisper back in amusement, 'I don't even go to bingo!'

Jenna leans even closer into the screen like Jason won't hear her if she does. 'Well, if my Jase asks, you do, mate, and ya fucking love it, especially after ya won big last week. So big that you treated me to a lovely little sequin skirt from Misguided, which I'm actually going to buy today on the emergency credit card, ready for my hen weekend!'

CHAPTER 47

Thursday 15th October, Evie Cottage

I don't know if this is just me, but it always seems like when one area of my life is going well, another turns to shit.

At the moment, though, that hasn't happened. I'm happy, work is good, everyone I care about is healthy, and my weight is now down to ten stone nine pounds. I still hope that I can teach Robert a lesson, though. I have thought about this a lot. Why I even have the desire for him to want me, when I don't even want him. A deep rooted need for acceptance maybe, or revenge. I am not entirely sure. I just know it will feel good to have the tables turned and for him to experience a snippet of how he made me feel. I want to feel like I am calling the shots.

I finally have a close group of friends. Even now I'm happy and don't have anything to worry about, I'm still anxious, waiting for the thing that will come along and cause the bump in the road. I don't know why I'm like this. I just can't help it.

Yana says I need to stop doing this; she is a firm believer in positive visualisation. 'What we think our universe returns back to us.' Easier said than done because anxiety has no stop button or rationale. I have been thinking about all this positive thinking, and to start with I did believe it was a load of rubbish, but it seems to work for Yana, so I have decided it is worth a go.

In light of this I've decided to try and be more thankful for what I have and try to look to the future in a positive way, by setting targets and planning for things that I can achieve or change to improve my life. Just things within my control.

I'm concentrating on feeling secure. As you become older, especially when you have a child, you realise it's so important to have a home to call your own. A base. I popped up to have a chat with my landlord, Tom the other evening, I told him how much I loved the cottage and how I never wanted to move. Tom said that he was glad to hear it and how I reminded him a lot of his sister, and how he loved seeing the place have a new lease of life. When I told him that one day I hoped to be able to buy it, he nodded and said, 'It's yours as long as you want it. If the day comes and you want to buy it then that'll be grand but you never need move. It's your home.'

Hearing that made me feel better. I had always got the impression Tom would never sell to anyone else, and that he wouldn't ever ask me to leave, but the confirmation was a massive step to settle my mind. I have since been wondering how much two-bedroom cottages go for. It's detached, but single-glazed and could do with a complete refurbishment including new kitchen and bathroom. I had a look online to see if I could get an idea of prices but there is nothing really to compare it to. Either way, I need a job that pays more if I am ever going to have a shot at buying Evie Cottage.

As a result of this, I have decided to take an access course from home starting in January to get the grades to go to university. Then I'm going to train to become a nurse.

I'd always thought having a career was beyond my reach, but now I think plenty of other people do it, so why not me? There is also a bursary, and student loans available, to help you afford to live while on the nursing course. I mean, it will be tight, but it's tight now so I may as well try and better myself.

I have also been thinking I'd quite like to meet someone in the near future. I was talking to one of the oldies at work about being single a few days ago and she said to me, 'Dear, just remember, looks fade. It's their personality you end up being stuck with, so take your time and choose wisely.'

This struck a chord. I want to be self-sufficient and never have to rely on a man. I want to be with someone because I can't be without them, not because I am dependent on them.

With a nurse's salary, I won't be exactly rolling in it, but with that and the inheritance I got from Uncle Ralph when he passed away, I may just about be able to get a small mortgage to buy here. I hope so anyway.

You have to try, don't you? I'm so glad I saved most of the nineteen thousand pounds of my inheritance. Unlike my sister, who blew all hers on a boob and nose job in Turkey and several holidays with her so-called friends. The same friends who then disappeared as quickly as Carly's inheritance did in the months after she cashed the cheque.

I knew that when I received mine that it was very unlikely that I would ever see money of that amount again, so I decided to save it until I could do something to make a real difference to mine and Chloe's lives. Like a deposit for a house, or something to make our lives better in some way in the future. I did consider driving lessons and a little run-around, but I knew that I would struggle to pay tax, insurance, and all the other running costs, so never bothered. Even when I have been boracic over the years – like having to scrape coins out from the bottom of my bag to get a loaf of bread until payday – I did it, rather than dip into it. Apart from a few emergencies, I have resisted the urge to dip into my mine. It's tucked away in an online savings account. That's one decision I'm proud of making. Very responsible even if I do say so myself.

The course and working full-time are going to be tough going but it will all be worth it to buy this place and have a career. At least the access course I'll be doing for the first year is distance learning from home, so I can do it in the evenings when Chloe is in bed. Let's hope I pass it so that I can apply to universities to start the following September. I will be trying to get accepted for either Peterborough or Cambridge campus. That way I'll be able to get the bus into Huntingdon then catch a train. It's going to take at least four years to qualify, but it will be worth it, to own my little bolthole that I've grown to love so much.

CHAPTER 48

Monday 26th October, Queensgate Shopping Centre, Peterborough

I feel a bit stupid writing this after me boasting about how frugal I am with money the other week. I have been shopping and ended up buying a whole new wardrobe. In my defence, I did need new clothes.

Before I lost weight, I lived in the same three pairs of black leggings, and a small selection of tops and cardigans. As I started dropping down sizes, I bought a few pairs of leggings and tops, mainly from Tesco or Primark each time I lost a stone or so.

But when I went out the other weekend wearing Jenna's dress, it highlighted how much better I felt in clothes I loved. I thought I felt good being slimmer but wearing that dress emphasised how much I needed a wardrobe update. In light of that, and to celebrate me now fitting into a generous size 12, I decided to go mad.

The five of us had planned to go over to Peterborough to

start looking for wedding outfits, so I thought it was the perfect opportunity to do my new wardrobe shopping. I reasoned that I also have Jenna's hen do coming up and so needed a few outfits at least.

We started in John Lewis because Yana wanted something smart for her stepson's party. As we browsed, Yana stopped in the Jaeger section and selected a bright print balloon-sleeve dress with a pleated skirt. 'I love this,' she said, holding it up to herself.

'Why don't you try it on?' I asked, after agreeing how beautiful it was. Yana looked down at the price tag and shuddered.

'It is one hundred and ten pounds! Simon say, "Yana, you are my queen. You must treat yourself" but I also need the outfit for the wedding of Jenna, so I don't think I should get it.' By the way Yana was clutching hold of fabric, it was obvious that she really loved it.

'You could always wear it to the party *and* Jenna's wedding,' Val ventured.

Yana bit her lip and took another look at the dress that was now draped over her arm.

'This is lovely dress. Do you think I *could* wear it twice?' she asked us.

'Of course you could. Who do you think you are? Zendaya? I have a French Connection maxi dress that has been to more weddings than my wedding planner,' joked Jenna.

Yana gives Simon a quick call to explain the situation. I hear him say, 'If you love it, sweetheart, then buy it. You're worth every penny.' Again, can we take a moment to say how lovely he is?

So off Yana goes in the direction of the changing rooms. Meanwhile, Val had found a Ted Baker shift dress with a bold floral pattern in the sale, reduced from over a hundred to forty-three pounds, and takes an instant shine to it. 'It's the last one, and it's a size fourteen. I'm going to get it,' she said, folding it carefully and placing it into the shopping basket.

'It will be a target dress for me, to help me stay on track. These trousers I'm in today are a sixteen so I should make it by your big day, Jenna, and I won't need anything else as I can wear it with my cream kitten heels and my favourite pashmina!' Val said, giving us a thumbs up.

Yana reappears smiling broadly as she skips towards us. 'I am getting! It looks, as Jenna say, banging! I love so much!'

While we are still in John Lewis, Jenna helps me select all the make-up that she used on me when we went out. You don't even want to know how much it all cost. I also got two new pairs of loungewear bottoms and vest top sets by DKNY. They were in the sale, though; I haven't completely lost the plot! In Primark I got two pairs of jeans and three tops.

While we were in H&M, Jenna got some body glitter for her hen weekend. I ended up with two cosy oversized jumpers, a chunky knit cardigan – much trendier than the shapeless market or Tesco ones I have always worn – and a denim dress. I wasn't sure about the dress, but then Jenna said how it would look flattering with tights and ankle boots so I went for it.

Afterwards I realised I didn't actually own any ankle boots, so I went into Zara and chose two pairs: one brown and one black. While I was in there, I also got some wide-leg trousers. Then I spotted some really lovely workout clothes so I got them as well.

Under the encouragement of the others I also decided that I needed a new jacket, so I chose a cream-coloured mac in Zara because, 'Zara does a shit-hot mac!' and also a lined winter wool coat, which will look lovely with my new gloves and a chunky knit scarf that I picked up to match, because, as you know, I walk backwards and forwards to work and the cold weather will be here before we know it.

Lastly, and I know this sounds ridiculously extravagant, I went into Marks and Spencer's and got five pairs of comfy Sloggi knickers, two pairs of work trousers – not leggings; ones with actual zips – and three new pairs of lacy underwear sets in white, black and a racy red in case, as Yana joked, 'you get lucky!'

I nearly stopped there but then I spotted two other dresses: a casual cream roll-neck jumper dress and a midi tea dress, which Nicky said I could wear with tights in the day or at night without.

That was definitely going to be it until Jenna came over with a long sleeve jade green dress, similar to her burnt orange one that I'd worn on our night out, and so I couldn't not have it.

'This is a great every occasion dress,' Jenna had declared, thrusting it into my arms.

I got caught up in the moment and bought them all, along with a pair of pointed, heeled court shoes in nude, just so I had all bases covered.

I fretted all the way back to the car that I had spent too much but Val tried to make me feel better by saying. 'You've worked hard for this moment. You deserve it. Just enjoy it.'

Then Jenna said, 'You have your capsule wardrobe now, so the big expense is over. You can just add a few new things as and when.'

I knew they were right: I have worked hard, and I did enjoy buying it all.

When we got back to the car, Nicky showed us her three new wrap dresses: a plum knee-length one in a size 18 for now, which will look classy with her calf-length patent croc-odile-style black boots; the other two are made of wool blend and will be perfect for the festive season at the end of the year as one is a berry red and the other a green tartan. They are both in a size 16. Nicky is confident that she will be in them by the end of the year, even though her weight loss has slowed. 'I can't believe I've lost all the weight I have! The feeling of being able to walk into a shop and pick up a size eighteen is worth every exercise class, and cutting back on the comfort food,' Nicky said as we drove out of the multi-storey carpark.

Val also treated herself. She'd picked up a new yoga outfit and a new pair of trainers from JD Sports.

When I was giving myself heart palpitations at the beauty counter paying for my make-up and the bottle of Creed perfume, which I chose – having never really worn any before – based on googling popular fragrances and liking that best out of a few testers the lady had sprayed on cardboard strips, Jenna had decided to treat herself to an Elemis skin care set, and some Aveda Blue Melva shampoo, both of which she paid for on the emergency credit card.

'For my wedding,' she had reasoned after.

Everything Jenna buys that she feels is extravagant, she makes herself feel better by telling herself, and usually us, that it's for her wedding.

I still feel bad that I have dipped into my savings for today's antics. The only time I have used some of it over the years before today was for proper sensible things that I couldn't do without. Like when Chloe had needed new school shoes just after a large energy bill, or when Alice jarred her leg and was limping, which resulted in an expensive trip to the vets. That kind of thing. Part of me feels guilty for spending so much money on myself; the other part of me can barely wait to try it all on and have a go with my make-up.

We called into McDonald's to have a late lunch on the

way home. Yana, Nicky and Jenna had Big Macs and Diet Cokes, Val had a coffee and a McChicken Sandwich, and I had a Hamburger Happy Meal with a Sprite Zero.

As we sat at the table savouring our rare treat I said, 'I would've never eaten this in public before. I would've been too embarrassed. I'd have gone through the drive-thru with Pam or Grandad and got a large Big Mac meal with large full-fat Coke and two apple pies and probably a McFlurry, then gone home and demolished the lot!'

We've all come a long way. Together we have realised that dieting isn't banning your favourite foods; it's about learning moderation and addressing why we are craving certain things. We are all still a work in progress, but we are on the right road.

CHAPTER 49

When we get back to Yana's that afternoon, we are all eager for Nicky to fill us in on the latest with her online dating.

'There are some really strange men on there, and some who are obviously just after one thing,' said Nicky coyly.

'One thing? What do you mean?' asks Jenna, pretending she doesn't know what Nicky is getting at.

'You know. The scoundrels that just want to make love. The ones that, once they'd had my flower, would disappear never to be seen again,' Nicky replies primly.

We all burst out laughing.

'Blimey, Nic! I really want you to find someone nice, so in light of that please don't ever say make love, scoundrels or my flower again!' says Jenna, shaking her head in mock horror.

Nicky nods slowly and says, 'Duly noted.'

Yana passes Nicky her laptop, so that she can log into her dating account and, after she's clicked on her inbox, she swings it round on the table so that we can all see. Nic, who takes an age to commit to any type of change, had finally decided to put her dating profile live the day before yesterday

— after weeks of her finding a variety of reasons not to. We had spent ages helping her get a good photo. In the end, we settled one of Nic in a white shirt and black jeans, sitting outside in her garden. Nicky had been keen to get an up-to-date one now that her hair has been coloured a lovely plum red. Jenna had straightened it and given it that Instagram wave effect.

It's a fantastic picture. We also helped write her 'about me' section, I think we've done a good job. That's what puts me off online dating. Having to write about myself. The thought alone makes me cringe. This is what we ended up going with.

> *'Nicky, 49, Cambridgeshire*
> *I am a voluptuous, long-divorced woman who is looking to meet someone to share my life with. I live alone with my two cats. I have a grown-up son, who lives with his girlfriend locally. I spend my weekdays working full-time in the care sector and my evenings and weekends exercising and socialising with my close group of friends. I would like to meet a man who loves animals, enjoys meals, films and gardening. I am a non-smoker but fine with smokers if they do not smoke inside the home.*
> *Ideally, I would like to meet someone taller than me, so 5ft 10 and above, although if you think you fit the bill but are an inch or two shorter then please still get in touch. Above all else, I am looking for someone kind and honest; someone who I can build a long-term partnership with. Looks, therefore, are secondary. I want to meet someone who is gentle and loving above all else.'*

Jenna wanted to write 'Do not contact me if you live in Algeria or anywhere that requires a visa for you to come to the UK. Also do not contact me offering me work as an escort, or money for snaps. NO DICK PICS!', but we felt it ruined the tone so decided to just help Nicky filter them out as and when they came through.

We deleted a few straightaway today based on them fitting into the scam or potential pervert bracket. Five more men were discounted because Nicky didn't like the look and/or sound of them, so we sent polite no thank you replies and then blocked them. One though, she did like.

'Wow!' Nic said as she leans closer to the screen to inspect him. Her glasses on chains are long gone. As part of her makeover, Nicky has ditched them in favour of golden-ochre-coloured prescription lenses.

Jenna leans over the table and clicks on the picture with a French-manicure-gelled finger, to enlarge the image and bring up his bio. A chubby, red-cheeked, freckled faced man, framed by a thick head of cinnamon-brown hair in a curtain-style cut that was popular among boy band members in the nineties stares back at us.

'Blimey Nic he looks like Johnny Vegas when he was on *Benidorm*,' remarked Jenna frowning.

'I know. Isn't he handsome?' Nic gushes as Val reads out his profile.

'Matthew, 33, Lincolnshire'
'I am looking to meet a woman who likes animals as much as I do. I am a full-time carer for my mum, so do not socialise a lot. I do not smoke or drink, but I love food. Hence my cuddly appearance. My main passion is Netflix and trains. People who know me would say I am placid and have a good heart. I am not interested in short-term dating and would rather meet one special person.'

Yana asks Nicky if she would be open to dating someone so much younger but Nicky doesn't respond. She is too busy gazing at the photo like a lovesick teenager.

'Take that as a yes then,' Jenna says, raising her eyebrows.

'What did his message say?' I ask when I realise we haven't even read what he sent her yet, having gone straight to his profile.

Nicky clicks back on to her inbox.

'Hello, Nicky. You sound just what I have been looking for. I am six feet, so I have the inches! Although I also have a few extra ones around my middle. May as well tell you that upfront! You look gorgeous. I hope to hear from you soon.'

As Nicky reads the last line she practically bursts with excitement. 'He thinks I'm gorgeous!'

Jenna wades in then with her notorious straight-talking. 'Right, Nic, babes. Play it cool. It's only day one. I know it's exciting, but you have only dipped your toe in so far. There's a whole ocean to swim in.'

The rest of us agree, including Nicky, who starts half-heartedly nodding, 'Play it cool. Yes, I can do that.'

But Jenna's words of wisdom clearly go in one ear and out the other as Nicky then starts frantically typing back and presses send before we get a chance to read it.

Jenna starts to read our friends response aloud. 'Matthew you sound so perfect to me, and I hope you don't mind me saying I am flattered you messaged me and believe me to be beautiful as I am a lot older than you, but I have to say you are the most handsome man I have ever seen!'

'Well, that was as cool as a house on fire, mate! Right, I think we're fighting a losing battle here, ain't we?' said Jenna before turning around and shrugging her shoulders at the rest of us.

'So, two more things and I'll leave you to it,' continues

Jenna as she leans forward to shut the laptop to ensure she has Nicky's full attention.

'Right so rule one, we do not send money to anyone we haven't met, even for sick animals or dying relatives, and two, under no circumstances should you send any pictures you wouldn't want your son to see, so no fanny, no tits, and no bum holes!'

Nicky looks alarmed and asks, 'Why on earth would I send a photograph of my private parts?'

'This is what concerns me, Nic. There are some right filthy fuckers on these dating sites. My mate Porsha once got offered ten quid and a half price KFC voucher to take a video of herself wearing rubber gloves and creaming her bum up with Nivea. She thought he was a nice bloke until that. Lured her on to a video call, he did, so just be alert babes,' said Jenna warning Nicky like a parent advising her naïve teenage daughter.

'I don't even have any washing-up gloves,' replied a confused looking Nic. 'I have a dishwasher. I mean, well, I do have some rubber gloves that I wear when I do the cat trays. They could pass for washing up gloves, but they're blue.'

Yana reassures Nic that she doubts anyone she meets will be a pervert who will ask her to get her body lotion out and her blue gloves on, so to just have fun, but to also be careful. As someone who met her husband online, Yana knows there are lots of scammers among the genuine people.

Nicky is far too busy however to discuss online safety any further – having already lifted the laptop lid – and begun typing away again to Matthew, a huge grin plastered over her face.

CHAPTER 50

Sunday 7th November, Fen Equestrian Centre, Warboys, Cambridgeshire

Despite Pam having a lot of lessons with Lynn down at the riding school, today was the first time I saw her in action.

Chloe and I still ride every Saturday and, a few times now, the ladies have also come with me. I expected Nicky to love it, but, since Matt has come on the scene, she is less keen, mainly because it involves her not being able to check her phone for messages every five minutes. Less than a week after their first inbox exchange, Matt and Nic both agreed it was time to remove their dating profiles, as they were only interested in each other.

This Sunday I decided to tag along and watch Chloe and Pam in action. Pam shunned the world-famous showjumper look in the end. Today she looks like she comes from good stock. Pam turns heads as she makes her way from the car, stepping over the piles of horse poo in her path, her cream breeches tucked into her gleaming rust-brown ankle boots, her porridge-coloured riding coat buttoned neatly, just a hint of a crisp, peach, high collar blouse and thistle brooch visible at her neckline.

I guffaw when Pam wastes no time in informing Lynn that she won't be wearing a riding hat on this occasion. She is not amused when Lynn tells her otherwise. 'You have to wear one for my insurance.'

'But I have my new Hermes silk riding headscarf on as Etta is here to record videos for me to show my friends. I want them to see my headscarf!' Pam whines in response while tilting her head to give Lynn, who is in her usual position in the Portakabin, sat at her filthy desk sucking the inside out of a cream egg, a better view.

Lynn, rightly, won't budge. 'And lovely it is too, Pamela, but it won't help if you take a tumble and land on your nut, luvvie, will it?'

A defeated Pam reluctantly unties the delicate cloth from under her chin and hands it to me. 'I hope your hands are clean, darling. Be an angel and pop back to the car and leave it there and get my crash helmet.'

I do as instructed, returning a few minutes later to hear Pam complaining about the horse she has been paired with. 'I just cannot see myself on a black and white crossbreed. I mean, I'm sure he's lovely, but it is all a bit secret lives of gypsies isn't it, darling? I wouldn't usually mind, Lynn, but, as I said to you already, Etta is going to film me today. My friends and Karen will be eagerly awaiting the photos and video as we speak. You remember, Karen, who I told you about my neighbour who lives at number twenty-four? Well, I know she would take great pleasure in seeing me upon a carthorse. So, have you got something a bit, well, classier, darling, please?'

Lynn shoots me a facetious look but manages to nod

straight-faced and reply that she's sure she 'can sort something out'.

Relief washes over Pam's face. 'Thank you. If possible, I really would prefer something a bit more well Burmese-ish, if you have it, darling.'

I look away as Lynn sucks her teeth and grimaces. Some of the other riders in the portakabin are frozen to the spot, seemingly shocked that anyone would dare challenge the formidable Lynn in any way.

'The thing is, Pamela, I don't think you are quite ready for a warmblood.'

Pam looks blankly as Lynn carries on. 'You mentioned Burmese, which was the Queen's parade mare. Well, she was a thoroughbred crossed with a Hanoverian – both breeds that need an experienced rider – so, as beautiful as they are, it would be dangerous for you and unprofessional for me to pair you with anything like her just yet.'

Lynn clocks Pam's unimpressed expression and offers up a compromise. 'What about Betsy? She is a Fell pony cross cob. The Queen rides Fell ponies, They are quite smart-looking, plus I am sure that Her Majesty also had a pony called Betsy at some stage.'

This sells it for Pam. 'That will do nicely, Lynn. Thank you,' she says, strutting off towards the barn.

Chloe has her half-hour lesson first. She is doing brilliantly and was so chuffed when she was told that she is ready to have no leader on our next hack. When Chloe finishes and disappears with some of the older girls to help with yard jobs, I have a coffee with Lynn and the others, who I have got to know well over the last few months.

Lynn drains her chipped mug of tea as soon as she hears the clip-clop coming from the barn. I follow her out of the Portakabin and try to gulp down my giggles as Pam appears, dragging along a very reluctant-looking pony.

Betsy has a bear-like brown coat with a coarse thick mane and tail. It reminds me of when Chloe takes a bristle brush to my dry curly hair. Betsy's ears are flat against her head, which at a guess I would say was due to her utter outrage at being taken away from her hay net, which, judging by her exceptionally podgy belly, she is very keen on.

'Oh, Betsy, stop it!' says Lynn, spotting her miserable face. 'She is a bit of a temperamental old troll. You'll learn a lot from her, though. She won't help you at all.'

Pam looks serious as she climbs up on the mounting block, gathers up her reins, takes the stirrup leather down and places her foot, and swings her leg over.

'Good grief!' shouts a surprised Pam, as a clunk of a shovel spooks Betsy, who darts forwards into the sand school.

'Oh, dear! She has one of her naughty heads on today. She's in one of her moods,' said Lynn. I follow on into the school to help Pam check Betsy's girth and adjust her stirrup leathers.

Before I leave, Pam leans down and whispers, 'Don't forget to film me, darling, will you? Then we can circulate it to all of my ladies. I've promised them. They'll be sitting by their phones on tenterhooks!'

As when any lessons are taking place, a small crowd forms by the arena gate as soon as Lynn somehow manages to heave herself up onto the three-foot-high flat pillar of the arena wall, where she sits on top of a saddlecloth. While the observers all look on with interest, listening to any words of wisdom Lynn shouts to her pupil. After a ten-minute warm-up, Lynn steps things up a little.

'Right, let's try a little canter, shall we? So, change reins at F to H,' Lynn calls out to Pam while pointing to the faded dressage letters on the wall. 'And then at K let's have a sitting trot, and after, when you're ready, at the next corner sit deep in your saddle, shoulders back, nice quiet hands, and ask for a canter.'

'Righto,' calls Pam in response. I start filming her, knowing she will be cross if I don't get this on camera. When Pam reaches K, she nudges Betsy with her heels, to ask for a trot. Betsy, however, isn't having any of it. Instead, she comes to a complete standstill and attempts to get her head through the fence to reach the grass on the other side.

'Right, she's taking the pee now!' says Lynn as she climbs down and unclicks the gate, shovelling down the other half of a cream doughnut that she had eagerly accepted from one of the livery owners while en route.

Lynn strides over towards Betsy, who now has a mouthful of grass hanging out of her mouth, entangled around her metal bit. I notice that behind Lynn's back in her right hand is now a long schooling whip. I am not the only one who has clocked it. Betsy takes one look at Lynn and the whip coming towards her, and jolts forwards, nearly unseating a startled Pam.

'Get on with it, Betsy,' Lynn growls in a low commanding voice.

The next thing I know, Betsy has dropped her shoulder and zoomed off into a fast, choppy trot. Pam, seemingly caught off guard, bobs about, hands see-sawing at the reins.

'I wasn't ready!' shouts Pam at no one in particular, as her panicked face shoots past us.

'Just shorten your reins, get her back on the track and stop messing about,' instructs Lynn calmly, who then turns around straight after and pulls an 'oops, that wasn't supposed to happen!' face in my direction.

'I can't! I'm panicking!' Pam shrieks as she flies back past Lynn.

Poor Pam is hanging on to Betsy's mane now, her face frozen in fear.

'Don't be pathetic, Pamela! Eight year olds jump that pony! Gather up your reins! You look like you're steering a motorbike, not a horse!' Lynn shouts as Pam bounds past her again on a now head down, proper tanking Betsy.

'Inside leg, outside rein! Lean back, deep seat! You know this! Just get on with it!'

Finally, Pam gets Betsy back on the track.

'Right, now, slow the trot and after C at the next corner ask for a canter,' instructs Lynn as she makes her way to C, schooling whip still in hand.

When Pam bounces past, she leans back in the saddle, and between her frantic kicking and high-pitched pleas of, 'Canter, Betsy, canter!' and Lynn growling, 'Get on with it, Betsy. You lazy greedy cow!' off they go like a rocket. Pam takes the precarious position of a jockey, leaning so far forwards that I think she may go out the front door.

Everyone watching takes big intakes of breath as horse and rider thunder past the gate. Pam, now having lost one stirrup, starts making panicked 'hurrah aarrgh!' noises.

'Lean back right now!' shouts Lynn coolly. 'That's it. Now stop moving about like that! Losing one stirrup is no excuse! You should be making love to the saddle, Pamela, not shagging it to death! I do hope you don't ride your husband like that!'

Pam's face goes beetroot. 'Stop filming! Do not send that to anyone!' Pam squeals at me the next time she flies past.

I do as I am told.

The lesson is cut short soon after when Lynn takes a phone call. 'Right, my straw delivery is just down the lane. We best get you dismounted before he gets into the car park. Betsy isn't a lover of artic lorries.' Lynn tells Pam.

Lynn must have noticed how defeated her pupil looked as she led Betsy out of the arena. 'Tell you what, Pamela. Get Betsy untacked and meet back in here in ten, luvvie,' Lynn said just before she sidles up to one of her staff and has a hushed conversation.

A quarter of an hour later, Pam, with her silk Hermes headscarf back in situ, is sitting astride Lynn's dressage stallion called Wilbert. At seventeen hands and a dapple grey, he is as eye-catching as he is a gentle giant.

Pam beams proudly as I snap away, making sure that I keep the groom, who is holding on to his bridle for extra safety, out of shot.

'Here, get hold of this one. That will make a brilliant photo to show your pals,' Lynn says, passing up one of her scruffy terriers. 'Very Princess Anne,' she confirms when Pam tucks the dog into her arm.

Pam is so over the moon with the pictures that she doesn't even wait to leave the yard before she sends them on a round-robin to everyone she knows.

'This one with me holding the terrier is the best photo of myself I have,' she declares as she proudly sets it as her WhatsApp profile picture.

I take a moment to quietly thank Lynn for being so kind before we head off.

'No bother, luvvie. If I can take ten minutes out of my day to make someone else's I will.'

Lynn is one of those amazing, truly formidable, no-nonsense women that people find intimidating, but really has a heart of gold.

Today was a good day.

It's later the same evening, and Jenna just rang me with news. Robert has seen photos of me on Jenna's Facebook. From the night out. He's told Jason we used to 'have a thing' and asked him for my number. I've said no. Not because I am playing hard to get; I have decided that I have no interest in speaking to Robert again. Even for the reasons I'd originally planned. I feel no need to have his approval of me now. Robert's opinion of me are now irrelevant. I value myself now and that's all that matters.

According to Jason, Robert plans to 'win me back' at the wedding. How ironic that for so many years I would have given my right arm for this scenario. Jenna still thinks I should go ahead with the plan. From what has been said this evening, it looks like I no longer have the choice anyway.

Now I have butterflies in my stomach for all the wrong reasons.

CHAPTER 51

Monday 8ᵗʰ November, Leisure Centre, St Ives

'Right, we only have four days until my hen do. Let's do ten more!' Jenna said as all five of us take a breather in the shallow end at lunchtime today.

'I don't think this is possible for me,' puffs Yana, her cheeks rosy.

'Me neither,' agrees Val as she dips her head back into the water.

'How many lengths have we done now?' Nicky asks me.

I look down at the Garmin watch I've borrowed from Pam. 'It doesn't measure lengths, but I've burned three hundred and ninety-six calories.'

'That's enough for me then!' Val laughs heading for the steps.

'Me too,' said Yana, wading off in the same direction.

'Ten more lengths?' Jenna asks me and Nic.

'Yeah, go on then. Slow breaststroke though or I may perish!' Nicky says, only half joking.

Off we go and by the time we get out, we have matching glowing post-exercise complexions and wrinkled fingertips. A month ago we decided to stop weighing ourselves every week; instead, just sticking to our calories and exercise, and going by how our clothes feel, then once a month do a weigh-in.

Today is our first step on the scales since we started our new approach. Jenna goes first. 'I'm eight stone ten pounds!' she squeals, so loudly that she makes a woman drop her hairbrush in shock.

'Sorry about that, mate!' Jenna says as she turns to the silver-haired lady, who's dripping wet, with a crispy lime green towel around her arms. The woman smiles politely, but continues to look on in confusion, while we all do happy dances and hug Jenna, celebrating her achievement.

'I'm back to my pre-baby weight. I'm so happy!' Jenna bellows.

I go next. My weight seems to have settled now and I am so content. 'Skinny, thick,' Jenna calls it.

'Nine stone exactly!' Seeing that number is enough to prompt me in taking my turn at startling strangers in changing rooms. I know I could get thinner if I really tried, but I'm happy feeling slim and strong. I still get to have the odd treat and join in on family dinners. I've found my happy weight. I'm a size 12 in most things, sometimes a 10, and, you know what? That's okay. I feel comfortable in my own skin; stretch marks, cellulite, wobbly bits and all. I am proud of how far I have come.

We all take a big intake of breath when Yana steps on the scales and the dial settles on twelve stone three pounds. 'Bloody hell, Yana! You've lost ten pounds in four weeks!' Jenna calls out after writing her latest weight along with mine in our now slightly tatty A Moment on the Lips notebook. The same book that we started right at the beginning.

Yana bursts into tears.

'What's wrong, you only have just over a stone to go before you reach your target weight, you must be chuffed sweetheart?' asks Nic as she places her arm around her.

'I cry because I am very happy. I knew I do the good job, because my gym leggings are the size fourteen but I'm so pleased that I see this weight!'

She takes a picture of her scale reading and sends it to Simon.

'Looks like you might need a new dress for my wedding after all!' giggles Jenna.

I know that Nicky has lost a lot, as she is in one of the wrap dresses that she bought on our shopping trip the other month, which I know is a size 16.

'Nic!' I say, gasping at the scales reading. 'You are in the fourteens!' She weighs fourteen stone two pounds.

'You've lost exactly eight stone in nine months!' Val shouts out excitedly.

'I never have! That can't be right.'

We watch as Nicky gets off the scales and then gets back on. 'I really have! I've lost thirteen pounds in four weeks!'

When Nicky steps off, Val gets on. Twelve stone one pound. 'I am bloody chuffed with that! I've lost six pounds this month and I have made my target, bar that one pound.' she beams. 'Goes to show, as long as we stick to it ninety per cent of the time, we've cracked it. We have done amazing! I am so pleased. It will be so satisfying wearing my Ted Baker dress at the wedding.'

Val looks very radiant lately. Since she got to the bottom of the whole Tim situation, you can tell she is positively moving on. Things have been very diplomatic. Tim, quite rightly, signed over the bungalow – which has no mortgage – to Val, as well as the rest of the items in it. Tim had reasoned that it was only fair Val got to keep her home. I think guilt had a lot to do with it. Her boys took the very shocking details about their dad surprisingly well. Val suspects that they may have had more than an inkling before they were officially told.

A few weeks back, Jenna finally got around to helping Val set up a Facebook account to reconnect with her old friends. One of those friends then put Val in touch with Adonis (yes, his real name). Adonis was Val's first love, back when she was a sixteen-year-old teenager. They had lost touch when he returned to Corfu in the summer of 1978 with his parents.

'You didn't have internet and mobiles in our day. It was near on impossible to have a long-distance relationship, especially with us being so young,' Val had explained. She is adamant that it is strictly platonic now, but every time he is mentioned you cannot fail to see how her eyes brighten.

Jenna had been really laid back about Jason's stag do since infiltrating his chat group, then a few weeks ago he blew it by giving in to his mates' jibes and agreed to go to a gentleman's club. This made Jenna demand furiously that her cousin tag along on the stag to 'keep an eye'.

Because of this, Jenna had to invite Gillian, her mother-in-law to her hen do. 'Jase said if he's taking my cousin then I have to take his mum,' Jenna had moaned to us at work last week. 'I've been fucked right over with it.' She then put on a deep, slightly dopey voice to imitate Jason. 'I told Mum it was your friends and close family only and the same with me. Now I'm taking your cousin she will feel left out if you don't take her.'

We all agreed that Jenna had drawn the short straw. 'It's

worth it though, for the peace of mind. Richie has promised he will intervene if things start to go too far,' Jenna told us.

The four of us smiled and agreed with her, then shot each other knowing glances. Richie is a thirty-five-year-old alpha male who, until he got discharged for medical reasons, served with the Special Boat Service. When Nicky had asked him at the wedding rehearsal what Special Boat Service meant he had replied, 'We are like SAS but much better and much harder!'

I must admit there is something incredibly manly about Richie. He has some serious Ant Middleton vibes. He's stocky and muscular with a thick head of flame-red hair and a full beard. Yana said Richie reminds her of the red-haired wildling in *Game of Thrones*.

However, as hilarious as he is (and he really is), and as much as I would want him by my side in a dangerous situation, I'm dubious after his performance at Jenna and Jason's wedding rehearsal, if he's going to be the best judge of someone going too far.

When the wedding planner, who, having failed to get Richie's attention for the third time, had cleared his throat and tapped him on the back, Richie had swung round and looked down at him from his towering six-foot two (at least) frame and said, 'Sorry, pal. I was just telling this lot about when my pal ate the contents of a pub ashtray for a pound.'

Richie then turned to Jason and all of his ushers in his booming upbeat Manc accent and said, 'Guess what my other pal did on a stag back in my twenties when he met a Kelly Brook lookalike?'

What followed was a graphic and wildly inappropriate account of how Richie's mate had 'shagged the little sort, right outside Yates in Leeds!'

This stopped everyone in their tracks. None more so than Jason's mum, Gillian.

I was shaking with laughter as Richie started describing how the girl had 'propped her burger tray on his friend's shoulder' as they had 'gone at it like rabbits'.

Richie had just picked up Jason to use him as a stand-in Kelly Brook lookalike to demonstrate how his pal had 'got her legs over his shoulders!' during the 'grand finale!' when Gillian thundered up the aisle towards them.

'How dare you be so crude! Have some decorum! You're making yourself sound like a sexual predator!' Gill had scolded before turning to the hotel manager. 'I am so sorry if you heard any of that. He belongs to the bride's side,' said Gill, as if that explained everything.

Within seconds, I heard Richie's deep voice start up again, obviously completely undeterred by being accused of being a sex pest. 'I made sure he got her a taxi after, like!' Richie chuckled, while holding out his hands in front of his chest as if to support his innocence, a mischievous grin forming from under his wild beard.

Yana and I shook with laughter for a good ten minutes afterwards. We had been separated from Val and Nicky due to lack of space inside the great hall, which was down to Gill requesting all family, key guests and suppliers to attend the rehearsal. Luckily Robert didn't fall into any of those categories.

When they re-joined us outside afterwards, Yana greeted them with, 'I made sure he got her a taxi after, like!' in the worst Manchester accent I have ever heard.

Jenna sulkily stomped over soon after and lit a cigarette. 'Fucking Gillian! She's doing my head in!'

She paused for a massive intake of nicotine.

'What is her problem? Trying to tell me where I can and can't have my own fucking flowers! And did you hear her have a go at my cousin? For no reason whatsoever. Like she's never shagged anyone in public before!'

Anyway, what I am getting at is that, as much as Richie is handsome, funny, chivalrous, and can 'swim better than anyone in the SAS', I'm unsure how valuable he is going to be in keeping Jase and his friends in line on the stag.

But at least Jenna is happy, and that's the main thing.

CHAPTER 52

Friday 12ᵗʰ November, Coach bound for Stansted Airport

I knew it was going to be a heavy weekend as soon as I climbed on board the hired coach wearing my cerise pink T-shirt with 'Hens do Dublin' printed across it.

'Isn't this festive?' Pam marvelled as she followed behind me wearing sparkly white jeans with a diamante belt and her hen top tied up at the belly button. When Jenna had sent Pam an invitation to join us in Dublin, I never in a million years thought she would accept.

A very flustered-looking bus driver nodded as we passed and uttered, 'Welcome to hell.'

Jenna's auntie then stood up and handed us both a gift bag. A grinning Yana waved at us as we made our way towards her and said, 'You two sit here opposite me. Nicky and Val are sitting over there,' as she pointed across the aisle to the set of four seats facing each other, separated by a table; an identical set-up to ours. 'Nicky and Val both disappear to get drinks down the back with mother and grandmother of

Jenna five stops ago. I not see them since. Ah, here they come. The wanderers do return!' Yana laughs, gesturing to Val and Nicky, who start waving their arms about and playfully pointing at us, while staggering back towards their seats holding on to the tops of the headrests to steady themselves as they go.

Pam, who has emptied her gift bag on to the table, picks up the bendy penis straw and pops it into her pink gin and lemonade can that was also in the bag.

Nicky leans over, kissing us all on our cheeks. 'Look what Maggie, Jenna's mum, gave me!' she slurs, holding up a bottle of Sunset Rum. 'You have to dilute it as it's eighty-five per cent booze. I've got it in this Coke bottle. Do you want some?' she asks me, now waving the half empty two-litre bottle in my face.

I'd decided I wouldn't drink on the journey or the plane, so I start to say no thanks just as Pam turns to face me, dick straw in mouth and shrieks, 'Look, it lights up and flashes when I suck it! Isn't that genius?'

I decide I might just have a small one after all.

'We don't have any cups. You'll have to just swig it out of the bottle,' Nicky says.

Val then adds, 'Try and get a few big gulps down quick before your throat feels like it's on fire!'

By the time we hit the dual carriageway, the noise levels on the coach are near deafening.

When the driver finally had enough, he paused the music playlist Jenna had plugged in and got on his loudspeaker to sternly bark, 'Could the woman in the nana-of-the-bride top and the girl in the wig dancing on the tables, both get down immediately!' An outraged Porsha throws her hands to her head, and shouts back at him, 'These are real Russian thirty-inch hair extensions, you cheeky prick! Wig! How dare you!'

Then Jenna's nana demands that he unpaused the music

immediately. 'I was in the middle of recording an Instagram story! I can't believe you paused my favourite song!' she bellowed. The driver gave up at that point and Cardi B 'WAP' restarted, as did Jenna's nana and Porsha's writhing about on the tables. I had almost forgotten that Gillian was even there until we pulled up outside Stansted Airport and she appeared at the front, grabbing hold of the driver's loud-speaker.

'Right, ground rules before anyone departs!' Gillian announces. 'Firstly, there is to be no shouting, screaming or flashing of body parts.'

She rolls her eyes disdainfully as everyone boos her and shouts things like, 'Who invited her?' and chants, 'OFF! OFF! OFF!'

Next, she goes all uptight primary school headteacher on a school field trip. 'You must walk in twos. Stay with your partner. If you lose them, you are to stand still and blow your whistle once.'

Everyone starts blowing their penis-shaped whistles, including Pam, who seems to be really enjoying the genital-based novelty items.

Gillian has just started informing us how many drinks we are permitted to have on the plane when Jenna marches to the front, rips the mic from her soon-to-be mother-in-law's hand and says, 'Oh, do me a favour, Gill. Get back to your seat and worry about yourself, mate. My hen do, my rules, and I only have one. What happens on hen stays on hen!'

We all start cheering and whooping.

Then the bus driver ruined the moment by shouting that it was time for us all to 'get the fuck off!' his bus.

Charming.

CHAPTER 53

Through some miracle, we all make it on to the plane. I end up sitting next to Porsha, who has taken a shine to me after I had agreed what 'rip-off merchants' WH Smiths are. I'd been in there buying some sugar-free Polos and browsing the magazines when I overheard Porsha scolding the shop assistant. 'You don't need to follow me round, babes. I ain't nicking nothing if that's what your problem is.'

The poor young cashier looked ashen as he continued to pick up and replace various items of confectionery that Porsha had obliviously knocked off the shelves as she lurched from aisle to aisle.

'I'm a level one beauty therapist! I've got money!' Porsha snapped at him as he tried to pass her the shopping basket that she'd just dropped on her own foot.

I decided to intervene before he called security or she started trying to force him to follow her Facebook 'Porsha Za Beauty' page as proof she wasn't casing the joint.

'Ah, Etta, babes! Fancy seeing you here! I'm so glad you're coming on the hen! I'll sit next to you on the plane!' Porsha informed me, stopping at the cold drink fridge and turning back to the member of staff, who had retreated back behind the counter.

'You can stick your drinks up your arse!' Porsha told the shop assistant loudly.

Several other shoppers looked at her in disgust, especially when she turned back at the exit and bawled at the worker again. 'Two quid ninety-nine for a bottle of Coke! I'd rather drink it neat! You piss-taker!'

～

The flight to Dublin was only an hour and fifteen minutes but, by the time we landed, I – alongside several rows of passengers, including many children, who were seated either to the side, front or back of us – had a new understanding of many intimate beauty processes, such as anal bleaching, thanks to Porsha's endless stream of foghorn anecdotes, my personal favourite being when she managed to 'remain pro-fess-ion-al' when an ex-boyfriend's dad had come into her salon for a 'back, sack and crack'.

There were tuts all round as she'd described in graphic detail how he had been on all fours 'stark bollock naked' and how she had almost gagged up her brekkie at the sight she was confronted with. 'Like two ostrich eggs flapping about inside a turkey's neck, they were!' Porsha had cackled, as I mouthed 'I'm so sorry' to anyone who glared in our direction.

I can see why Jenna likes Porsha so much. She's really funny, without meaning to be.

Porsha also offered to give me a Kylie Jenner face filler makeover before the wedding. 'I'll sort ya jawline right out for ya,' she'd told me between gulps of wine that she was knocking back at a rate of knots. 'I did the course a few months back. I nearly passed it as well. Going well it was then I got distracted watching a row on Facebook. My mates half brother gave their ex-auntie-in law an STD. In all the excitement, and because I was hungover and a bit shaky, I went in wrong doing a brow lift. It was only a little bit of blood and bruising. The course leader was just being an awkward cow when she refused to give me my certificate. It wasn't that bad. Well, fuck her! Experience means more than bits of paper, don't it babes?'

I agree and say, 'Yeah, definitely.'

Obviously, there is absolutely no chance of me letting Porsha loose on my lips, cheeks, or jawline with 18 ml of facial filler that she won on eBay. But really kind of her to offer all the same.

CHAPTER 54

The Dublin hotel was like *Fawlty Towers*, but with internet access and lots of animal print. The owners, a friendly couple who had one of those part-wild Savannah cats on a lead, welcomed us in reception wearing matching zebra print shirts and showed us straight to our rooms. I'm sharing a triple bedroom with Yana and Pam. Nicky and Val are next door in two singles. All of us have animal print sheets and faux gold taps. On the pillows they have placed little treats of Nestle Animal Bars. Nice touch. I've saved mine for Chloe.

'Good grief!' said Gillian as she traipsed up the stairs with her suitcase. 'I do not believe this! No bellboy, no room service! I told Jenna we should have booked that little boutique hotel that I printed out from the *Hitched* magazine website. The rooms all had rain showers and Cowshed toiletries and lifts.'

Maggie, Jenna's mum, shot Gill a death stare and replied, 'Feel free to fuck off there then! I still owe you one for making my little girl cry, so don't push your luck!'

The rest of the day passed in a blur of pubs, bars and restaurants; mainly of the all-you-can-eat-for-a-tenner variety.

We all had a great time. Even Gillian didn't complain. She just mainly sat with a haughty expression – sometimes reading an intellectual-looking book – whilst we all had fun around her.

We went to the Temple Bar the following evening. We'd stood outside whilst a friendly passer-by took loads of photos of us, Jenna at the front, hand on hip, her bare tanned legs covered in gold glitter, looking amazing in a white tutu and corset, which did an excellent job of showing off all her hard work over the previous months.

The bar was like nothing I have ever seen. It's an impressive corner-plot building painted a cherry red and, being mid-November, it looked stunning. The windows and upper storey were completely decked out in icy-blue fairy lights between old-fashioned lanterns, and a massive Christmas tree was already suspended above the entrance with thousands of red twinkly lights sprawled across every branch.

Inside it was cosy with beer hop garlands draped around the bar and from the ceilings, and a heaving mix of locals and visitors gathered around the heavy wooden tables. Even Gillian said it had a 'certain charm' and let her hair down ordering herself a 'small, sweet vermouth' in a 'ladylike glass, please'. The bar had every bottle of alcohol you could imagine; not on optics, just standing illuminated by shelving lights.

No one wanted the night to end, especially Pamela and Jenna's nana who, having formed an unlikely friendship, had parked themselves up at the bar happily accepting the endless stream of slippery nipple shots that the charismatic barman poured for them. The pair refused point-blank to move when we told them it was time to go.

'We're waiting for the strippers!' they announced, their bloodshot eyes darting around the room expectantly.

'Nana, there aren't any strippers. It's time to get back to the hotel,' Clemmie, Jenna's sister, said.

'Well, that's a let-down. In my day, if you didn't get an eyeful, it wasn't a hen party,' Jenna's nana had grumpily muttered to Pam as they staggered out of the door, arms linked before sloping off down the street towards the taxi rank.

When Val and I popped inside to ask for four taxis to transport all sixteen of us back to our hotel, we walked back out to utter carnage.

'For fuck's sake! Someone help her up!' said a howling-with-laughter mother-of-the-bride. I looked down at what, or should I say, who, Maggie was pointing at and gasped, as I saw Jenna's nana lying in the road, giggling away.

'How about stop barking orders and get her up yourself,' Gillian said primly. 'A woman of her age lying in a gutter, drunk. What an embarrassment!'

As Clemmie and Yana helped lift a still laughing nana back on her feet, and guided her over to a nearby bench, a red- and bleary-eyed Maggie squared up to Gillian and gave her an aggressive shove.

'Now who's an embarrassment lying in a gutter?' Maggie goaded smugly.

Us all being so drunk, none of us fully grasped what was happening at first. A few of us had witnessed the shove and took large intakes of breath, and the next thing we knew Gillian had got back up off the floor and flew at Maggie's hair, swinging away in the fashion of a Morris dancer – Maggie being the maypole, her clumps of hair the ribbons.

'I've had enough of you! You will not ruin my special day! This ends now!' Gillian screeched.

By the time everyone had fully cottoned on to the fact

that both mothers of the wedding party were acting like opponent's on the *Hunger Games*, Maggie had already managed to shake off Gillian and had charged back at her like a raging bull, screaming, 'Come on then! Let's be having you!' She then tore Gillian's blouse wide open, exposing her bare chest. Which prompted some kind of rolling about on the pavement, during which Gillian sunk her perfect veneers into Maggie's hand.

'For fuck's sake!' Jenna said, sighing like it was the most normal thing in the world. Between us – well, the ones who were able to stand up unaided – we managed to separate them. I say all, I am not including Porsha in that statement, because she could stand but didn't help. Porsha done nothing whatsoever apart from screaming, 'Go on, Mags, babes! Fuck her up! Go for her eyes!' in-between bites of a steaming hot dog, which she'd bought from a burger van opposite the pub we'd just left.

After we managed to separate them, Clemmie lent her jacket to Gill, as she was struggling to keep her boobs under wraps because Maggie had ripped not only all her buttons off of her blouse but had also torn her camisole straight down the middle.

Jenna stomped to the opposite side of the road and stood on her own, smoking. When she finished her fag, she came back across and rejoined us. She then lit another, turned in the direction of Gillian and her mum, and said, 'If you two don't make up now then you ain't coming to my wedding. And, by the way, Gill, mate, the day you keep calling your "special day" is actually my special fuckin' day. I am so sick of this shit!'

For a few minutes after we all stood shivering in silence waiting for our transport. Gillian was the first to relent. Probably because she was worried what her posh friends would think if she were banned from her own son's wedding for attacking the bride's mother. Gill looked down at the ground and muttered, 'Maggie, I apologise for calling your mother an embarrassment, alongside biting you, and pulling out your hair.'

She sniffed quietly, still not looking Maggie in the eye.

Jenna then narrowed her eyes at her mum until Maggie huffed and said, 'Yeah. Fair dos, Gill. No harm done on the hair front. They're just clip-ins.'

Gillian forced a tight smile.

Then things got a little weird. Maggie smiled back and said, 'And I'm sorry for ripping your top and exposing your tits, Gill, mate. But I have to say I was gobsmacked at how perky they are! I couldn't believe you had no bra on!'

Only for Gill to reply smugly, 'I know. Dr Fisher is more than a cosmetic surgeon; he's an artist.'

Pamela and Jenna's nana joined in the conversation then, saying how they can't believe they're fake as they looked so pert and bouncy.

'Where the fuck are these taxis?' mutters Jenna a few minutes later while grimacing at the sight of her mum copping a feel of Gillian's pair.

When the taxis finally arrive, someone asks Maggie if she wants to go to A&E for stitches and tetanus for the gaping tooth-shaped hole in her thumb.

'Nah, Pamela Etta's step-nan has said she has some Savlon and some wound closure strips in her case. That'll do. Plus I want to get back and get these washed out with some travel wash ready for the morning,' replies Maggie whilst holding out her straggly pink and white-blonde hair strands. 'Quality they are. Designed by the girls off of *Geordie Shore*. Hundred per cent manmade. Takes years off me 'n' all. Clemmie, don't my hair extensions take years off me?'

～

We all headed straight to bed when we got in. Just as I thought the night had reached peak weirdness, Gillian called down the hall as we was about to disappear into our room, 'Oh, Pamela. Don't forget to come to my bedroom in the morning. I'll give you my surgeon's details and show you my areolas. Stunning they are. You will be amazed. Honestly, the man is a genius!'

As fun as it was to be away, I was glad to get back on Sunday afternoon. My grandad and Chloe had just returned with two warm rotisserie chickens, crusty tiger baguettes, and a selection of fresh fruit from Sainsbury's. When Pam and I troop through the door, Pam gazes at grandad like I used to look at the cake counter during a rare trip to Waitrose.

'Aren't you clever, darling. So thoughtful,' she said upon spotting the tablecloth spread across the sun lounge table and the butter dish and knife next to a neat stack of plates. She rushes over to him to stamp a Rimmel Coral Shimmer seal of approval on his cheek.

We all sit together, the floating log burner crackling away, while Pam and I share the tamer parts of our trip and Chloe divulges snippets of her 'best weekend with her best grandad ever!'

Later on, I take one look at the dark drizzly night and accept Grandad's offer of a lift home. I hurry Chloe along in collecting up all her various books and dolls, knowing he will want to be back and settled in his favourite chair in time to watch *Countryfile* with Pam.

Delicious warm spicy notes of my favourite mulled wine diffusers greet us as we cross the cottage threshold; the scent even more pleasingly pungent after a few days' absence. A heavy-eyed Alice looks up briefly as I run my hand down from her head to her chocolate bushy tail, before resuming the scrunched-up ball position in her beloved radiator seat. Grandad and Chloe had been calling in all weekend. Therefore I am certain that she wouldn't have run low on her two favourite things – fuss and food – in my absence.

My grandad has had a busy weekend, between looking after Alice, Charles and Diana the corgis, along with Chloe and also calling in on Nicky's Siamese cats. He came to the rescue when Nic sent a tearful voice note to our AMOTL WhatsApp group the day before our departure date.

'I won't be able to come tomorrow now,' Nicky said between sobs, going on to explain that her son had let her down on his promise to look after her cats at the last minute due to 'relationship stuff'. I was out walking with Pam when it came through and she'd sprung to the rescue, calling Grandad to explain Nic's predicament.

Grandad, being the good egg that he is, didn't even hesitate in offering his help. 'That's no problem. Ring Nicky and let her know that me and Chloe will pop round twice a day, or as often as she needs us to,' he said before adding, 'And, Pamela, make sure Nicky knows I said she can leave me instructions and I'll do everything exactly how she needs it to be done.'

He knew all too well from being around Nic several times over the months that her cats are her babies. Nic was so grateful and had dropped her spare keys round to him the morning we left, together with a surprisingly short list of dos and don'ts. I was even more taken aback when Nic told me on the coach that she had decided that she wasn't going to check the pet cam while we were away. 'I trust your grandad, so I am going to let my hair down!' Not that her decision meant that she was on her phone any less than usual. Things with her toy boy have moved fast. Anyway, more of that later.

After I get the fires going, Chloe and I both sit sipping mugs of Options hot chocolate, all cosy in our fleecy PJs and slippers (complete bargains from Primark!) Afterwards, I wash up our mugs, put a load of washing on and take Chloe up to bed. Her room has become a pony lover's paradise, with her Black Beauty bedding and various cute horse and unicorn cuddly toys lined up on every surface. As I lean down, I wipe away the last residue of minty blue specks around her mouth with my finger, before planting a kiss on both of her cheeks.

'Mummy, stop it,' she giggles as I tickle her.

Our messing about is interrupted by a loud knock on the front door. Chloe and I exchange puzzled looks. No one ever calls in on us apart from Grandad and Pam, who we've only just seen, and the ladies, who I'd only just said goodbye to a few hours ago when the coach dropped me and Pam off at the top of Willow Road.

'Right, you get cosy and I'll go see who it is,' I say, leaning down to plant one last kiss on her forehead. When I get downstairs, I peer through the curtains at the front of the lounge. Although a bush – known only as 'the bushy bush' – blocks my view of seeing who is standing by the front door, I can see a battered Toyota truck parked up by my picket fence and that's enough to reveal my visitor's identity.

'One minute, Tom! I'll just grab my keys!' I call out, dashing into the kitchen and then back again, leaning down to pull the draft excluder cushion away from the bottom of the door.

'Hello, Tom!' I greet my landlord warmly as the cold air instantly chills my face.

'Ah, grand. Ya home,' Tom says, wasting no time in turning around and ambling back down the path towards the gate. I stand frowning, a bit confused as to what is going on. When Tom gets to his truck, I tug my dressing gown around me and hunch my shoulders, and watch as he disappears round to the passenger side.

'Fecking thing!' he shouts out as several bangs ring into the night in response to his struggle to open the rear door. I gasp as he reappears, and attempts to boot my gate open because his hands are no longer free. My mouth falls into an 'O' as he stumbles back. His head and torso are completely lost behind a humungous bouquet of uniform perfect, blousy parrot tulips.

After trying and failing to balance the offering on a knee of his oil-stained jeans, which are tucked inside his muck boots, Tom turns around and shoves my gate open with a thrust of his bottom.

I gulp down my amusement as Tom then assumes the position of a crab, side-stepping up the path with his head cricked sideways.

'The girl came up the farm this morning and left them. Said you wasn't in, so I took them for you.'

I was taken aback, by both the surprise of the gesture and the utter luxuriousness of the gift. The flowers are so delicate, each one blemish free and wrapped in layer upon layer of cream, sumptuous purples and gold paper. I manage to say thank you and offer him a cup of tea. I'm also about to ask if they are definitely for me when I notice a little envelope with my name on it.

I'm relieved when Tom replies, 'Ta, but I'd betta get back up mine. Have a stew on the stove. But I'll be seeing you.'

Not because I don't like my landlord's company but because my heart felt like it was about to pump out of my chest and, despite the evening being so bitter, that my lips had started chattering involuntarily when I had opened the door, only to stop the second I clapped eyes on the bouquet. My cheeks now feel almost on fire and my hands are clammy.

You're probably rolling your eyes at this, but I have never received flowers, unless you count the ones my grandad picks up for me from Tesco. Robert almost bought me a rose in a plastic tube once in Chicago's in Peterborough when a man approached us with a bag full of them. He'd accepted one and handed it to me, but after he'd asked how much they were, he'd scoffed, 'Three quid! Fuck off, pal!', taken it from out of my hand and thrown it back at the seller's chest.

So I'm not sure if you would count that. I would be inclined to say probably not.

CHAPTER 56

I plonk the tulips down on top of my coffee table, almost abashed by their beauty. Luckily, they are in their own plastic water bag vase, which reminds me of when the koi carp arrived. It's a good job that they don't need to be put in water as I only own one vase, which barely holds eight stems. There are at least a hundred in the arrangement; probably more. I cringe as my mind drifts to what Pam and Grandad will say when they see them, which they will because you can't exactly miss them. Oh god! Pam will definitely hyperventilate with excitement at the sight of them and probably faint if they're from a man. I'll be the talk of the Slim With Us meeting on Tuesday!

I resist the temptation to open the card straightaway; instead savouring the anticipation. I creep back up the stairs into Chloe's room then slide *The Saddle Club* paperback out of her hand and put it back on the packed shelf above her desk, smiling at the sight of her soundly asleep. The busy weekend must have caught up with her. I leave the door ajar, clicking on the hallway light as I pass. Both actions I have done so many times before that they are almost carried out on autopilot.

I practically gallop back downstairs into the lounge. A sweet, heavy, honey-like smell has seeped from the periwinkle and plum petals and has overpowered the winter diffusers. With closed eyes, you would believe yourself to be in a flower-filled meadow, straight after a summer downpour. As I carefully slide out the note from inside the little shiny aubergine envelope, I realise that my hands are shaking.

Etta,
I just wanted to say that I hope you had a good weekend in
Dublin. All went well in Vilnius. Jas is back in one piece. Look
forward to seeing you on the big day.
R xx

My heart thumps in my chest. 'R'. That must stand for Robert. I can't think of anyone else who would be sending me flowers.

For a few seconds, I wonder how he knew where to send them, then I remember that we have mutual friends. Jenna would have never given out my address, so it must have been Jason.

I take a picture of the flowers and the note and post them on our group chat.

CHAPTER 57

Within seconds we are all on a video call.

'Oh my God!' Jenna squeals, throwing her hands over her mouth as she appears on the screen, her hair piled up on top of her head, her face make-up free.

'I know,' I say, shaking my head in bemusement.

'Now that is a bunch of flowers!' says Val, who is sitting at her kitchen table, holding half a tuna salad wrap, which becomes a quarter when she finishes her sentence.

Yana's washing machine can be heard approaching the end of a spin cycle in the background as she makes herself a cup of tea in her gleaming kitchen. She asks me. 'Do you think they are sent from Robert?'

Before anyone can answer, Jenna, who is no doubt keen not to miss any of the conversation, rolls her eyes and says, 'Hold that thought. Sorry, these are being little fuckers as usual!'

As she marches into her downstairs hallway, her phone still in hand, I laugh as I see Yana, who – like the rest of us – knows what's coming next, reaching down to the side of her propped-up device to adjust the volume just in time before Jenna launches into action.

'Erm, sorry. You're what, Jase? You're sick of putting the boys back in bed *for me*! Are they not your kids as well then? And I am fuckin' sick of a lot of things, mate, but that's a whole other convo!'

We all stay silent as Jenna then props up her phone on an oak sideboard while she picks up the various coats and shoes dumped on the floor and throws them into a cupboard. I see Maxwell dart across the upstairs landing wearing a pair of *Jurassic Park* PJs and a green hero's dress-up cape. Jason follows in close pursuit, pausing at the top of the stairs to give his two cents' worth. 'Well, it wasn't my dad who fed both of them a diet of sugar, white bread and crisps for three days solid and let them watch *Tremors* as a bedtime film, was it, Jenna? Jesus Christ, Maxwell! You can't jump from the bed to the TV stand, little man. You'll break your neck! There are no worms that live under the ground! No one's gonna eat you, pal!'

A lively debate breaks out between the couple, and then Jenna comes up with her winning trump card. 'Well, at least my dad offered to look after them! Seeing as your bloody mother was too busy ruining my hen do and taking chunks out of my family members' body parts!'

Before Jason can say any more, Jenna retreats into the utility room 'because the tumble dryer drowns out the boys' demands and Jase's whinging.'

'Right, where was we!' Jenna asks, sitting down on a car booster seat and rubbing her hands together.

For the next five minutes the four of them dream up make-believe scenarios of how Robert will want to sweep me off my feet at the wedding, and how I will stand up for all women who ever have been treated like shit by a man and tell him to dream on. Finally, they all agree that the flowers must be from him, as there is no one else whose name begins with R who went on the stag do.

Val disappears for a few minutes during our discussion then returns to the camera, which is nothing unusual; she has a habit of placing her iPad in a room and carrying on her activities.

'Well, now I think about it,' Val says, with a metal watering can in her hand, 'we have missed someone. Jenna's cousin, Richie. He went on the stag, didn't he?'

I feel my belly flip.

Nicky's eyes widen and Jenna frowns.

'Richie is the proper alpha man, so if it is him who send them, I think this is good, Etta! Did you see how he picked the grown man up? When he pretend he do the shagging of the woman! Imagine what Richie would do with you Etta. And his hands! Big like shovels!' Yana jibed while belly laughing.

Jenna chuckles but then pulls a disgusted face and starts to make gagging noises. 'As a blood relative of his, I can only say that is fuckin' gross! Plus I doubt Richie even knows how to order flowers! He is far too Rambo for feelings and shit.'

My thoughts spiral as the woman debate between themselves before jointly deciding that it must be Robert. A strange, hopeful feeling washes over me, and I change the subject. 'Anyway, Nic, enough about all that. How are the cats?'

'Happy as sandboys,' Nicky replies, her eyes elsewhere. 'Sorry, I was just sending a message to Matt to let him know we're all chatting.'

When Jenna asks Nic if she has spoken to him about having a video call, Nicky shakes her head. 'I'm going to, though,' she replies.

Since Nic and Matt started speaking, they haven't Face-timed or met up in person even once. We've tried to tentatively share our concerns about this with Nicky over the last few weeks but each time she became a prickly and defensive. Especially when Yana directly questioned her if he'd asked for money at any time.

'Of course not! He isn't an immigrant after a new life or a meal ticket,' Nicky had snapped.

Poor Yana had looked hurt and said that she had come from Russia as she'd met a man she loved; not for a free life.

I jumped to Yana's defence and told her to stop explaining herself and that Nicky was out of order. Val and Jenna also said that it was uncalled for.

Nicky apologised straight after, but since then I have noticed that Yana is much quieter when Matt is mentioned. Nicky seems oblivious to this. She is too wrapped up in her relationship. Even after the discussion all five of us had yesterday.

~

The day before, Dublin, Ireland

It had been at the table of an all-you-can-eat buffet, during Jenna's hen weekend, that things had come to a head.

It was one of those all around the world set-ups. At one food station was a man in a puffy white hat shredding crispy Chinese duck with a huge knife; opposite was a team pan-frying authentic Asian noodles, both just a few feet away from a line of hungry diners waiting to have a full English carvery handed to them.

I ended up with pan-fried sea bass in a tomato-based sauce from the Italian section, after wandering around. The choice was overwhelming.

Pam had joined Jenna's mum and nana in attempting to try a little taster from each of the many stations.

'Around the world in sixty plates!' Maggie had joked after they'd sampled everything from chicken curry to lasagne.

'I feel like a judge on *MasterChef*.' Pamela had said, while grinning for a picture between Maggie and nana, as all three of them animatedly held up lobster tails as I'd clicked away.

During the meal, Matt had phoned Nic to see how she was getting on. Narrow-eyed glances were swapped when she ended the call with, 'Love you too, baby.'

Val looked taken aback as she shot me her 'did you hear what I heard?' look.

Jenna also seemed far from impressed. 'I need a fag. Will you four come with me? I need to have a chat,' she said while gesturing to our little group.

Porsha went to rise from her seat to join us, but Jenna put her hand on her shoulder. 'Just give us five minutes, mate.'

Porsha shrugged. 'No bother, babes,' and went back to devouring her profiteroles.

It was hammering with rain, so we huddled under the restaurant's canopy. Yana sheltered Jenna's cigarette with cupped hands as she struggled to light it between the strong wind and her cheap plastic lighter.

'Nic, I'm saying this because I care 'bout ya. I have to tell you that I think it's so strange. How can you and Matt say that you love each other when you ain't even clapped eyes on one another?'

I bite my lip as Nicky's cheeks flush. She looks at the floor and offers nothing in response.

'We are your friends, Nic,' I say, knowing that she's feeling ambushed. 'And we wouldn't be very good ones if we didn't speak our true thoughts when we were worried about each other, would we? But whatever you're happy with, we will support you.' I glance at Jenna, who bulges her eyes at me and turns her palms over, waving them in frustration. I respond by pulling an 'I know but be gentle about it' face. Isn't it funny when you know someone? Like, really know them? A single look between you is all that is needed to convey thoughts and feelings.

'Etta is right. If you're happy, that's enough for your friends. We just don't want you to get the hurt heart.' Yana tries to reassure Nicky, reaching her hand out to grasp her arm and squeeze it warmly.

The atmosphere still feels quite heavy, so I'm relieved when a group of men, who look to be in their twenties, spot us while coming out of a bar opposite. Eyeing our hen do sashes, and Jenna's clip-in veil that is swirling around in a kite-like fashion above her head in the breeze, they bellow across to us, in their delicious, carefree, rich Dublin twang. 'Happy hen to yous!'

We all return their gesture with warm shouts of, 'We will, thank you!'

The realisation that we are English only increases their enthusiasm. 'Yous are English!' they call back. They are still marvelling over how much they love our accents, blowing us kisses and bowing at us before they disappear into another pub a few doors down.

'And that, ladies, was a real-life example of the saying Irish charm!' says Val, grinning at the unexpected and much-welcomed respite from the heavy-going conversation. With that, Val stubs out her dog-end on the wall and places it in the bin. Yana and Jenna follow suit and we are just about to head back inside when Nic speaks. 'I have asked him to meet up, and FaceTime. He always lets me down last minute, or says he has no connection.'

Nicky blinks back tears.

We all form a protective scrum around her.

'The thing is, Nic,' Jenna says, her voice softer now, 'no one is that busy that they cannot meet someone they claim to love. And to not even FaceTime, saying they have no connection, well that's bollocks. Even Etta manages to FaceTime from her cottage broadband, which as you know is slower than Val swimming breaststroke.'

Val feigns outrage and sticks her tongue out in Jenna's direction. This makes us all laugh.

Nicky's inner battle is written all over her face. Her mind knows that we are right, but her heart hopes that we aren't.

Val digs around in her handbag and retrieves a travel packet of Kleenex. She removes a single tissue and wipes away the eyeliner that is now streaming down Nicky's cheeks.

'I know,' Nicky agrees quietly. 'But he's said he's coming to the wedding. That it will be romantic for us to meet for the first time there. Plus he hasn't asked me for any money.'

We all agree that that is some positive news at least.

'I would rather have video chatted or met before, if I am being honest, though,' Nicky confides in us later that day after a few drinks.

'Then you insist that's what happens,' declares Val.

Nicky agrees and says that, as soon as we get back, she will.

Present time, Evie Cottage

'When we hang up, I'm going to give him a call and explain how I feel and ask to switch to video call. Well, as soon as I've put some lipstick on!' promises Nicky when Matt becomes the subject of our conversation again.

Our chatter soon drifts back to my flower mystery.

'God, imagine if it was my cousin, though. I'd be horrified!' said Jenna, shuddering at the thought.

I chuckle along with the others, even managing to say, 'Christ, yeah! Can you imagine?'

When I ask Jenna not to mention it to Jason, she agrees enthusiastically. 'Good call, babes. Play it cool. Besides, we already know it's deffo Rob, don't we?'

After we all hang up, I realise that I could actually imagine them being from Richie. A bit too easily. Hopefully even. I try to brush the thoughts away. As Jenna said, it's doubtful that they're from him. Plus it's her cousin and that would be weird for all involved. No point daydreaming and getting excited about things that are never going to happen. That said, how Robert has enough money to buy a bouquet like the one sitting on my table is anyone's guess. He never had any money before. Maybe he has a replacement me with a bigger bank balance.

Richie really does have a brilliant beard, though, and there's how chivalrous he was when he held the door open for Val when we arrived at the wedding venue, and how he stood up from his seat to pull out a chair for me at the bar area when Yana and I had a coffee before heading home. Such good manners, and he smelt good! I got several wafts of his fresh citrusy aftershave during that day.

Anyway, enough of that. I know that I should be over the moon that the man that I lusted over so much that it caused me to have years of self-loathing and a public meltdown when I saw him with someone else has now possibly sent me flowers, but I'm not.

I'm starting to think that Robert was always more of a conduit, and that I didn't ever really want him for myself after all. Not him as a person; just his acceptance. He, my toughest critic, deeming me beautiful, would have proved to myself that I was good enough. I am sure my thing for him has always been about that now. But I no longer need his or anyone else's approval. I know that I am good enough.

When I'd seen Rob at the River View, I didn't get that rush of excitement. I mean he's eye candy but is he ever going to be the love of my life? Grand gestures or not, I can say with utmost certainty no. Richie however! Oh well a girl can dream.

CHAPTER 58

Friday 4th December, En route to Sandringham, Norfolk

There is something about weddings that never fails to bring out both the best and the worst in people. Estranged family members coming together, calling a truce 'for the good of the day'. New relationships hatching as a result of being swept along by the intoxicating spell of true love and romance that floods the air. But it is that same love and romance, combined with the free bar, that also triggers old grievances to rise to the surface and come to a very public head.

For every radiant bridesmaid hanging off a ruddy-faced usher, you can guarantee that there will be as many distressed singletons in tears before the cling film has been lifted off of the evening buffet.

So, I can see why Jenna is so nervous this morning about someone potentially ruining her day. In her words, 'I'll only be doing this once, so I don't want it fucked up by Gillian and my mum brawling during the speeches, Jason's pals having a punch-up on the dance floor, over one feeling up the other's bird, or one of my mates bawling her eyes out as I cut the cake because she is thirty-five, single and living alone with her cat.'

I will admit I did feel momentarily personally attacked by the last scenario but then I realised I was only thirty so I knew she hadn't meant me.

Jenna must have seen my wide-eyed face because she gasped straight afterwards and said, 'Oh, I don't mean you mate! You don't live alone with your cat! You have Chloe. Plus you could have any man you wanted!'

I laughed then, and said, 'Don't worry. I promise not to give myself a stress-related nosebleed during the sit down meal about the state of my love life and ruin the speeches!'

This makes Jenna snort with laughter.

'God, yeah! Please don't. Not everything is about you, babes. Plus the tablecloths are rented and Gill will have a shit fit if we don't get the deposits back. She's already enforced a blanket ban of red wine at the tables.'

Jenna and I share a dark sense of gallows humour. I think that if you can't laugh at yourself then you may as well just give up.

CHAPTER 59

Jenna and Jason's wedding weekend, the Cliffe Country Hotel, Sandringham, Norfolk

The venue looked even more spectacular than when we had visited for rehearsals. We arrived the day before the wedding, early on a misty mid-December Friday morning.

I love that time of day; no noise or signs of life; the fog that had set in the night before rising just enough to spot the deer through the sunlight, grazing the still frosty parkland in the distance.

The ivy-covered stately home hotel was always going to be a magical wedding venue. When we arrived, the staff were already hard at work.

In the grand entrance hall stood two towering bushy real Norway spruce Christmas trees either side of a roaring fire, which was so big I suspect that both Jenna and I could stand inside it on the grate side by side. Above the fireplace hung luscious garlands; the smell was divine. Decorated with cream roses, larkspur and Scottish thistle – a nod to Jenna's deceased, much loved grandad. Jenna had felt strongly that she wanted a subtle Scottish theme so, when she had viewed the venue, the blue and green tartan carpet that runs down the middle of the vast oak staircase had sold it.

'How perfect will your photos be tomorrow with you and Jason standing here!' Yana marvelled, looking on at the foot of the stairs as a team of florists wound eucalyptus and spruce garlands around the handrail.

'Pretty amazing, ain't it?' Jenna agreed, taking in the busy scene.

Her moment was broken by Gillian appearing at the top of the stairs, clipboard in hand, with a very panicked-looking Liam, Jenna's wedding planner, at her heels.

'Will those carpet runners be polished?' Gill barked. 'And what about the trees? Is the watering schedule I faxed over in August being adhered to?'

Before a flustered Liam has a chance to answer, Gillian spots us. 'Ahh, finally! I need to run a few things by you!' Gill said while trotting down the stairs. 'So, disasters first. There has been a last-minute change to the menu. The chef has ordered organic local chicken thighs instead of breasts! I simply cannot allow thighs. I mean, what will people think? The only slight consolation is that we have offered pheasant as an alternative,' said an exasperated Gillian.

'But I don't like pheasant and neither does Jase,' replied Jenna.

Gillian sighs and rolls her eyes. 'It's not really about what you two like, though, is it? Jason's father has Edward from bowls coming. He is a dentist! I simply cannot serve him chicken thighs!'

Jenna turns to Liam. 'The thighs are fine. Tell the chef we will be keeping the chicken.'

We all follow Jenna as she makes her way past Gill and up towards the bridal suite. 'Right, before you disappear, there is also an issue with the seating plan,' said Gillian as Jenna swipes her key card at the oak-panelled bridal suite door. 'It has been brought to my attention that your friend Porsha and her plus-one have been moved at the last moment. This must be an error as they are now on the same table as Saskia and Ruben Parker-Wells. This simply won't do. I mean, Porsha is, erm…entertaining, but, I do not think it is a suitable personality combination. Saskia and Ruben are close family friends and, well, they have a second home in Tuscany and two full-time housekeepers,' pleaded Gillian to a disinterested-looking Jenna.

'I am not changing the seating plan, Gill. Just chill out, will ya, and leave it all to Liam? Go have a sweet vermouth at the bar!'

As the door to the plush chintz suite closes, Jenna falls back on to the heavily draped four-poster bed.

'You did that on purpose, didn't you? That table seating thing?' I ask, laughing.

Jenna sits back up and throws her hand to her neck in mock outrage then breaks into a massive grin. 'Yeah, I did!'

The four of us join Jenna in lying back on the regal-like bed.

'What time will your man arrive?' Yana asks Nicky.

'He will be here by ten in the morning,' Nic replies with an excited grin.

'Are you nervous, Nic?' asks Val.

I know that Nicky is disappointed that she and Matt still haven't Facetimed. Despite her best efforts, the excuses continued to flow.

'I am, yeah. Nervous but also really excited. He sent me a picture of his suit last night. He got a tie to match my dress. He's made a real effort.'

It's nice to see Nicky so happy. I just hope it isn't short lived.

CHAPTER 60

Jase and his groomsmen arrived that afternoon and disappeared to shoot clay pigeons, while us five plus Jenna's mum, nana, sister and Porsha hit the spa. Out of good manners, Jenna had invited Gillian, but she had waved her off haughtily. 'I am eyeballs deep in disasters. I have no time for massages and nail painting! The white doves have just arrived and one of them has a grey chest. Plus I have just rejected four chair covers. Creases galore! In short, everything is falling apart!' Gillian had rambled with a manic look in her eye. 'Now where is my espresso? I haven't slept in twenty-six hours. Liam! I need caffeine now. I am feeling light-headed!'

Maggie then looked at Gillian with a perplexed expression and said, 'Blimey, Gill! Just leave it all to the wedding planner. He knows what he's doing. Come and have a facial.'

To which Gill replied indignantly, 'I am not leaving my little prince's wedding day in the hands of someone whose most used phrase is "that'll do, I suppose"!'

We gave up and left Gill to it after that because, in the words of Jenna's nana, 'Some people just aren't happy unless they're miserable.'

Possibly the wisest words ever spoken.

We kept separate from the stag party that evening but I did catch a glimpse of Robert when I went down with Yana when she wanted to smoke. He didn't see me. Far too busy flirting with one of the pretty receptionists. Some things never change.

We had such a good evening, all of us piled in the plush bridal suite eating wood-fired calzone and salad from room service. We resisted the minibar, knowing we all – especially our bride – needed an early night, before a long busy day ahead tomorrow.

Just after nine, I'd said my goodbyes along with everyone else, bar Clemmie, who was sharing Jenna's room tonight in Jason's absence.

As I made my way back to my room, I decided to be lazy and take the lift so pushed the call button and stood waiting in my bridal party matching shorts and vest top set and flip-flops. As it pinged open, there he was.

I felt my belly flip as his icy-blue eyes met mine, and, as they did, a warm, genuine grin spread all over his face.

'Fancy seeing you here,' said Richie.

I hadn't ever thought a Manchester accent to be particularly attractive before I'd met him.

Conscious that I had been standing at the lift, I felt that I had no option but to take his place as he stepped out – as much as I didn't want to – and so I smiled coyly and said hello as I passed.

Then something happened that's hard to explain.

As the lift doors started closing, Richie turned and glanced back and held my gaze. I felt more exposed in that moment than I ever have, but in a good way.

He looked at me like no one ever has before.

When I got back to my room, my heart was still racing. I decided to ring Pamela to check that she was all set for tomorrow. It had been decided, with her having grown close to Jenna, that she and Grandad would come for the ceremony and the sit-down meal, and then leave after the speeches. Because they were both anxious to get back for Charles and Diana and to call in on Alice at mine and check Nicky's cats on the way home.

I was still thinking about Richie when I ran myself a bath, pouring in a generous glug of the Molton Brown Ylang Ylang bath gel from the complementary toiletries that had been placed next to the roll-top bath in my en suite.

After I dried and covered myself in body oil, I reached for the fluffy oversized robe on the back of the door and took a deep intake of breath, enjoying the feeling of being swathed in baby-powder-soft Egyptian cotton. My mind was still wandering back to the lift long after I had sunk into – hands down – the comfiest bed I have ever been in, with *Bridesmaids* on the television.

I thought that the knock at the door would probably be Nicky giving me a Matt update, or Yana, who, knowing that I would most likely be the one out of all five of us alongside her still awake, had come to ask me if I wanted a nightcap, but I let my hair tumble out of the high bun it had been in since before my bath.

Just in case it was a certain someone else.

CHAPTER 61

'Sorry, mate, I know it's late, but can I come in?' said an animated-looking Jenna, standing opposite me in a matching dressing gown.

'Of course, you can,' I said, anxiety rising in my chest.

'What's happened? Is everything okay?' I ask her, stepping aside.

As Jenna sat down on the edge of the bed, she turned to me and said, 'I've got some good news.'

I sit on the dressing table stool opposite her.

'So, my Jase texted me half hour ago and told me that it was Rob that sent the flowers. You reeled him in hook, line and sinker. The even better news is that Rob has got well pissed tonight and confided in Jase that the bird…the blonde one—'

'Clara,' I say.

Jenna nods. 'That's her, yes. The one who helped Yana. Well, she is supposedly pregnant. Rob is fuming, saying that she has done it to trap him and that he is going to still try and get back with you. Clara being pregnant and him reacting like he has proves he hasn't changed at all,' said Jenna as she beams at me expectantly.

I am not sure what reaction she was expecting but my non-reaction clearly wasn't it.

'What's up with you, babes? You looked upset when I said that the flowers were from Rob. I mean, I know you don't want him, but this is the outcome you wanted! You get to tell him to fuck off now,' Jenna says, frowning.

'The thing is, Jen,' I venture, 'have you ever thought you really wanted something but then realised afterwards that you didn't want it after all? You just thought you did, when really you just didn't want what you had.'

Jenna narrows her eyes at me again.

'Um, I think so. Like when, if I'm sick to death of cooking and decide I really fancy a takeaway, so I order one, then it comes and it's cold, greasy and a massive let-down?' she asks.

'Yeah, kind of,' I say with a small chuckle.

'So, Rob is the kebab that you thought you wanted, because you had nothing in, but really you just needed to get down Aldi and sort your empty fridge out,' says Jenna.

We are both laughing now. But she has summed it up perfectly.

'Yeah, exactly. I mean, I never wanted him back, but now I don't even want him to want me. I was so miserable before I got healthy and I wanted him to feel as shit as I did. Now I would just rather move on.'

Jenna goes over to my minibar and takes out two glasses, a can of Diet Coke and a vodka miniature.

'One to help us sleep,' she says as I watch her untwist the vodka lid and crack open the can of Diet Coke, before dividing them both equally between the glasses.

'So, now your own fridge's full, Rob's greasy doner can be binned!' Jenna cackles, handing me one of the soda tumblers.

I take a sip as she sits back down.

'I think you had a lucky escape, to be honest. He clearly ain't changed at all since he was with you,' Jenna tells me, looking relieved.

I feel a pang of empathy for Clara, knowing from bitter experience that babies should be the result of a committed, loving relationship; not a tool to use in an attempt to achieve one. It also feels weird that my daughter may soon have a half brother or sister.

When Jenna leaves to make her way back to the bridal suite, she turns back to me.

'You are right not to settle for someone who is not the love of your life, mate. When you meet the one for ya, you will just know. Look at Jase and me. Yeah, he is a bit of a goon, and we bicker, but it has always been him for me, and always will be. I would want him if he lost his legs and he would want me if I weighed thirty stone. Real love is blind.'

I call after her as she heads off down the long wide corridor, back towards the lift. 'I'll be seeing you in the morning! I cannot wait to see the dress, Jen!'

Jenna shoots me one last smile and shouts back, 'Remember, when you know, you just know, and from that moment onwards it will always be them.'

CHAPTER 62

The big day…

'What time is it?' Nicky asks as she paces up and down like a caged tiger.

'Five minutes later than the last time you ask,' Yana replies as she bends down to put on her shoes. 'You look so lovely, Etta!' Yana says, glancing up at me.

I feel good too. I'd pondered over the silky wide-leg trousers one Monday lunchtime in Zara when Val had appeared in the changing room with a cream crossover blouse.

'This will work a treat with them!' she'd said, passing it through the gap in the curtain of the cramped changing room cubicle. As soon as I tried it on and tucked it into the waistband of the berry red trousers and stared at my reflection, I knew it was a perfect outfit for the day ceremony.

'I don't think he's coming,' Nicky tells us fretfully, reappearing from the bathroom after checking her appearance for the tenth time in the last half hour.

'He might just be running late. You know how traffic can be,' offers Val.

'And if he doesn't turn up, it will be his loss!' I say, before seeing Nic's crestfallen face and adding, 'But I'm sure it's traffic.'

All of us have scrubbed up well. Nicky's emerald-green peplum dress is the perfect cut for her shape. Yana has done a brilliant job of curling her hair and pinning it back off her face to show off the make-up Jenna's artist had expertly applied to her – and indeed all four of us when she visited our room – at the bride's insistence earlier.

I have gone with a different look today with my hair. I've straightened it and tied it back in a high pony, no longer feeling the need to hide behind my curls.

Val is in her dress; the Ted Baker one she got in the sale. She did end up treating herself to a pair of red kitten heels, a little 'divorce pressie' to herself. The make-up lady has given Val a vixen red lip, to match the print on her dress and shoes. It's the best Val has ever looked. So classy and confident.

Yana…well, where do I even start! As Jenna had predicted, the dress that Yana loved from John Lewis has made way for a forest green, velvet pencil skirt and matching puff sleeve top, teamed with tights and black pointy-toed court shoes.

'Simon say I look like the sexy solicitor,' said Yana as does a twirl for us to give our verdict. Her new dark locks have been teased into a perfect bun.

'You do!' I say, taken aback by how different she looks. 'You look so amazing!'

We all group into the mirror together to take a photo.

'I wonder how she's getting on,' says Val, taking the words out of my mouth, our photo highlighting the missing piece of our friendship jigsaw. In that moment, the old-fashioned hotel phone starts to ring, making us all jump.

Nic answers, then calls out to us excitedly, 'It's Maggie! Jenna wants us to go up to her suite!'

CHAPTER 63

'Will I do?' Jenna asks us nervously as the four of us stop dead upon setting eyes on her. Jenna is standing in the middle of her suite, in the centre of three floor-length mirrors, facing us. Kenny G's 'Songbird' playing in the background gives me a rush of warm nostalgia.

One evening, a good few months ago now, the five of us had been sitting watching *Pretty Woman* at mine and the scene where Julia Roberts greets Richard Gere wearing nothing but a tie came on and Jenna had said, 'This is the most romantic song I have ever heard. I'm going to have this playing when I'm getting ready on my wedding day.'

I had forgotten all about it, but she clearly hadn't. I know that when everyone describes a bride's wedding dress, they always say, 'Oh, it fitted her like a glove!' but when I tell you that Jenna's did just that, I mean it.

Her usual blonde extensions were gone in favour of her natural freshly balayaged hair that had been plaited loosely to the side over her slender shoulder. Delicate diamond and pearl drop earrings hung from each ear, and a floating diamond necklace glistened on her shimmery clavicle.

The dress was even more exquisite than Jenna had described. Long-sleeved, off-the- shoulder lace that hugged in her waist and gave way to a spectacular fishtail satin train that fanned out like a peacock's tail behind her.

I had never really understood the whole crying at someone else's wedding but there wasn't a dry eye in the house at that moment.

'You will more than do. You will take his breath away,' I said, dabbing my eyes with one of the tissues that Val had just dished out from her seemingly never-ending supply.

'I told ya, my girl, didn't I! You're a knockout!' Maggie cries out between sobs.

'Right. Enough of all that,' Jenna's nana announces between sniffs into her tissue when Jenna starts to look misty-eyed.

'Nana's right. Maria took over an hour to do your eye make-up. We don't want your falsies falling off, do we?' said Maggie as she plunges her hand into a watery ice bucket and pulls out a Moët bottle.

'Let's have some booze, shall we?' she adds jovially.

I then heard something I never thought I would. Jenna refusing an alcoholic drink. 'Nah, not for me mum. Those trays of shots we had for elevenses really had a kick. I'm struggling to stay upright to tell ya the truth!'

As Bon Iver 'Skinny Love' gives way to 'Clair de Lune' everyone collectively turns and gasps at the sight of Jenna making her way down the white, rose-petal-laden aisle. Jason looks at her as if she were the only one in the room, tears streaming openly. As she reaches him, I see him mouth, 'You look beautiful.'

Everyone got caught up in the emotion of the moment;

none more so than Nicky, who was openly sobbing next to me, although I am sure that Matt being a no-show may have contributed heavily. Nic had given up at midday as we took our places in the great hall for the ceremony. She did check once more, then switched her phone off and tucked it inside her bag, without comment. As Jenna and Jason are pronounced husband and wife, cheers erupt. I squeeze Nic's hand, and she manages a watery smile.

Despite her own disappointment, Nicky did Jenna proud during the photos with her wide grin and raucous laughter as we all try and fail to catch the bouquet. The five of us get emotional again when Jenna asks all four of us to join just her on the staircase for a photo.

'Look how far we've come,' she whispers. 'We did it.'

And she's right. We have.

When we take our seats for the meal, Jason surprises everyone with a heartfelt speech about the 'love of his life', the 'most amazing mother to my boys'. Maggie also made a lovely toast to Gillian for all her hard work in bringing together 'a perfect day'.

Talking of Gillian, a close friendship seems to have formed between her and Pamela. Since the hen do, there have been several 'coffee mornings' in each of their respective houses. When we sat down for the meal today, Gill had scooted over before the first course and said, 'Etta, would you mind awfully if Pamela was to join me up at the top table?'

Pam, who believes herself born to be sitting at every top table, had already arisen from her fabric-covered chair before Gillian had even finished her sentence.

In the end, you see, my grandad decided to stay home. He isn't really a social occasion person, and he was really fretting about leaving the corgis for so long, especially after how upset they were when they had to have a dog-sitter when we went down to Cornwall. Chloe, when given the option, jumped at the chance to stay with Grandad. Being able to go on an afternoon hack had been the winning factor. So, he had driven and dropped off Pam, just before eleven-thirty, and turned around and gone back home. I'd already offered to share my room with her; it having a pull-out sofa bed. No prizes for guessing which one of us will be sleeping on that!

Anyway, as Pam trundled off with her new friend, I did feel a pang of endearment as Pam paused briefly to kiss Maggie and Jenna's nana on their cheeks as she passed them.

Pam is quite loveable really.

After the meal, there were a few hours' break before the evening do started and the evening guests (the ones that Jenna and Jase – as Jenna put it so well – 'don't like enough to pay for them to eat') arrived.

Some of the day guests disappear into the bar, lounging on the Chesterfield sofas and sharing bowls of expensive handmade crisps. Others dash off outside to smoke or make calls. The rest who have rooms retreat to freshen up and change for the evening.

Nicky had disappeared a little while earlier, apologising to Jenna and explaining that she was going to pop upstairs to get some headache tablets and have a little lie-down 'to be fresh for this evening'.

I whisper to Jenna that the rest us of are going up to check on Nic as I pass her posing by the side of her triple chocolate layer wedding cake.

'Okay, I won't be far behind,' Jen whispers back, as her husband leans down and kisses her forehead.

I get as far as the staircase when a familiar voice calls me back. I don't need to turn round to discover who wants my attention.

Robert.

CHAPTER 64

When I turn round, there he is. In all his handsome, hubristic self. I move to the side of the staircase and hold his gaze, waiting for him to speak. This seems to unsettle him. Probably because the Etta he knew was eager to please and accommodating.

Finally, he speaks. 'Hear me out before you say anything.'

He goes to touch my arm and I recoil. A look of sheer confusion at my reaction spreads over his face.

'I know you don't want anything to do with me but just hear me out. When I saw you in the River View, I couldn't believe it was you. You look so beautiful and thin, and I know I made a massive mistake not settling down with you. Then I found out you was coming today and knew it was fate. I am older now and I am ready. I was stupid to not realise that you just needed time to sort yourself out. I should have stuck it out.'

This is a red rag to a bull.

'Sorry. What?' I challenge him. 'You should have stuck it out? I needed time to sort myself out, did I? Are you taking the piss?'

The glances in our direction make me realise that my voice is raised.

'Yeah. No. Well you know. To get your looks back, I meant, after…You well know what I mean,' says Robert, awkwardly running his hands through his hair. I notice his hairline is receding.

'After you deserted me during the whole pregnancy? Or after you reappeared briefly after I had our daughter, only to take money from me, tell me how awful I looked and then disappear again? Which 'after' are you referring to, Robert?'

I glare at him as he shuffles about and pulls a pained 'poor me' expression.

'Can we draw a line and try again? I have a good job now. Look, I just got a new watch!'

I feel a stab of revulsion for the man flashing his wrist in my direction. A father to a seven year old, who he hasn't even asked about or to this day paid a penny towards, and here he is showing off his 'rose gold Rolex that cost the same as a new family car!'

'That's good to know. I'm happy for you. I'm sure the CSA will be glad of this information too. At least now you can start contributing to your daughter's life. Financially, at least.'

'What! Well, let's not be hasty. I'm not completely on the books. Anyway, what about us?' Says Robert, winking at me.

'Tell me something, Robert. If we were back together and I started piling the weight on again and I got back to the size I was at my heaviest…and that, for your information, is a lot bigger than when you last saw me. I was a size twenty a few months ago—'

Robert's disgust is clear. It is written all over his heavily Botoxed face.

I couldn't care less. I carry on. '—So, if I was a size

twenty, what would you do? Would you still want to be with me?'

I already know the answer.

'Like fuck you would get to a size twenty with me! My mates would rip the piss, like they used to when I was with you before. I'd have to get your jaw wired!'

Robert is chuckling now.

I am not.

'The thing is, Rob, and I mean this exactly how it sounds, I would rather become a fucking nun, and never touch a man again, than ever have you in my life or in my bed again. I deserve more – a lot more – and so does your daughter. You are welcome to set up visits to see Chloe, if you can be consistent. I will be instructing a solicitor to help me get child support now you have a good job, but, other than that, I want you to stay as far away from me as possible. Now, if you don't mind, my friends are waiting. Enjoy the rest of your day.'

I turn back a second or two later and see he's planted to the spot, noticeably gobsmacked.

I call back to him. 'Oh, I nearly forgot. I heard congratulations are in order. Send my love to Clara. I really hope you treat her better than you treated me. She's a lovely girl, who also deserves a lot more. You have a chance to do things right this time.'

I walk up the staircase with my head held high. Feeling everything I have ever wanted to feel about myself, and more.

CHAPTER 65

When Nicky lets us in her room, she is sobbing again, mobile in one hand, a half-eaten chocolate bar in the other. I take one look at the other two Wispa Gold wrappers at her feet and say, 'Well, you don't need any more of those for a start!' taking the half bar and chucking it into a nearby bin.

'I feel so stupid! You all knew he was going to do this. I really thought he was going to come,' sobs Nicky.

'Putting your trust in someone is nothing to be embarrassed about,' Val replies, as she walks over to the window.

We all watch as Val kicks off her shoes and wastes no time in lighting up a ciggie, completely ignoring the gold 'no smoking in rooms' signs dotted around on multiple surfaces.

'Bloody hell, Val! You'll get us thrown out!' I say as I watch her lean out of the window to exhale thick cloudy smoke. Before I can protest any further, Yana takes Val up on her offer of a drag.

'You don't know what it's like for us!' Val says, chuckling. 'We need our fix!'

When Nicky says, 'bugger it! Give us a go,' we all raise

our eyebrows, but Yana passes her cigarette to her without comment.

'I used to love smoking, but Theodore said it was common, so I stopped. I'm not starting back up – not with my asthma. I just really need one today.'

Yana and Val nod in understanding.

Our sympathetic pep talk to Nicky is soon interrupted. Urgent pounding on the door makes all three of them jump like naughty schoolgirls.

'Shit! I think staff see us puff out of the window!' Yana shrieks as Val starts waving her arms around like a human windmill.

Yana darts into the bathroom and comes back, frantically spraying Nicky's Ralph Lauren Romance perfume.

'Open up! It's me! Come on, it's urgent!'

I shoot over to the door and let Jenna in. She's breathlessly waving her arms about.

'We only had one very small cigarette for the nerves!' Yana says sheepishly.

'He's here! He's here!' Jenna shouts, finally getting her breath while pointing in the general direction of outside.

'Fudge! They'll charge us for a deep clean!' said Nicky, picking up a pillow from her bed and attempting to fan the room.

'Have you all gone mad? He's here. Him for her!' Jenna screams, jabbing her finger at Nicky like she's on fire. 'Online man, Matt, is downstairs! It's definitely him. I recognised him from his photo, and he's wearing the emerald-green tie!'

We all stop and stare at Nic.

'Jason is stalling him! You lot best make yourselves scarce. I'll go back down and send him up. He'll be up in five, okay, Nic, mate?' Jenna says, glancing at Nicky's vacant expression.

'He's here? Matt is downstairs?' Nic repeats slowly.

'Yeah, mate, he is, so you had better get the windows

open 'cos it smells like my nana's kitchen in here!' Jenna replies.

Nicky lets out an excited scream and starts hopping about to try and get her shoes back on. 'Do I look okay?' she asks us when she dashes out of the bathroom.

Yana hands her a little plastic glass brimming with a bright-green liquid. 'You must swig this before your man comes here,' she says, handing it to Nicky. We all burst out laughing as Nic downs it in one.

'I give you mouthwash, Nicky! Why do you swallow?' Yana laughs.

'Oh, I thought it was a shot from the mini bar for my nerves!' giggles Nicky.

We help her air the room and adjust her hair.

'Good luck!' I bellow as we head back to our own rooms.

As soon as we are out of Nicky's earshot, Yana turns to us and says, 'He better have the good excuse. There is something about all this that does not sit right with me. I think he is no good man for our friend.'

Val says that she agrees but that we should give him the benefit of the doubt, until we meet him.

'Umm, yes, but we must find out who is this man,' replies Yana, clearly unconvinced.

CHAPTER 66

I feel a bit nervous as Jason leads Jenna through the crowd for their first dance, him only having had one job in the whole planning of their wedding. That being choosing their first dance song. Jenna had high hopes that he would choose something meaningful, so I hope she won't be disappointed.

I sigh in relief when the lights go down and the gentle spotlight beams on the newlyweds as Ryan Adams' acoustic version of Oasis's 'Wonderwall' rings out on the speakers. The crowd claps as Jenna throws her head back giggling and then wraps her toned arms around Jason's neck as he lifts her off the floor and swings her around.

When they start snogging like a pair of teenagers as the chorus starts up, Jason's friends all start chanting the lyrics, their pints of lager swishing about everywhere as they punch the air in solidarity and the joy of reliving their lost youth.

I had to laugh when I heard Gillian mutter to Jason's dad, 'Good grief! What will the Anderson-Patrick Jones think? I give up! I *told* him he was to go with Frank Sinatra 'The Way You Look Tonight'!'

After a lot of dancing, I manage to have a chat with

Nicky and the others. I'm dying for Nic to fill us in, although things are obviously going well, judging by all the slow dancing and canoodling that has been going on between her and Matt since his late entrance.

'The agency carer for his mum let him down!' Nicky tells us in the toilets. 'He couldn't just leave her. He had to ask his neighbour to look after her in the end. Bless him. Too scared to tell me, he was. And guess what else? His car conked out on the motorway and he had to wait three hours for roadside assistance,' Nic adds as she dabs on her face powder in front of the mirror and straightens her dress. 'He rang her, his mum, Dot, on speakerphone from my room phone to let her know he'd arrived safe and sound, and I spoke to her! She said that she can't wait to meet me and invited me to join them for Christmas! I can even take the cats!'

I don't need to look in Yana's direction to know her facial expression.

It's Jenna who says what I, and I am sure the other two, are thinking. 'That was a run of bad luck, weren't it!'

I can tell that Nicky takes it as an innocent comment and replies, 'I know. Bless him. He's had a terrible time, but he's here now, and that's all that matters.'

As we leave, Nicky practically skips off to Matt, who's waiting right outside the toilet for her. As Nic and Matt head towards the bar, and we're sure that Nic is out of earshot, Val turns to us and says under her breath, 'There is a lot more to that man. We need to keep a close eye on him. I don't buy into any of it.'

'Yeah. It's sketchy all right,' Jenna replies.

And it brings me no pleasure whatsoever to have to say that I completely agree.

CHAPTER 67

Despite tucking into scrambled eggs and grilled bacon at breakfast and devouring three scrumptious courses of Welsh rarebit (posh cheese on toast), stuffed chicken thighs with roasted vegetables and a cinnamon apple pastry basket with double cream for dessert, my belly, now accustomed to small but regular refills, has been rumbling since the first dance. Therefore, I practically galloped to get in line for the hog roast and jacket potato station and was happily loading up my spud with tons of salad and tuna sweetcorn when a familiar voice boomed from behind me.

'That's what I like to see. A woman with an appetite!'

I turn round and there Richie is, looking all dishy in suit trousers, his shirt sleeves rolled up.

Broad men always look better in suits, don't they?

The gazing at each other thing was back in action. I smile what I think would be described as a flirty smile. I don't really know what one of those is, but I did think flirty smile in my head as I did it.

'Have you had a good day?' I ask him as he forks heaps of cheese-laden jacket potato into his mouth.

'I have, yeah. It's been good. I'm not looking forward to the drive back tonight though,' he says before joining me at a table as we both continue to eat.

I learn that Richie runs a weight-loss camp in Wales.

'Me and a few ex-marines run it. Week-long residential courses mainly,' he tells me. 'That's why I have to get back. I have a course that's full to capacity starting in the morning so gotta leave shortly. People want to get festive season dress ready.'

He chuckles.

Why Jenna never thought to mention this is beyond me, given we were all clueless when we started looking into losing weight and she had an expert at her disposal.

I'd be lying if I said I wasn't bitterly disappointed when Jenna's mum, Maggie, appears a short while later, swaying as she pesters Richie for his attention. 'Come on. You owe your auntie a dance!'

He gives up protesting when Maggie starts trying to drag him from his seat by his beard.

'Nice to see you again, Etta,' he calls back to me as the crowd swallows him up.

I try to brush my disappointment aside, telling myself that we will cross paths again.

A while later, I spot him from across the room. He is shaking a few men's hands and kissing Clemmie, Jenna's sister, on the cheek. I'm standing with Jenna at the time, attempting to loosen her heavily pinned hair, which had started to give her a headache, when Richie makes his way over to us and gives Jenna a warm hug.

'I'm off now, Jen. You look stunning,' he says. 'I'll text you tomorrow and I will see you soon anyway, for Christmas, when you're fresh back from paradise.'

'Ah, so soon, dear cousin! I haven't even gagged at the

sight of your tongue down some random's throat yet! You're slipping!' Jenna jokes.

'Yeah. New me. I'm far too old for all that. Time to find the one and stick to her.'

As Richie says that he holds my gaze. He then puts his hand on the small of my back and kisses my cheek.

'I'm off, Etta, but hopefully see you again soon.'

As Richie breaks away from the embrace, his hand falls next to mine and for a very brief second our fingertips touch. I see him look right back at me twice through the crowd before he reaches the exit, and then he's gone.

Jenna is narrowing her eyes at me quizzically. I'm sure that she is going to say something. I can tell by her face that she's considering it, but instead she just smiles, links her arm through mine, and says, 'Come on mate. Let's get a drink and grab the others. The fireworks are going to start soon.'

When we've rounded up all our group, we follow Jenna's lead, soon falling about laughing as she lets out high-spirited shrieks with a bottle of bubbly in each hand as Jason scoops her up in a fireman's carry and jogs towards a small hill. Val and I link arms behind them. Thankfully, the ground is too hard for our heels to sink in.

I glance back at Nicky and Matt, who are each carrying a basket of blankets, which they've grabbed from the hallway next to the leather sofa where we'd found them deep in conversation.

Yana isn't far behind with Simon, who had arrived this evening, coming via taxi straight from Norwich train station to join his wife after being away in Newcastle on a four-day work course. The pair are chatting happily, carrying armfuls of champagne flutes between them.

As we reach the top of the small mound of grassy earth, Jason, Simon and Matt drag three benches together and spread the wool blankets on the damp seats while Yana pops open a bottle. Fizzy spray launches into the air as she rushes to direct it into the glasses that Val and Nicky are holding, poised in anticipation.

Muffled sounds of the DJ announcing fireworks starting momentarily prompt the rest of the guests to flood out of the orangery attached to the reception room and congregate in small groups in the gardens below us.

The sight of Porsha chatting away to her earlier table companions, thrusting her hips and demonstrating I dread to think what, while the couple look on at her like deer frozen in headlights, makes me chuckle because I know that I'm observing Gillian's worst nightmare.

When all of our little group are seated on the bench, glasses in hand, Val clears her throat and gets back on her feet.

'I would like to make a toast.'

Everyone shuffles up to join Val.

'To our special friends, Jason and Jenna; the happy couple. May you always be as happy and in love as you are today.'

Glasses clink as a chorus of 'To our special friends Jason and Jenna' rings out. Rainbow bursts of fireworks explode above us, Jenna turns to the four of us.

'We made it together! Look at us all. Not just how we look – and we are all banging! – but we are all in a better place than when we found each other, ain't we? And that is what real friends are about,' she says, embracing us all.

Jenna's right. As much as we have all transformed our bodies – It is the emotional support we have given each other that has profoundly changed each one of our lives.

Knowing you have a team behind you that has your back regardless is an extremely empowering thing.

A few minutes later I glance round me and take in the scene: Jason's arms draped around Jenna; Val's rapturous expression as she types away on her mobile, no doubt responding to her long-lost first love, Adonis; Nicky tenderly holding hands with Matt, the one she was (hopefully) right about all along; and Yana perched on Simon's knee, wrapped up in a blanket on one of the benches.

I lean down and pick up a cork from one of the champagne bottles. My little token of assurance that I will be able to revisit this memory; my snippet of happiness shared with the four best friends anyone could ever dream of having.

CHAPTER 68

'Shall I order some decaf, darling, before we turn in?' Pamela asks me as she reappears from the bathroom, just before midnight, wearing her ankle-length black satin and lace nightgown.

'Yeah, go on then,' I said, flicking the television on to Netflix. I shuffle about trying to get comfortable. Predictably, I ended up on the pull-out.

We are laughing away at *Schitt's Creek* when a light tap tap on our door alerts us to what must be our room service arrival. I make my way towards the door and my heart drops to my feet upon hearing a drunken jubilant slur from passers-by in the corridor. 'Oi-oi, it's the red-haired aqua man! I thought you'd left!'

I stand on tiptoe and peer out of the spyhole. My hair, having showered between the day service and the evening party, is back to its wild curly self. I rake my fingers through the tangles and scrunch. I wish that I'd been lazy and not removed my make-up. Never mind.

He swings around as I open the door.

'Hello, you,' Richie says, his voice quieter than usual, the twinkle in his eyes ever present.

'Richie! I thought you'd gone back to Wales,' I reply, smiling.

'I did. Well, I left but I came back.'

Richie shifts about then and looks down at the carpet then back at me.

'Look, the thing is, Etta, before Rob sent you those flowers, I'd told him that I was going to send you some, then, when I rang Jase when we got back to get your address, he said that Rob the knob had beaten me to it and about your history with him, so I decided to back off.'

I feel light-headed, like I'm in a dream.

I nod as Richie continues. 'But then when Jenna texted me after I left tonight to tell me that you didn't like Rob at all and that, well, she thought that maybe you actually liked me, like I do you...' He pauses again, lifting up his left hand and running it over his hair that's in a messy but very manly ponytail bun. 'So, when I was told that, I decided to turn back so I could give you these,' Richie says as he produces some very battered-looking, glitter-covered chrysanthemums in a cellophane sleeve from behind his back.

He raises his hand to his forehead as I take them.

'I know they're dire, but I had to work with what I could find at half-eleven on a Saturday night.'

I laugh as I accept them.

'They're perfect,' I say, not laughing any more.

I attempt to kiss him on the cheek but his height makes it more than a little out of my range. I feel very delicate as he leans down to allow me to brush my lips against his stubble.

'Could I take you out for dinner when I'm down over Christmas?' Richie almost whispers.

My hands look so tiny as I glance down at them now that they've somehow naturally found their way inside his.

'I would love that,' I manage to reply, beaming at him.

'I'm glad. I really don't want to, Etta, but I have to go now. Can I ask for your number?'

Before I can answer, Pamela sprints past me. 'No need! Here you go! I've been carrying these in my purse for years just in case I ever bumped into a gentleman suitable for her!' she says breathlessly, whilst thrusting a white business card into Richie's hand. I'd forgotten all about Pam until then. Caught up in the moment, so to speak.

Richie looks as amused as I do mortified.

'Henrietta's mobile and email address are on there and also mine and her grandfather's landline, just in case!' Pam says, beaming up at him like a maniac.

I am saved by a tired-looking woman in a blue waistcoat arriving with our tray of refreshments. Pamela signs for them, before retreating out of sight, although no doubt well within earshot.

'So, Etta, five foot three, curly black hair, hazel-green eyes with a shapely figure and excellent natural teeth,' says Richie, comically reading off the little printed card while I groan and laugh. 'I guess this is goodbye for now,' he says, cupping my face in his hands.

What happened next is a blur. I remember hearing Ben Howard 'Only Love' in the distance and Richie leaning down to kiss me and taking a deep breath as his lips touched mine.

The next thing I knew he had lifted me up and my legs were wrapped around his waist.

Completely lost in the moment, I can honestly say that it was the most romantic moment of my whole life. Admittedly, it wasn't a completely perfect moment; mainly due to Pam reappearing next to us relentlessly huh-humming until she gained our attention.

'I just wanted to say, don't leave on my account young

man. I have my earplugs. I'll even take the sofa bed. We are all adults, after all!'

But the real love stories are never completely perfect, are they? Because life isn't ever going to be like the stories we read as a child. There are no princes who will ride up on their white horse and whisk us away to live happily ever after but there are some decent men; some of whom have been kissed by fire, who will turn up when you least expect it, to present you with the most perfect, awful flowers. And kiss you in a way that confirms that everything you have been through before – every struggle and disappointment – had to happen in order for you to meet the person you were destined to be with.

We just have to keep that faith until our time comes. And know in our hearts that, in the end, we will all end up where we're supposed to be, with who we are supposed to be with.

In the words of Jenna, 'When you know, you just know. And from that moment onwards, it will always be them.'

If you would like to know what happens next for the ladies of A Moment on the Lips please consider visiting my author page on Amazon and pressing the 'Follow' me button. Amazon will then update you via email when I release my next book. As a debut author reviews and star ratings are so appreciated, so please also consider leaving one. Thank you for reading!

If you would like to hear my A Moment on the Lips playlist, you can find it here.
https://open.spotify.com/playlist/
5HdpfLLUBr5QJMBnrk7JbS?si=i3dyG-
oETHqMzLgAXp6Wzw&utm_source=copy-link

Printed in Great Britain
by Amazon

23512369R00202